The Deployment Toolkit

MILITARY LIFE

Military Life is a series of books for service members and their families who must deal with the significant yet often overlooked difficulties unique to life in the military. Each of the titles in the series is a comprehensive presentation of the problems that arise, solutions to these problems, and resources that are of much further help. The authors of these books—who are themselves military members and experienced writers—have personally faced these challenging situations and understand the many complications that accompany them. This is the first stop for members of the military and their loved ones in search of information on navigating the complex world of military life.

1. *The Military Marriage Manual: Tactics for Successful Relationships* by Janelle Hill, Cheryl Lawhorne, and Don Philpott (2010)
2. *Combat-Related Traumatic Brain Injury and PTSD: A Resource and Recovery Guide* by Cheryl Lawhorne and Don Philpott (2010)
3. *Special Needs Families in the Military: A Resource Guide* by Janelle Hill and Don Philpott (2010)
4. *Military Finances: Personal Money Management for Service Members, Veterans, and Their Families* by Cheryl Lawhorne-Scott and Don Philpott (2013)
5. *Sexual Assault in the Military: A Guide for Victims and Families* by Cheryl Lawhorne-Scott, Don Philpott, and Jeff Scott (2014)
6. *Raising Children in the Military* by Cheryl Lawhorne-Scott, Don Philpott, and Jeff Scott (2014)
7. *The Deployment Toolkit: Military Families and Solutions for a Successful Long-Distance Relationship* by Janelle B. Moore and Don Philpott

The Deployment Toolkit

Military Families and Solutions for a Successful Long-Distance Relationship

Janelle B. Moore and Don Philpott

ROWMAN & LITTLEFIELD
Lanham • Boulder • New York • London

Published by Rowman & Littlefield
A wholly owned subsidiary of The Rowman & Littlefield Publishing Group, Inc.
4501 Forbes Boulevard, Suite 200, Lanham, Maryland 20706
www.rowman.com

Unit A, Whitacre Mews, 26-34 Stannary Street, London SE11 4AB

British Library Cataloguing in Publication Information Available

Library of Congress Cataloging-in-Publication Data
Names: Moore, Janelle, 1972– author. | Philpott, Don, 1946– author.
Title: The deployment toolkit : military families and solutions for a
  successful long-distance relationship / Janelle B. Moore and Don Philpott.
Other titles: Military families and solutions for a successful long-distance
  relationship
Description: Lanham, MD : Rowman & Littlefield, [2016] | Series: Military
  life | Includes index.
Identifiers: LCCN 2016003349 | ISBN 9781442254282 (cloth : alk. paper)
Subjects: LCSH: Soldiers—Family relationships—United States—Handbooks,
  manuals, etc. | Deployment (Strategy)—Psychological aspects. |
  Long-distance relationships—United States. | Military spouses—United
  States—Handbooks, manuals, etc. | Families of military personnel—United
  States—Handbooks, manuals, etc. | United States—Armed Forces—Military
  life—Handbooks, manuals, etc.
Classification: LCC UB403 .M673 2016 | DDC 355.1/20973—dc23 LC record
available at http://lccn.loc.gov/2016003349

♾™ The paper used in this publication meets the minimum requirements
of American National Standard for Information Sciences—Permanence
of Paper for Printed Library Materials, ANSI/NISO Z39.48-1992.

Printed in the United States of America

Dedications

As a child I couldn't understand why my father wouldn't take us to see the fireworks. I really couldn't understand what self-medication looked like because I didn't have anything else to compare it to. We weren't allowed to talk about certain things in my household. There were no labels for what we know today as Post Traumatic Stress Disorder (PTSD). It starts with deployments and separations in many cases.

"That Others May Live"

For my dad, Captain E. Roy Moore, USMC, CallSign "PlayBoy 13," the Mustang who participated as the first A-1 Pilot on the scene in the daring search, extraction, and rescue of wounded fellow pilot and Marine officer Capt. Gary Bain USMC (Ret.) on May 11, 1969. It was not until I was in my forties that I learned of one of my father's brave acts of heroism in the line of duty. I understand that he nearly or did exhaust the fuel in his jet, as well as his ordnance, protecting Captain Bain, who was severely injured in the crash when shot down in hostile territory. I'm told that he would not leave despite being called back; while protecting and providing cover for Capt. Bain. He chose to stay despite the risk to himself and his aircraft, and despite the fact that the inbound rescue party was being recalled due to heavy fire and weather. I'm grateful for his bravery as well as that of the equally courageous pilot of the refueling jet, who risked his life and his aircraft to come in from the ocean to refuel my father's jet so that he could continue to provide cover fire and a deterrent presence from surrounding enemy fire for Capt. Bain until he could be reached for extraction by the Jolly Greens. Sometimes the real heroes never talk of what they've endured, or decades later still endure; and we have to acknowledge how proud we are of their selfless acts of service and valor for our country as well as for their fellow servicemen and women and provide them the support they need when they come home. Stories like these need to be told and shared, but in the case of many of these individuals, their time in war affected them so deeply they could not, even if they relive some part of it every single day decades later. If you'd like to know more about the rescue mission, Capt. Bain tells some of the incredible story

of his survival in the face of certain captivity or death here: http://www
.videoexplorers.com/2nd_ejection.htm.

Thank you, Roy Moore, for having Savannah's and my six; my contribution to this manuscript is dedicated to your service, your bravery, and your sacrifices.

Don Philpott dedicates this book to Mary Osterman Mai, who passed away on October 13, 2015, three days after her thirty-fifth birthday. Mary, daughter of Jenny and Bob Osterman, was a disabled veteran having served two tours of duty in Iraq. We owe her and her fellow warriors so much.

Contents

Acknowledgments

Many thanks to all of those who contributed their trust, confidence, and experience on—but mostly off—the record; with special acknowledgement to Michelle "Mo" Barrett and Jennifer Crossman; Dr. Barbara Van Dahlen, Give an Hour foundation; the NCSU MCF Brothers, Callsign "Draino" D.T., L.E., M.C., R.B., and C.B.; and L. Mazucca.

Introduction

Since September 11, 2001, more than 2 million service members have deployed to Iraq or Afghanistan. Many have been separated from their families for extended periods. Only recently have we started to fully appreciate the extent of the mental and physical strains that these separations and deployments impose on both the service members and their families and friends.

Any separation from loved ones is an emotionally difficult time for all concerned, especially when children are involved—but separation is now a modern day military reality. Homesteading—where a military family stays in place for an extended period of time—is a thing of the past. The average Permanent Change of Station (PCS) is three years in duration, meaning career military can expect to be in a near-constant state of transition.

As a result, military families must learn to adapt to long-distance relationships as well as how to adjust and positively cope with separations for various training deployments and real-life exercises. On the positive side, there is a lot of help available. The military is a huge family with scores of support groups, both official and unofficial, to help families prepare for separation and the stresses associated with the long absences. More importantly, help is usually available if needed, for when the service member returns home after the separation. Even under the best circumstances, if the separation has been a long one, reintegration into full family life can be very difficult for all concerned.

The duration and the frequency of deployments in the last two decades has been unprecedented. Apart from the very real and complex issues of family relationships, there has been increased exposure to battlefield injury and combat stress. There has been a growing number of service members with post-traumatic stress disorder (PTSD) and traumatic brain injury (TBI).

The Medical Surveillance Report found that almost 10 percent of service members interviewed between 90–180 days after returning from deployment self-reported PTSD symptoms and 27 percent reported symptoms of depression. Additionally, more than 19 percent of service members returning from combat reported potentially experiencing TBI during deployment.

Deployment does not just impact the service member. Military families are not immune to the stresses of deployment. There is a growing body of research on the impact of prolonged deployment and trauma-related stress on military families, particularly spouses and children. There are approximately 700,000 military spouses and an additional 400,000 spouses of Reserve members within the United States Armed Forces. More than 700,000 children have experienced one or more parental deployments.

The cumulative impact of multiple deployments is associated with more emotional difficulties among military children and more mental health diagnoses among spouses. Reducing these negative effects requires a robust psychological health plan, including better data collection, reducing stigma-related barriers, and stronger involvement from the chain of command.

While many military families are thriving, common stressors can further erode their resilience. However, many of these stressful situations are preventable. The compounding effects of deployments, occasional financial stress (including housing and home ownership), substance abuse, and incarceration have caused excessive stress for certain military families. For instance, in surveys conducted by the Department of Defense (DoD), military families have listed personal financial management as number two in their list of biggest sources of stress.

Furthermore, homelessness and home foreclosure can be realities in some veteran families, although this is not widespread. In the direst situations, families must cope with incarceration. According to the Department of Justice's (DOJ) most recent survey of incarcerated veterans, it was found that an estimated 60 percent of the 140,000 veterans in federal and state prisons were struggling with substance use disorders, while approximately 25 percent reported being under the influence of drugs at the time of their offense. Self-medication is frequently a symptom of the pain of stress-related experiences in veterans who, candidly, may not be receiving proper care and attention from the system designed and funded to support them. In some cases, the mental health of the veteran has deteriorated to the extent that veterans can become unable to "raise their hand" to the medical or military community in terms of asking for help and/or struggling to be their own advocates in a system that is extremely difficult to navigate. They can become withdrawn and isolated at the very times it's most important to keep reaching out and seeking help, and being consistent in terms of finding the right mental health care choices that fit their individual needs. Unfortunately, drug-related crimes and incarceration are an output of failures to identify, intervene, and continually support our veterans who may be silently struggling and self-medicating.

Coping with the effects of separation and deployment and the many issues arising from them requires a comprehensive plan and a network of skilled professionals and facilities to support it. This book looks at the types of separations a serving member can face and the tactics needed to successfully prepare for them so that family relationships remain as strong and vibrant as before, during, and following these extended absences. It is clear, however, that much more is needed. In particular, we must call out the extreme, potentially negative long-term effects that correlate to the stressors of deployments, which are often left unrecognized and untreated for extended periods of time. It is our intention that our readers will be informed and subsequently motivated to be more prepared. It is our intention to empower our readers to become able to recognize and identify the types of positive mental health approaches and services that are available and to seek them at the first signs of trouble. Furthermore, it is our intention to encourage our readers to seek alternatives if something isn't working well, particularly as we share the benefit of the communicated experiences from servicemen and women, and our veterans; many of whom did not meet with success through "standard" protocols for mental health care.

In the course of writing this book—between April and September 2015—a number of interviews were conducted with military couples and families who had experienced long-term separations and deployments. Those interviewed represented serving members of different ranks and multiple services. In many cases the subjects asked not to be identified and that request has been respected.

After completing the interviews Janelle wrote, "It's been the real deal interviewing multi-ethnicity couples and families, LBGT spouses, families with kids, long-term married couples who survived full careers—not just military but those in federal service on the civilian side with the same challenges. Several things astounded me: the humility of our servicemen and women who would only talk off the record with no attribution, and the horror stories of how the system has failed them in terms of mental health services beyond a 'check in the box process.' I had a wonderful interview with Dr. Van Dahlen of Give an Hour foundation this week, and the work she is doing with the highest levels of rank to devote time to awareness is so worthy and so impressive. I am truly in awe of the sacrifices, wisdom, and contributions that have gone into this process."

Of the couples interviewed, three were long-term marriages and one couple was comprised of a military service person, divorced, and his girlfriend, who had previously been a military wife—the latter couple had also been through years of a long-distance military relationship together due to his duty station assignment being nearly six hours away from her residence. Though the latter couple is not remarried, they are domestic partners and cohabitating, raising a blended family that includes a special needs child of an active-duty former spouse.

In addition, "conversations" rather than formal interviews were held with several enlisted, retired, current, and prior active duty military members and some spouses who offered the insights that they had gained from their separation experiences. Their comments are quoted throughout this book and many of their tips have been incorporated into the manuscript. At other times the authors have interviewed many other military couples about a wide range of military life issues and these attributed interviews are also included throughout.

Having received all this information, it is the authors' contention that none of the individuals talked to fully received the appropriate therapeutic help or the intervention required for the challenges caused by deployment or the aftereffects of them, other than procedural or temporary "stop gap" measures from the systems currently being operated by the military or government.

In many cases the right help was not available to the people when it was needed and in most cases self-help—ranging from religious or spiritual practice to alternative medicine—tended to be a better coping mechanism for many situational experiences. Physical exercise and movement was another common theme for coping.

While individuals were generally compliant in reporting to their commands or authorities, it appeared from the interviews that many institutional practices might cause more harm than good. Getting through deployment is one issue that has to be addressed, but there are also many other long-term consequences caused by and directly correlated to deployments such as impact on careers and ongoing family issues and relationships.

It is our earnest hope that this book provides the information needed for serving members, their families, and friends to cope with and successfully overcome the challenges of separation and deployment. Remember that you are not alone and that millions of others have gone through this as well. Reach out to these people. Find out what they did—what worked for them and what didn't. Get the help that you deserve.

Finally, we would urge the authorities to reflect on some of the issues raised by our interviewees. Health and social workers are constantly discovering new areas of concern that are a direct result of deployment and long-term separation. Institutional practices must be flexible enough to accommodate these new concerns and help our serving members and their families tackle them.

Chapter One

Types of Separations and Deployments

There are many types of separation and deployment, and scores of factors involved in both of them. How serving members and their families respond will, to a great extent, depend on the nature of the separation—the duration, whether it is a safe or hostile environment, and so on. Other factors that come into play include the nature of the serving member's assignment, rank, and experience in the field. Every serving member is different and their reactions—and those of their families—will likely vary accordingly.

INTERVIEW SUMMARY: A BRIGADIER GENERAL

"There are many levels of deployment that can include being sent away from families. These can include being in another state, completely safe, working a desk, to being in a hostile environment in a setting where they can fire at you (and do) but you can't fire back (but want to), to 'Being in the shit.'

"The point is that what the Active Duty service person goes through and what the family will go through really depends on what type of separation it is, and for what reasons, and to address the material as such.

"Preparing for separation where a [certain type of] job assignment is away or abroad is very different than a separation with high risk and hostile forces. It is also different for enlisted ranks and officers, and different for various age groups and experience levels."

Stanley Kubrick's 1987 movie *Full Metal Jacket* is an extreme example of the some of the worst experiences of a war-time deployment. Starting from "boot camp," the viewer watches the psychological strains of an indoctrination of draftees. They are being "broken down" to be rebuilt as "killing machines," and the viewer sees one recruit who experiences a full psychological "break" and the devastation resulting from it.

Another more recent film, *American Sniper* (2014), directed by Clint Eastwood, tells the story of U.S. Navy Seal Chris Kyle and the toll his deployments took on him and his family, and ultimately what the deployment and wartime experience did to other veterans, including the one who took Chris Kyle's life. While these are examples of the entertainment industry's version of stories of war, they are also stories about the psychological impacts of service and deployment in extreme situations and can be used as opportunities to call attention to the ongoing need for readiness and proactive mental health services rather than ad hoc services that are generally voluntary after the fact.

TRAINING

From the day you enter the military, you are going to be separated from your family because you will be heading for boot camp, Officer Candidates Schools (OCS), or Career Schools—for many people their first real experience of being away from home. In this chapter we will identify the various types of initial activities that involve separations, and provide more information about each by branch of service.

Boot Camps, Officer Candidates Schools, or Career Schools:

1. Basic or OCS
2. Schools at the early part of the military career

Boot Camp

Recruit training, more commonly known as Basic Training and colloquially called "boot camp," is the initial indoctrination and instruction given to new military personnel, enlisted and officer. After completion of Basic Training, new recruits undergo Advanced Individual Training (AIT), where they learn the skills needed for their military jobs. Officer trainees undergo more detailed programs that may either precede or follow the common recruit training in an officer training academy (which may also offer a civilian degree program simultaneously) or in special classes at a civilian university. During recruit training, drill instructors do everything possible to push a recruit to his or her physical and mental limits.

Recruit training is oriented to the particular service. Army and marine recruits are nearly always trained in basic marksmanship with individually assigned weapons, field maintenance of weapons, physical fitness training, first aid, and basic survival techniques. Navy and coast guard training usually focuses on water survival training, physical fitness, basic seamanship, and such skills as shipboard firefighting, basic engineering, and signals. Air force training usually includes physical fitness training, military and classroom instructions, and field training in basic marksmanship and first aid. In all training, standard uniforms are issued and recruits typically have their hair cut or shaved in order to meet grooming standards and homogenize their appearances. Recruits are generally given a service number. Recruit training must merge divergent trainees, often from different levels of culture and society, into a useful team.

Recruits are typically instructed in "drill": to stand, march, and respond to orders. Historically, drills are derived from eighteenth-century military tactics wherein soldiers in a fire line performed precise and coordinated movements to load and fire muskets. Although these particular tactics are now mostly obsolete, drilling trains the recruit to act unhesitatingly in the face of real combat situations. Modern militaries have learned that a service member often must make critical decisions on behalf of his team and nation.

Drill also serves a role in leadership training. Combat situations include not only commands to engage and put one's life in danger, but also commands to disengage when military necessity so demands. Drill is essential for military function because without the ideally instantaneous response to command that drill conditions, a military unit would likely disintegrate under the stress of combat.

Some aspects of basic training are psychological: instructors reason that recruits who cannot reliably follow orders and instructions in routine matters will likely be unreliable in a combat situation wherein they may experience a strong urge to disobey orders or flee and thereby jeopardize themselves, their comrades, and the mission. Volunteers in a combat unit will experience a unique level of "agreement" among participants, termed unit cohesion, that cannot be equaled in any other human organization because each team member's life may depend on the actions of the recruit to their right or left. Special forces and commando units fully develop this unit cohesion.

In the United States, recruit training in the U.S. Army is called *Basic Combat Training* (BCT); U.S. Army Infantry undergoes OSUT (One Station Unit Training) which involves BCT, Infantry Advanced Individual Training, and Specialized Infantry Training (such as Bradley, or Mortar School) all in one. In the U.S. Air Force it is called Basic Military Training or "BMT." In the U.S. Navy and U.S. Marine Corps it is called Recruit Training, and in the U.S. Coast Guard, it is called "Basic Training."

Some services present a badge or other award to denote completion of recruit training. The United States Army typically issues the Army Service Ribbon (issued after completion of Advanced Individual Training), and the United States Air Force presents the Air Force Training Ribbon and the Airman's Coin. The United States Marine Corps issue the Eagle, Globe, and Anchor once initial training is complete to signify that the recruits are now Marines. The United States Navy replaces the "RECRUIT" ball cap the recruits have worn throughout training with the "NAVY" ball cap upon successful completion of "Battle Stations." The United States Coast Guard's basic training graduates place a Coast Guard Medallion on their ball cap.

For honor graduates of basic training, both the U.S. Air Force and Coast Guard present a Basic Training Honor Graduate Ribbon. The Navy and Marine Corps often meritoriously advance the top graduates of each division one pay grade (up to a maximum of E-3).

U.S. Army

In the U.S. Army, recruits are sent to Basic Training in a location chosen by the Military Occupational Specialty, or MOS, which is selected upon enlistment.

Basic training is divided into two parts, which commonly take place at two different locations, depending on the chosen MOS: Basic Combat Training, or BCT, is a ten-week training period. Advanced Individual

Training, or AIT, is where new soldiers receive specific training in their chosen MOS. The length of AIT training varies depending on the MOS and can last anywhere from six weeks to one year.

Several MOSs combine both basic training and AIT in a back-to-back combined course called One Station Unit Training (OSUT), which can last up to twenty-two weeks.

The U.S. Army has four sites for BCT: Fort Benning in Columbus, Georgia; Fort Jackson in Columbia, South Carolina; Fort Leonard Wood in St. Robert, Missouri; and Fort Sill in Lawton, Oklahoma.

U.S. Marine Corps

United States Marine Corps Recruit Depots are located at Marine Corps Recruit Depot Parris Island, South Carolina, and Marine Corps Recruit Depot San Diego, California. All female enlisted Marines go to Parris Island. Men go to either, depending on whether they were recruited east or west of the Mississippi River. Marine Corps boot camp is considered to be the longest and arguably the most demanding basic training regimen in the U.S. Armed Forces.

Marine Corps Recruit Training is divided up into three 4-week phases and further broken down into individual training days. While there are sixty-nine individual training days, recruits also go through pre- and post-training processing where recruits are afforded relatively little freedom in comparison to recruits of other branches. Phase 1 mainly consists of learning recruit life protocol, physical training, MCMAP training, academic classes, initial drill, a series inspection, and the confidence course. West Coast recruits also do swim qualification during this phase.

Phase 2 is completely in the field at Camp Pendleton for West Coast recruits, with the first two weeks being spent on marksmanship training and qualification with the M16A4 service rifle, and the last week in the field is devoted to learning skills such as fire-team formations, land navigation, and hikes. For East Coast recruits, phase 2 is swim qualification, rifle qualification, and Team Week, a week of maintenance duties for the island as a show of how to perform base support tasks while still keeping military bearing and attention to detail. Phase 3 brings the San Diego recruits back to the recruit depot where they finish up with final drill, final inspection, more physical training (PT) and confidence courses, and graduation. During the third phase, West Coast recruits also go back into the field one last time to do the Crucible event. Parris Island recruits finish with field training, final drill and inspection, the Crucible, and graduation. Note that recruits going to either depot receive exactly the same training, if in a different order.

Recruit training for Marines is a thirteen-week-long program, and is followed by ITB (Infantry Training Battalion) or MCT (Marine Combat Training) at SOI (School of Infantry) military occupational specialties (MOS) located at Camp Lejeune in Jacksonville, North Carolina (for Parris Island graduates) and Camp Pendleton in San Diego, California (for San Diego graduates). Marines with an infantry MOS (03XX) receive fifty-nine days of training at ITB (Infantry Training Battalion) and then are assigned to a unit, while Marines of other specialties receive twenty-eight days of infantry training at MCTB (Marine Combat Training Battalion) before proceeding to their MOS-specific school.

U.S. Navy

The U.S. Navy currently operates boot camp at Recruit Training Command Great Lakes, located at Naval Station Great Lakes, near North Chicago, Illinois. Instead of having drill sergeants or drill instructors like other branches of the U.S. Armed Forces, the U.S. Navy has RDCs (Recruit Division Commanders) that are assigned to each division. Training lasts approximately eight weeks (although some recruits will spend as many as nine weeks in training due to the somewhat complicated processing cycle). Days are counted by a system that lists the week and day that they are on, for example 7-3 for week 7, day 3. The first approximate week is counted P-1, P-2, and so on, which denotes that it is a processing day and does not count as part of their eight-week training period.

Recruits are instructed on military drill, basic seamanship, basic shipboard damage control, firefighting, familiarization with the M9 pistol and Mossberg 500 shotgun (the Navy no longer gives instruction on the M-16 in boot camp), pass the confidence chamber (tear-gas-filled chamber), PT, and the basic essentials on Navy life. Recruits also attend many classes throughout boot camp on subjects such as Equal Opportunity, Sexual Assault Victim Intervention, Uniform Code of Military Justice, recognition of naval aircraft and vessels, and more. In order for recruits to pass boot camp, they will be physically and mentally tested on a twelve-hour exercise called Battle Stations which consists of twelve different scenarios consisting of firefighting, first aid knowledge, survival at sea, mass casualties, shipboard flood control, bomb detection and many other skills that they have been learning in the past seven weeks.

After completion of boot camp, freshly minted sailors are sent either to various "A" schools located across the United States, where they begin training to receive their ratings (jobs) or to apprenticeship training, where they then enter the fleet without a designation.

The Navy formerly operated Recruit Training Centers in San Diego, California; Orlando, Florida; Meridian, Mississippi; and Port Deposit (Bainbridge), Maryland. From 1942 to 1946 the Navy had two additional training sites: Naval Training Station (USNTS Sampson; in 1950 renamed Sampson Air Force Base) near Seneca Lake, New York, which trained over 400,000 recruits, as well as Farragut Naval Training Station in Bayview, Idaho.

U.S. Air Force

The U.S. Air Force's Basic Military Training (BMT) is eight and a half weeks long, as they do not count the first week ("Week 0"). BMT is sixty-three calendar days long. It is conducted at Lackland AFB in San Antonio, Texas. Formerly, trainees were referred to as "Airman" from day one of BMT. This has been changed; now, personnel are referred to as Trainees until the Airman's Coin Ceremony in the eighth week of training, when they receive their Airman's Coin.

Trainees receive military instruction (including the Air Force core values, flight and individual drill, and living area inspections), academic classes (covering topics such as Air Force history, dress and appearance, military customs and courtesies, ethics, security, and alcohol/drug abuse prevention and treatment), and field training (including protection against biological and chemical attack, basic marksmanship on the M-16 rifle as well as first aid). Following BMT, Airmen go to a technical school (or "tech school") where they learn the specifics of their Air Force Specialty Code (AFSC), which is similar to the MOS (Military Occupational Specialty) in the Army and Marines, the Navy's NEC (Naval Enlisted Classification) code, or the Coast Guard's ratings.

All non-prior-service enlistees are required to complete BMT, including those enlisting in the Air National Guard and Air Force Reserve Command. Reserve component enlistees receive the same training as their active-duty counterparts. Credit can be given on a case-by-case basis for enlistees with college credit. Eagle Scouts and service in the Civil Air Patrol qualify for promotion to E-2 (Airman) or E-3 (Airman First Class) upon graduation from BMT. The stripes are not worn until graduation, though trainees are paid at the higher pay grade.

Lackland AFB has been associated with BMT for almost the Air Force's entire history. From 1950 to 1956, 300,000 airmen received BMT at Sampson Air Force Base in New York. In 1951, Parks Air Force Base in Dublin, California, became a BMT center, with training beginning in March 1952. BMT at Parks AFB ceased later in the decade and the installation was transferred to the U.S. Army in 1959. For a brief time between 1966 and 1968, the Air Force operated a second BMT at Amarillo AFB, in Amarillo, Texas.

Unlike the Army and Navy, but like the Marine Corps (throughout boot camp) and Coast Guard (during the first section of boot camp), trainees are required to refer to all Airmen, enlisted and NCOs (noncommissioned officers), as well as commissioned and warrant officers, as "sir" or "ma'am." Trainees are required to preface speaking to Military Training Instructors with their "reporting statement": "Sir/Ma'am, Trainee (the recruit's surname) reports as ordered." or "Sir/Ma'am, Trainee (the recruit's surname) reports," depending on who initiates the conversation.

An additional two weeks of BMT was added to the program on November 1, 2008, extending the duration of BMT from six-and-a-half weeks to eight-and-a-half weeks. BMT has been tailored to incorporate some of the additional warfighting skills to coincide with increased Air Expeditionary Force (AEF) rotations, and more frequent support of its sister services during those rotations.

U.S. Coast Guard

Recruit training for the U.S. Coast Guard is held at the Coast Guard Training Center Cape May in Cape May, New Jersey. The training lasts eight weeks. The U.S. Coast Guard is unique in that it fires the SIG Sauer P229R pistol during the training. The training also covers basic seamanship, drill, military bearing, and firefighting. The Coast Guard base on

Government Island (now known as Coast Guard Island) Alameda, California, was also used as a second major recruit training center until it was closed in 1982 and converted into the base for the USCG Pacific Area Command, the Eleventh Coast Guard District, the Marine Safety Office San Francisco Bay, the USCG Maintenance and Logistics Command Pacific and the Integrated Support Command Center–Alameda.

Although the Coast Guard is a part of the Department of Homeland Security, rather than the Department of Defense, it is by law and tradition a branch of the United States Armed Forces. As with all military members, Coast Guard personnel are subject to the Uniform Code of Military Justice (UCMJ). Due to the Coast Guard's unique mission set—including CONUS and OCONUS defense operations, search and rescue, and maritime law enforcement—there are added requirements to maintain high physical fitness standards and intense military bearing. Due to its extremely unique, diverse, and difficult mission, the U.S. Coast Guard is the most selective in recruiting and training standards. (As an example, the Coast Guard Academy is the only service academy that uses competitive admissions for prospective officer candidates.)

During their time at Cape May, recruits are subjected to the usual "boot camp" atmosphere of direct instruction and intense motivation. The recruits are designated as Seaman Recruits (SR; E-1) and, uniquely to the Coast Guard among the services, advanced to the rank of Seaman Apprentice/Airman Apprentice/Fireman Apprentice (SA/AA/FA; E-2) upon graduation. They must adhere to strict rules such as hygiene and uniform regulations and obey all lawful orders. Coast Guard drill instructors are called "company commanders" and hold a rank ranging from Petty Officer 2nd Class (E-5) up to Senior Chief Petty Officer (E-8). Coast Guard companies have approximately two or three company commanders and anywhere from twenty to over one hundred recruits.

After completing boot camp, recruits can select their rate and then attend an "A" school. Not all graduates go straight to "A" school; many spend time in the fleet as "non-rates." "A" school is a long-term technical school providing specific instruction about a rate. The "A" schools last two to six months and usually occur at TRACEN Yorktown, Yorktown, Virginia, or TRACEN Petaluma, Petaluma, California. Some rates have an available apprenticeship training option instead of attending an "A" school; this is known as "striking."

Advanced Individual Training, or AIT, is where new soldiers receive specific training in their chosen MOS. The length of AIT training varies depending on the MOS and can last anywhere from three weeks to nearly two years. The current longest AIT training lasts eighty-four weeks (one year and eight months).

Just like in BCT, AIT progressively allows trainees more privileges and independence. Trainees begin AIT in Phase IV. After a varying length of time and satisfactory performance, trainees are awarded Phase V. Phase V often includes the privilege of applying for off-post passes or use of a cell phone. Phase V+ is awarded after a similar length of time and continued good conduct. Phase V+ trainees may walk about the base without having a battle buddy present, be able to drink alcohol on weekends (provided one is of legal drinking age), and even stay off-post overnight on weekends. These privileges vary.

Federal Service Academies

The colleges operated by the U.S. Federal Government are referred to as the Federal Service Academies, and they are as follows:

- United States Air Force Academy, Colorado Springs, Colorado
- United States Coast Guard Academy, New London, Connecticut
- United States Merchant Marine Academy, Kings Point, New York
- United States Military Academy, West Point, New York
- United States Naval Academy, Annapolis, Maryland
- Uniformed Services University of the Health Sciences, Bethesda, Maryland

Senior and Junior Military Colleges

There is one all-military state-sponsored military academy: the Virginia Military Institute (VMI), Lexington, Virginia.

In addition, there are five institutions that were military colleges at the time of their founding and still maintain both a corps of cadets and a civilian student body. Many of these institutions also offer online degree programs:

- University of North Georgia, Dahlonega, Georgia—Formed by a 2013 merger with Gainesville State College, its main predecessor institution, last known as North Georgia College and State University, was chartered as a military college. However, when NGCSU was founded in 1873 as North Georgia Agricultural College, it had both a corps and a civilian student body, and was also the state's first coeducational college.
- Norwich University Corps of Cadets, Norwich University, Northfield, Vermont
- Texas A&M Corps of Cadets, Texas A&M University, College Station, Texas
- The Citadel, The Military College of South Carolina, Charleston, South Carolina
- Virginia Tech Corps of Cadets, Virginia Polytechnic Institute and State University, Blacksburg, Virginia

Along with VMI, these institutions are known as the Senior Military Colleges of the U.S.

Today five institutions are considered Military Junior Colleges (MJC). These five military schools participate in the Army's two-year Early Commissioning Program, an Army ROTC program where qualified students can earn a commission as a second lieutenant after only two years of college. The five Military Junior Colleges are listed below:

- Georgia Military College, Milledgeville, Georgia
- Marion Military Institute, Marion, Alabama
- New Mexico Military Institute, Roswell, New Mexico
- Valley Forge Military Academy and College, Wayne, Pennsylvania
- Wentworth Military Academy and College, Lexington, Missouri

Staff colleges (also **command and staff colleges** and **war colleges**) train military officers in the administrative, staff, and policy aspects of their profession. It is usual for such training to occur at several levels in a career. For example, an officer may be sent to various staff courses: as a captain they may be sent to a single service command and staff school to prepare for company command and equivalent staff posts; as a major to a single or joint service college to prepare for battalion command and equivalent staff posts; and as a colonel or brigadier to a higher staff college to prepare for brigade and division command and equivalent postings.

Air Force

- Air University, HQ at Maxwell AFB, Alabama
  - Air Command and Staff College
  - Air War College
  - Air Force Institute of Technology (Wright-Patterson AFB, Ohio)

Army

- Command and General Staff College in Fort Leavenworth, Kansas
- School of Advanced Military Studies
- U.S. Army War College (Carlisle, Pennsylvania)
- U.S. Army Warrant Officer Career College

Navy

- Naval War College in Newport, Rhode Island
  - College of Naval Command and Staff
  - College of Naval Warfare
- Naval Postgraduate School (Monterey, California)

Marines

- Marine Corps University
  - Marine Corps War College
  - Marine Corps Command and Staff College
  - School of Advanced Warfighting
  - Expeditionary Warfare School

Joint

- Defense Acquisition University—five campuses—HQ at Fort Belvoir, Virginia
- National Defense University in Washington, D.C.

o National War College
o Industrial College of the Armed Forces
o Joint Forces Staff College in Norfolk, Virginia

Attendance at Service Schools

There are strict rules governing attendance at service schools with regulations covering all aspects of the stay. As an example, see the following extract from the Army Manual.

4–1. Applicability a. This chapter applies to— (1) Active Army enlisted Soldiers. (2) Army National Guard of the United States and USAR Soldiers only when they are serving on AD or ADT to attend Service school. b. This chapter does not apply to combat-disabled Soldiers who have reenlisted under AR 601–280 or have continued on AD under AR 635–40. They will be processed under AR 635–40.

4–2. Application submission a. Applications for attendance at Service schools will be submitted to the appropriate approval authority listed in table 4–2. b. Soldiers serving on a stabilized tour must serve at least 56 of that tour prior to submitting an application for attendance at a Service school. c. Soldiers assigned OCONUS may submit an application for attendance at a Service school not less than 5 months or more than 12 months before DEROS.

4–3. Selection criteria a. Soldiers must meet the prerequisites (see AR 350–1 and ATRRS course catalog) and MOS requirements (see DA Pam 611–21) to attend a Service school. However, as an exception, Soldiers who possess other significant civilian acquired skills or qualifications may be accepted for entry in the specific course for which applying. If it is later determined that enlistees are qualified for more advanced courses, they must waive their enlistment commitments in favor of the alternate course. Refer to AR 601–210, paragraph 8–3 for processing procedures. b. Selection criteria for attendance at Navy and Air Force schools or for courses not listed in ATRRS course catalog will be announced by the HRC. c. Selection of Soldiers will be based on the best-qualified method. Selection of the best-qualified Soldiers will be based on the requirement for technically trained personnel and the projected assignment for the Soldier. When excessive numbers of Soldiers apply for the same course or a limited number of quotas are available, the HRC will select the best-qualified personnel. Major CDRs will not establish additional selection criteria. d. Soldiers selected to attend

Service schools must be able to complete the SRRs in paragraph 4–6. e. Normally, Soldiers will be selected for schooling in the same CMF in which classified. A Soldier will not be selected for a course in the same career group that trains at a skill level lower than that for which the Soldier presently qualifies. School training should be in progressively higher skill levels to promote career progression of the Soldier. The following grade standards apply in selecting Soldiers for MOS training: (1) Specialist E4–level courses. (a) Privates enlisted twos and PFCs may be selected for E4–level courses without regard to grade authorization. (b) Only SPCs in pay grades authorized in the MOS (including skill level) that the course trains for may be selected. (2) Noncommissioned officer–level courses. Only Soldiers in the grade of E4 or higher will be selected for an NCO–level course. To qualify for selection, Soldiers must be in a grade equal to or lower than the highest grade authorized for the school-trained MOS (including skill level). f. Soldiers will not be selected for successive attendance at courses in different entry groups unless training in one course is a prerequisite for the other or training is directed by HRC. g. Soldiers who have successfully completed a Service school course will not be selected again for the same or an equivalent course unless such training is required to maintain proficiency in the MOS. Soldiers will not be selected to attend a course if, because of prior training or experience, they already possess the knowledge and skills that would be obtained through successful completion of the course. Requests for exception must clearly explain why school training is necessary if the Soldier— (1) Holds, as primary, the MOS containing the skills taught in the course. It must be assumed that, if pertinent regulations have been followed, a Soldier who has been awarded a PMOS is fully qualified in that MOS. (2) Does not hold the MOS for which the course trains but has performed duty in that MOS and is qualified for award of the MOS. (Unless otherwise prohibited by this regulation, a Soldier who has performed in an MOS for an extended period of time should be considered qualified and awarded the MOS.) Those MOSs that require formal training are identified in DA Pam 611–21. (3) Is drawing SDAP and holds the MOS as a verified MOS. h. Except as authorized in paragraph e, above, Soldiers who have completed a school course will not be selected again for school until they have served in their MOS for the time required by the SRR. i. Commanders who are OCONUS will select Soldiers to attend Army Service schools during the term of service in their command only when qualified Soldiers are not available through normal replacement channels. Selectees will attend the school in a TDY status. On completion of the course they will be returned to the OCONUS command. Temporary duty attendance at NCOES courses and return to the OCONUS command is authorized provided the Soldier will have at least 6 months remaining to serve in the OCONUS command after completing the course. j. Soldiers may be involuntarily selected for schooling for retraining in shortage MOSs or to further their career development. k. Soldiers who enlisted under the Stripes for Skills Program are ineligible to attend any MOS-producing school course until completion of 1 year of service in the accelerated grade awarded under the program. l. Soldiers who do not meet the body composition standards of AR 600–9 will not be authorized to attend professional military schools. Professional military schooling, as defined in AR 600–9, includes all individual training courses beyond IET. This IET includes entry-course nonprior Service personnel, BT, AIT, one station unit training (OSUT), or one station training level. m. The immediate CDR will ensure Soldiers have the security clearance required for— (1) The course of instruction. (2) Award of an MOS following the course if it differs from that required for attending the course. Before the Soldier departs for school, the immediate CDR will ensure that the Soldier has applied for a security clearance of the level required for award of the MOS.

4–4. Waivers Soldiers may apply for waiver of course prerequisites in technical MOS-producing courses if they have previous related training and have demonstrated that they are capable of completing the course. a. Waiver requests will be forwarded to the appropriate personnel proponent as defined in ATRRS course catalog. Application should include— (1) Appropriate justification. (2) All aptitude area scores. (3) The course prerequisite(s) to be waived. (4) Any outstanding facts to support the request. b. Granting waivers for prerequisites is authority for the Soldier to be enrolled in the course for which applying. c. Soldiers desiring to waive an enlistment commitment to attend a school course or to select an alternate course must sign the following statement: "I voluntarily waive enlistment choice made at the time of my enlistment in favor of attending (course number and title). I realize and fully understand that on school completion, I will be assigned according to the needs of the Army." d. Soldiers desiring to waive a reenlistment commitment should refer to AR 601–280, paragraph 4–4.

4–5. Administrative guidelines a. Soldiers ordered to Army Service schools from organizations in CONUS will take clothing and equipment required by AR 700–84. Special clothing required for the course (see ATRRS course catalog) will be furnished to Soldiers before they depart for school. Soldiers ordered to schools directly from an OCONUS command will be furnished required clothing and equipment that are available in the command. Items that are not available will be furnished to Soldiers on arrival at the school. b. Soldiers will be advised that Family member travel and shipment of household goods to schools at Government expense is not authorized under Joint Federal Travel Regulations (JFTR) unless the Soldier is being assigned PCS to a school or installation to attend one of the following: (1) A course of 20 weeks or more. (2) Two or more courses for a cumulative period of 20 weeks or more at any one duty station. c. Family members will not accompany Soldiers ordered to schools from OCONUS commands at Government expense when they are scheduled to return OCONUS, regardless of the length of the course. However, if Family members do accompany or join them at their own expense, Soldiers must be advised that they may encounter some of the following hardships: (1) On-post Family housing is not available. Students normally are not permitted to live off-post. (2) In many areas, housing near schools or installations is unavailable or extremely costly. In some areas, if it is available, it is substandard. (3) Rigid training schedules often preclude regular visits away from school or installation.

(4) Soldiers in CONUS who are entitled to Family member travel and shipment of household goods and who are selected for a course or courses of less than 20 weeks will sign the following statement, which will be filed per AR 600–8–104. "I have been advised of the provisions of JFTR, which restrict Family member travel and movement of household goods to schools at Government expense when scheduled course is less than 20 weeks in duration. I understand that if my Family members accompany me to the school, it will be at my own expense. I also understand that PCS orders for assignment on completion of course, when applicable, will authorize Family member travel and movement of household goods only from the station at which I attended school to the new PCS assignment. I further understand that if my PCS orders are canceled and I am returned to my old permanent station, I am not entitled to a dislocation allowance. Failure to complete the course satisfactorily will result in cancellation of the PCS portion of the orders." d. Guidelines for assignment or attachment of Soldiers selected to attend Service schools will be specified in their orders. e. Any leave en route to the school or on completion of the course will be granted under AR 600–8–10.

4–6. Service-remaining requirements a. Unless the HRC directs otherwise, in-Service Soldiers must meet the SRRs appropriate for the selected courses. This applies to Soldiers who attend Service schools in a PCS, TDY pending further orders, TDY en route, or TDY and return status. It also applies to those who attend functional courses, seminars, and so forth, at civilian institutions (on a contract or reimbursable basis) for training not available in the Service school system and where no other established SRR exists. Soldiers who do not meet the SRR must be processed in accordance with AR 601–280, paragraph 4–6, before they comply with orders directing movement to the school. b. Service-remaining obligations for Soldiers who recycle for academic or disciplinary reasons, or who voluntarily recycle, will be computed from new course completion date. Extension of enlistment will be accomplished under AR 601–280 prior to restart of training. c. Service-remaining requirements for Soldiers who complete training but do not possess required security clearance for award of CMF 18 will be computed from the date MOS is awarded. This does not apply if delay in granting of required security clearance can be attributed to processing delays. d. The amount of SRRs will not be changed for students who meet prerequisites at the beginning of a course and are recycled through no fault of their own. Approval must be obtained from the HRC (AHRC–EPF–R) for reclassified Soldiers (or Soldiers who have reenlisted for retraining) prior to placement in the next available course. Enlistment commitments will be honored without any additional SRRs. e. Soldiers selected for additional schooling under special training programs before completing BT or AIT must meet the service-remaining obligation prescribed by the regulation for that program. f. The required amount of the SRR will be computed from the completion date of the course. When Soldiers are selected to attend two or more successive courses, the combined course lengths will be added to obtain the total SRR. This combined amount will not exceed 36 months. Service-remaining requirements will be based on the course length shown in table 4–1, unless otherwise stated. Soldiers eligible to, but refusing to take action to satisfy the SRRs must be processed in accordance with AR 601–280, paragraphs 4–11 and 4–12. g. Soldiers attending the following NCOES courses will incur a 6–month service-remaining obligation upon graduation: (1) Advanced Leaders Course. (2) Senior Leaders Course (SLC). h. Soldiers attending the following courses will incur a 24–month service-remaining obligation upon graduation: (1) The U.S. Army Sergeants Major Course (USASMC). (2) Training associated with entry into and award of a CMF 18 MOS. Soldier must be able to serve 24 months AD in a CMF 18 MOS duty position upon completion of MOS training (including completion of any required language/ specialized skill training). (3) Training associated with entry into and award of a CMF 37 MOS. Soldier must be able to serve 24 months AD in a CMF MOS duty position upon completion of MOS training (including completion of any required language/ specialized skill training). i. Soldiers attending the following courses will incur a 36–month service-remaining obligation: (1) Middle Enlisted Cryptologic Career Advancement Program. (2) Military Electronic Intelligence Signals Analyst Program. (3) Military

Intern Signal Intelligence Analyst Program. (4) Training associated with MOS 15R, 15S, 15T, 15J, or 15X (excluding ASI Q2 training). (5) Training associated with MOS 25B (Information Systems Operation Analyst). (6) Training associated with MOS 89D (EOD). (7) Apprentice Special Agent Course.

j. Soldiers attending the Battle Staff Course will incur a 12–month service-remaining obligation upon completion of training. k. Regular Army Soldiers who will become eligible to retire under 10 USC 3914 or 10 USC 3917, must agree to meet their SRR to attend the selected course. Soldiers will be required to sign a statement before movement to the school acknowledging that they have been informed that voluntary retirement will not be approved until the required service has been completed after either graduation or termination of class attendance (see AR 635–200, para 12–9c). l. Soldiers in the ARNGUS and USAR units on AD who are selected to attend Service schools must sign an agreement that they will remain on AD to complete the course although their units may be released from AD earlier. m. Soldiers scheduled for training as a result of participation in the BEAR must be extended for the number of months stipulated in AR 601–280, chapter 6, prior to departure for training.

4–7. School assignment and classification a. Soldiers' records will be evaluated upon arrival at school in a PCS status. Soldiers' qualifications will be evaluated to— (1) Ensure input of qualified personnel to school courses. Evaluation will include verifying Soldiers meet course SRRs prior to start of training. (2) Preclude unnecessary training of Soldiers already qualified in the skills and knowledge taught in the course. (a) Soldiers who meet course prerequisites or those for whom a waiver has been obtained will be entered in the selected course. (b) Soldiers may be assigned by the school commandant to a course other than that for which selected only after approval by HRC, (AHRC–EPF–R). A different assignment will be considered when a student fails to qualify for the selected course or is exceptionally qualified for a course other than the selected one, particularly a more advanced course. The HRC (AHRC–EPF–R) is the approval authority for requests to assign Soldiers to another course (see table 4–2). However, if the Soldier is attending school TDY, the CDR shown in the TDY orders must grant approval first. (c) Soldiers who, because of prior training or experience, possess some of the skills and knowledge of the course will be entered in the course. They will be given only the training needed to qualify for award of MOS, ASI, SQI, language identification code, or other qualification identifier. (d) Soldiers found to be fully qualified in all skills and knowledge in the selected course and who require no additional training will be classified into the appropriate MOS or awarded the ASI, SQI, language identification code, and reported for assignment. The HRC will be advised of these actions. b. If Soldiers are erroneously ordered to school or if a course has been relocated, Soldiers will be reassigned as appropriate. Travel will be chargeable to Military Personnel, Army Funds (see Defense Finance and Accounting Service (DFAS)–IN Regulation 37–1). c. In exceptional cases, to correct serious misclassification in original selection, a school commandant may recommend to the HRC that a Soldier be assigned to another school (course) that is better suited for the Soldier by qualification and interests. If the HRC approves, assignment will be chargeable to Military Personnel, Army Funds (see DFAS–IN Regulation 37–1). d. On successful completion of an MOS-producing course, graduates will be awarded the school-trained MOS. Reclassified Soldiers must possess an RCN to be awarded the new MOS.

Allowances and Benefits

Family Separation Allowance. Married members are entitled to a Family Separation Allowance when they are separated from their dependents due to military orders. The tax-free allowance begins after separation of thirty days. This means married people in basic training and technical school (if the technical school duration is less than twenty weeks) begin to receive this pay thirty days after going on active duty. Single personnel do not receive this allowance.

Job Training. If technical school, AIT, or A-school is twenty weeks or longer in duration (at a single location), one is entitled to move their dependents to their school location at government expense. They are then (usually thirty days after arrival) allowed to live with their dependents after duty hours. Single members, of course, cannot move their girl/boy-friends at government expense, nor will they be allowed to live off base (even at their own expense) at job training locations.

In such cases, if the military member elects not to move his or her dependents, the Family Separation Allowance stops, because the member is not being forced to be separated (the dependents are allowed to move at government expense, so if they don't move, that is the member's choice). Of course, if the dependents do join the member, Family Separation Allowance stops as well, as the member is no longer separated from his or her dependents due to military orders.

If the job training is less than twenty weeks, a married person can still elect to move his or her dependents (at his or her own expense) but would (usually) be allowed to live with them, off base (beginning thirty days after arrival), with the school commander's permission (as long as the student is doing okay in class, such permission is routinely granted). If the dependents do move to the member's school location, Family Separation Allowance stops.

OTHER TYPES OF SEPARATION

Temporary Duty Assignment (TDA)

A temporary duty assignment (TDA), also known as "temporary duty travel" (TDT), "temporary additional duty" (TAD) in the Navy and Marine Corps, or "temporary duty" (TDY) in the Army and Air Force, refers to a United States Government employee travel assignment at a location other than the employee's permanent duty station. This type of secondment is usually of relatively short duration, typically from two days to two months in length but it can be almost six months. Some government agencies including the Defense Department mandate they be less than six months in duration. Temporary duty assignments usually come with per diem pay, covering lodging, meals, and incidental expenses. Many nonmilitary employees value the per diem aspect of a TDA, since that money is guaranteed, even if they spend less than their allotted daily value. However, some agencies handle the lodging per diem separately from the meals and incidentals, and employees may not make money by staying at cheaper accommodations, or putting more than one person in a room. Typically, an employee may request a cash advance of 60 percent to 80 percent of the total value of the meals and incidental expenses before the TDA per diem takes place, in order to prevent the employee from having to use his or her own money, or putting money on a personal credit card. Government travel cards are also typically available, though these sometimes carry restrictions on the types of goods or services that can be purchased with them.

Some locations have furnished apartments for long-term stay. These apartments have fully equipped kitchens so TDA recipients have the option to cook rather than always eat out, and some may have free washing machines and clothes dryers.

Those agencies that do not mandate a six-month limit consider longer durations to be a Permanent Change of Station (PCS).

Permanent Change of Station (PCS)

In the United States Armed Forces, a Permanent Change of Station (PCS) is the official relocation of an active-duty military service member—along with any family members living with her or him—to a different duty location, such as a military base. A Permanent Change of Station applies until mooted by another PCS order, completion of active-duty service, or some other such preemptive event. This should not be confused with a Permanent Change of Assignment (PCA), which describes the reassignment of active-duty personnel to a new unit within the same military post.

Allowances and Associated Leave

Temporary Duty (TDY). Military members are allowed a permissive TDY for up to ten days in conjunction with a permanent change of station (PCS) move between and within the fifty states and District of Columbia. "Permissive TDY" means there is no transportation or per diem paid, but members are not charged for leave.

Military members may request (from their commander) this permissive TDY any time after they receive their written reassignment orders. However, because there is no travel entitlement, most military members elect to use this benefit, after signing out of their old base, but before signing into their new base. In other words, they plan to arrive at their new base ten days early, which then gives ten days for house-hunting, which is not charged as leave. The "house-hunting" entitlement only applies for members who will not be living in the barracks/dormitories after arrival at the new assignment.

Temporary Lodging Expense (TLE). TLE is designed to partially offset lodging and meal expenses when a member and/or dependents need to occupy temporary lodging in CONUS (Continental United States) in connection with a PCS. The member receives reimbursement (for member and family members) for temporary lodging and meal expenses, up to $180 per day.

If the member is moving from one CONUS base to another, he or she is authorized up to ten days TLE, either at the losing duty station or at the new duty station (or any combination, up to ten days total).

If the member is moving from CONUS to overseas, they can only receive up to five days TLE at the losing duty station. If the member is moving from overseas to CONUS, they can receive up to ten days TLE at the new CONUS duty station after arrival. TLE is not paid for lodging made during the actual travel days from one duty station to another (this is claimed as a "per diem"—see below); rather it is for temporary lodging (in the states) at the old duty station, before departure, or at the new duty station, after arrival. The legal authority for TLE is 37 USC 404a.

Temporary Lodging Allowance (TLA). TLE applies to CONUS, TLA covers overseas. Up to sixty days (can be extended) may be paid for temporary lodging expenses and meal expenses after a military member (and his or her family) arrive at a new overseas location, while awaiting housing. Up to ten days of TLA can be paid for temporary lodging expenses in the overseas location, prior to departure. The legal authority for TLA is 37 USC 405.

Dislocation Allowance (DLA). Military members may be entitled to a DLA when relocating their household due to a PCS. DLA is intended to partially reimburse relocation expenses not otherwise reimbursed. The legal authority for Dislocation Allowance is 37 USC 407.

Per Diem for PCS travel. Military members receive a "per diem" allowance, which is designed to partially reimburse for lodging and meal expenses when traveling from one duty station to another. When traveling by Privately Owned Conveyance (POC), military members are paid a flat rate of $85 per day for each day of authorized travel used. When the member travels by commercial means, they are paid the established per diem rate for the new Permanent Duty Station (PDS), or the rate for the delay point if the member stops overnight. Per Diem for dependents is three-fourths of the member's applicable rate for each dependent twelve years old or older and half of the member's rate for each dependent under twelve years. The legal authority for PCS Per Diem is 37 USC 404.

Travel by Privately Owned Conveyance (POC). When members elect to travel to their new duty station by POC (auto), they are entitled to receive a mileage allowance, in lieu of the cost of an airline ticket. The reimbursement rate depends on the number of authorized travelers in the vehicle. The legal authority for POC Travel is 37 USC 404(d).

Dependent travel within CONUS by other than POC. Within CONUS dependents may be authorized to travel by commercial means (air, rail, bus), unless they elect to travel by POC, from the old PDS to the new PDS. The military member can be reimbursed for this travel, up to what it would have cost the military to purchase an airline ticket. The legal authority for Commercial Travel of Dependents within CONUS is 37 USC 406(a).

Dependent travel outside CONUS. Dependents can travel to overseas assignment locations either via military aircraft or by commercial means. Warning: If one purchases their own commercial airline tickets for travel to an overseas assignment location, one may only be reimbursed if the aircraft is an American-Flag Carrier, if any AMCs (Air Mobility Commands) fly to that location.

The only time one can be reimbursed for flying on a commercial foreign carrier is if no AMC services that overseas location. The legal authority for dependent travel outside of the CONUS is 37 USC 404. If there are special medical considerations that require additional space or upgraded travel and necessitate that a family member cannot travel long distances by automobile, there are certain additional protocols that are driven by physician's recommendations that can be accommodated to ship an automobile and pay for alternate transportation.

Household Goods (HHG) transportation. Military members can ship household goods from their old duty station to their new duty station. Authorized up to 18,000 pounds, but varies by grade and whether or not the member is with or without dependents. In addition to allowing the military to arrange for movement of HHG, the member can elect to move it themselves, and receive reimbursement if the move is within CONUS. The legal authority for Household Goods Transportation is 37 USC 406. Military members facing a move may want to look into exceptions for weight allowances and restrictions, such as Professional Gear (ProGear), which is not included in the overall shipment calculations and can cover things specifically needed for military duty if labeled, weighed, and reported properly.

Damage claims. A member has two years from the date of HHG delivery to make a claim. Claims are processed through the Personal Property

Office responsible for the area where the HHG were delivered. Claims are limited to $40,000 depreciated value of the shipment regardless of weight. At his own expense, the member may purchase full replacement coverage. The additional cost is based on the weight of the HHG shipment.

Limited household goods transportation overseas. If the military member's orders state that government furnishings are provided at the overseas location, the member's Household Good Weight Shipping Allowance is limited to 2,500 pounds or 25 percent of HHG weight allowance, plus non-available items. Additional items (up to the weight allowance) are allowed to be placed in non-temporary storage. The legal authority for limited household goods transportation is set by various military service regulations.

Non-temporary storage of household goods. Military members can elect to have the military store all, or part of their household goods on a permanent basis during the assignment, up to their maximum weight allowance. The legal authority for Non-temporary Storage of Household Goods is 37 USC 406(d).

Additional consumables allowance. This is a separate allowance for annual shipment of up to 1,250 pounds per year of consumable items. Weight is in addition to the household goods weight limit. The legal authority for additional consumables allowance is 37 USC 406(b)(1)(D).

Mobile home transportation. When moved by commercial transporter, reimbursement includes carrier charges, road fares and tolls, permits and charges for the pilot car. If towed by POC, reimbursement is for actual costs. For self-propelled mobile home, reimbursement is at agreed cents-per-mile rate. May be transported by GBL (Government Bill of Lading). Reimbursement is limited to what it would have cost the government to transport member's maximum HHG weight allowance. Transportation of mobile home is in lieu of HHG transportation and is authorized only within CONUS, within Alaska, and between CONUS and Alaska. The legal authority for Mobile Home Transportation is 37 USC 409.

Transportation of Privately Owned Vehicles (POV). Military members can ship POVs in conjunction with many overseas assignments (and, of course, can ship them back to the CONUS upon completion of the assignment). The military services can apply restrictions on this entitlement. For example, for assignments to Korea, military members must be "command sponsored" (allowed to be accompanied by family members) or must be in the grade of E-7 or above in order to ship a vehicle. Members may also be authorized shipment for a replacement POV during any four-year period while assigned overseas.

Members are also authorized mileage reimbursement when driving the vehicle to the authorized port for shipment and when picking up the vehicle from the authorized receiving port.

There is only limited authority for POV shipment within CONUS. Shipment within CONUS is authorized only when medically unable to drive, homeport change, or not enough time to drive. The legal authority for Privately Owned Vehicle shipment is 10 USC 2634(h), 10 USC 2634, and 37 USC 406(h).

POV storage. A member is authorized storage of a POV when (a) ordered to an overseas assignment to which POV transportation isn't permitted, or (b) sent TDY on a contingency operation for more than thirty days. The legal authority for Privately Owned Vehicle Storage is 10 USC 2634.

DEPLOYMENT

There are various stages before military are deployed. First there has to be mobilization.

Mobilization is the act of assembling forces (usually Reserves) for active duty in times of war or national emergency. Generally, the type and degree of emergency determine the level of mobilization. Regardless of level, recall procedures and phases of mobilization remain the same.

Selective Mobilization responds to natural disasters or civilian disturbances that do not threaten national security. Examples of a domestic emergency that might require a selective mobilization would be a postal strike, an earthquake, or other natural disaster.

Partial Mobilization occurs when the president mobilizes forces in response to external threats to national security for no longer than twenty-four months.

Full Mobilization occurs when Congress mobilizes all Reserve units in response to a declaration of war or national emergency. Mobilization can last for the duration of the emergency plus six months to meet the requirements of a war or other national emergency involving an external threat to the national security.

Total Mobilization occurs when the president and the Congress activate the entire Armed Forces, as well as all national resources, to meet the requirements of war or other national emergencies involving an external threat to the national security.

Members of Reserve units are given the maximum time possible between the date alerted and the date required to report for active duty. Some units may be alerted but will not actually begin active duty for several weeks. However, under mobilization conditions, an emergency situation may require extremely short active duty notice.

Phases of Mobilization for Reservists:

1. **Preparation:** Reservists plan, train, and prepare for mobilization at their home unit. This phase takes place during normal peacetime.
2. **Alert:** A reserve unit receives notice of orders to active duty. The unit prepares for a transition from Reserve Component to Active Component status.
3. **Mobilization at Home Station:** The reserve unit assembles at home station and begins active duty.
4. **Movement to Mobilization Stations:** The reserve unit departs from its home station and travels to the mobilization site—either in the United States or overseas.
5. **Operation Readiness Improvement:** The reserve unit makes final preparation before actual deployment at mobilization site.

Deployment is the next step for a service member after mobilization. Deployment is the assignment of military personnel to temporary, unaccompanied tours of duty. It is the actual sending of soldiers somewhere by some means. Like mobilization, deployment has five phases:

1. Pre-deployment Activities
2. Movement to Ports of Embarkation
3. Strategic Lift
4. Reception at Points of Debarkation
5. Onward Movement

Our service members continue to be deployed around the world and few have much advance notice that deployment orders are on the way.

There are, however, many things that service members and their family can do to prepare and be ready for that day when the orders do come.

First you have to acknowledge that there will be many challenges and a whole gamut of emotions from all involved. For the family these emotions can range from sadness that a loved one is leaving to anger, resentment, and apprehension. These emotions are natural, but they have to be put to one side as you all look at the challenges that deployment will bring and discuss constructively how best you are going to meet them.

In the period leading up to deployment, it is important to understand that emotions and tensions will run high and that because of these, a wrong word can quickly lead to arguments. Understand that everyone is under stress and you must all make every effort to rapidly defuse any situation that looks as if it might get out of hand. If despite that you do have an argument, make up as quickly as possible. There are far more important things to be focused on.

Planning for deployment allows you and your partner to sit and down and work out how, in the absence of the other, you will run the home, look after the children, pay the bills, and really important—how you plan to stay in touch with each other during the separation. Ironically, in civilian life very few couples actually sit down to discuss these vital issues. The time to make these decisions is before the deployment. Trying to discuss critical matters long distance is never a good idea and can lead to harmful miscommunications.

Tips for Couples

- Discuss expectations for managing finances, children, and personal conduct before deployment.
- Expect changes in departure and return dates.
- Accept growth and change in all family members.
- Reserve disagreements for face-to-face encounters with your spouse.
- Put existing and unresolved marital issues on hold until the serving member returns home.
- Communicate regularly and creatively with your serving member. End communications on a positive note.
- Keep the serving member's parents informed and give mutual support.

Tips for Parents

- Establish and maintain supports that help the family cope.
- Plan for family stress relievers like fun outings and get-togethers.
- Plan opportunities for the at-home parent to get breaks from the children to revive emotionally and physically.
- Encourage family members to share feelings and give assurances.
- Honestly discuss the serving member's deployment. Share information about the serving member's work and what the parent is doing for our country.
- Answer questions openly and honestly, using words your children can understand.
- Provide a calendar or some measure to help your child count the days the parent has been deployed.
- Maintain a structured and safe emotional and physical environment for your children.
- Make sure the deployed parent is part of everyday conversations.
- Help your children sort out what they hear and see in news reports.
- Find out what your children know and understand and talk with them about their feelings. Follow your child's lead. Give a small piece of information at a time and see how your child responds before deciding what to do next.
- Provide your children with a method to communicate to the deployed parent, such as letter writing or e-mail access. Make it creative and fun.
- Maintain family routines and traditions during the other parent's absence.
- Keep children involved with outside activities and maintain communications with schools.

SUPPORT

Remember you are not alone. There are other families who can offer support and comfort and groups and organizations available to step in, if needed. For instance, the Army has Family Readiness Groups.

Family Readiness Groups

A Family Readiness Group (FRG) is an organization of family members, volunteers, soldiers, and civilian employees belonging to an Army command. They provide support, assistance, and a network of information among its members, the unit, and community agencies. Unit FRGs consist of all assigned and attached soldiers, their spouses, children, extended families, fiancé(e)s, boyfriends or girlfriends, and retirees. Even interested community members are welcome as well.

For spouses and family members, being active in an FRG will help give a sense of belonging to the unit and the Army community—the Army family. It will also provide you with a way to develop friendships, share important information, find needed Army resources, and share moral support during any unit deployments. It is during the preparation for deployment, during the deployment itself, and in the homecoming that FRGs best show their full value.

The FRGs help every family to keep up to date on what is going on, and in addition to sharing information, the group chooses goals and activities centered on supporting soldiers and families.

Family Separation Allowance

Being separated from your loved ones can take a much greater toll on a family than just an emotional one. To try to care for families during these trying times, there is the Family Separation Allowance (FSA). This is a benefit typically payable to serving members with dependent family members when they are required to be away from their family for greater than thirty days due to military orders. In order to be payable, the separation must be "involuntary," that is, a dependent is not allowed to accompany the soldier at government expense. The rationale for Family Separation Allowance entitlement is that forced family separation results in added household expenses when the serving member is absent for a period greater than thirty days.

Army

Army Community and Family Support Center. The Army Community and Family Support Center serves as the headquarters for Army MWR (Morale, Welfare, and Recreation).

Army Family Action Plan. The AFAP program seeks input regarding critical issues that affect the well-being of soldiers, Army families, retirees, and Department of the Army (DA) civilians. All components are included—active duty, Army National Guard, and Army Reserves. AFAP

issues are solicited directly from Army constituents through annual conferences convened at installations, major Army commands, and HQDA.
The results from AFAP conferences are reported to leaders who ensure
the issues are worked toward resolution.

The Army's Well-Being Division. The Army's Well-Being Division
(AWBD) provides a central source of compiled human dimension data
(both objective and subjective) with the commensurate analytical capability to inform Human Capital Strategy, policy and program decisions, and
to provide assessments of issues related to the well-being of the force.
AWBD is a key measurement tool for senior Army leadership, providing
the capability to use metric analyses and assessments to inform Strategy,
policy, Core Enterprise Activities, Task Force operations and Army Staff
Action Plans.

Army Family Team Building. Army Family Team Building (AFTB)
is a volunteer-led organization which provides training and knowledge to
spouses and family members to support the total Army effort. AFTB's
mission is to educate and train all of America's Army in knowledge,
skills, and behaviors designed to prepare our Army families to move successfully into the future.

Navy

LIFELines. The LIFELines Service Network provides online resources
in areas such as deployment readiness, family support, transition assistance, and MWR.

Morale, Welfare, and Recreation Headquarters. The Navy MWR
administers a varied program of recreation, social, and community support activities on U.S. Navy facilities worldwide. Their mission is to
provide quality support and recreational services that contribute to the
retention; readiness; and mental, physical, and emotional well-being of
sailors and their families.

Navy Family Ombudsman Program. This program is dedicated to
support the volunteers who comprise the Naval professional Ombudsman
team. This includes Ombudsmen, Ombudsman Assembly members, and
Naval Services Family Line staff.

Navy Services FamilyLine. Naval Services FamilyLine is a volunteer,
nonprofit organization dedicated to improving the quality of life for every

sea service family. This is achieved by answering questions from spouses about the military lifestyle, referring spouses to organizations that may be able to assist them, publishing and distributing free booklets and brochures that contain very helpful information, and developing successful educational programs for the sea service spouse.

Family Support and Relocation. Family Support and Relocation provides a comprehensive resource for sailors and their families enabling them to access information about the Navy communities in which they reside or to which they may be relocating.

Air Force

Air Force Crossroads. Crossroads is the official community website of the U.S. Airforce. This site (www.afcrossroads.com) provides information on numerous topics including Air Force installations, family separation and readiness, medical and dental, and relocation.

Air Force Services. Air Force Services exists to provide combat support to commanders directly in support of the Air Force mission. They also provide community service programs that enhance the quality of life for Air Force members and their families. These programs indirectly support the mission by improving morale, productivity, and retention. They offer a full range of military and community support programs at most major Air Force installations.

Marine Corps

Marine Corps Family Readiness Conference. Recognizing the family as one of the "pillars of readiness," the U.S. Marine Corps held a Family Readiness Conference at Marine Corps Base Quantico July 11–13 in Virginia. Family members, Marine Corps leadership, and support organizations from all over the world came together to discuss the challenges of today's military lifestyle. The conference highlighted the unique programs offered to Marines and their families, as well as provided a forum for people to share ideas and suggestions for improving those programs. The initiatives and changes discussed will be brought forward to the Commandant and Marine Corps Community Services leadership for consideration and implementation.

Marine Corps Community Services. Marine Corps Community Services (MCCS) exists to serve Marines and their families wherever they are stationed. MCCS programs and services provide for basic life needs, such as food and clothing, social and recreational needs, and even prevention and intervention programs to combat societal ills that inhibit positive development and growth.

Marine Corps Family Team Building. This service provides educational resources, services, and a roadmap to the Marine Corps lifestyle to foster the personal growth and enhance the readiness of Marine Corps families.

Coast Guard

Coast Guard Ombudsman. The Coast Guard Ombudsman is a Coast Guard spouse who serves as a member of the Command, and functions as a liaison between families and the Commanding Officer.

National Guard

Army National Guard Family Readiness Program. The mission of this program is to help bond Guard families together and promote a sense of comradeship; relay vital information from the director and the Family Readiness Program in order to lessen the feeling of isolation and convey the director's concerns for the well-being of Guard families; aid Guard families in better understanding the mission of the Army National Guard (ARNG); keep Guard families informed about activities sponsored by the director and/or the Family Readiness Program; and provide an avenue for Guard families to share some of the common rewards, tensions, and frustrations of military life.

National Guard Bureau (NGB) Family Support. In the aftermath of the Cold War, members of the Guard and Reserve are being called to active duty to an unprecedented extent. In recent years we have repeatedly called reservists to duty involuntarily for missions in Bosnia, Kosovo, and Southwest Asia. Contingency operations like these have placed enormous strains on our service members and their families. The NGB provides information on the steps it is taking to enhance family support and readiness.

The National Guard Family Program Community. The National Guard Family Program helps military personnel and their families prepare for deployment. This program offers useful information on topics such as education, employment, benefits, and financial and legal issues.

Reserves

Guide to Reserve Family Member Benefits. This guide provides an overview of military benefits and how to access them. It identifies eligibility requirements associated with some entitlements and provides guidance for obtaining assistance on specific questions and problems.

Army Reserve Family Program. This program provides information on family program support offices, reserve family member benefits, family readiness handbooks, and reserve family news.

Navy Reserve Ombudsman Online. The Reserve Ombudsman provides a volunteer force which is able to offer support and guidance to families.

National Guard and Reserve Family Readiness Strategic Plan. Prepared by the Office of the Assistant Secretary of Defense for Reserve Affairs and the Office of Family Policy (within the Deputy Assistant Secretary of Defense for Personnel Support, Families and Education), this plan seeks to ensure that reservists and their families are prepared to cope with the strains associated with long or repeated deployments and are adequately served by military family care systems, networks, and organizations.

Air Force Reserve Family Readiness. Families of deployed reservists will be assisted and supported by the Family Readiness office. The types of deployment assistance services the family can expect include family support groups, reunion information, and volunteer opportunities.

Marine Corps Reserve Community Services. Marine Corps Community Services (MCCS) is the by-product of merging the Corps old Morale, Welfare, and Recreation and Human Resources programs and tailoring them to better meet today's needs in personal and family readiness. MCCS is designed around five essential, required capabilities: Marine Corps Family Team Building, Personal Services, Semper Fit, Business Operations, and General Support. Marine Forces Reserve, due to the Force's unique challenges, will focus on the first three.

U.S. Coast Guard Reserve. This page (http://reserve.uscg.mil) has been designed to aid the Coast Guard Reservist, their families, and employers to better understand the benefits and nature of reserve service.

Office of the Assistant Secretary of Defense for Reserve Affairs. This office is dedicated to today's Reserve force. It provides information about the policies, programs, and initiatives that OSD/Reserve Affairs manages for the National Guard and Reserve Components of the United States Armed Forces. This includes family support/readiness issues.

All Services

Deputy Assistant Secretary of Defense for Military Community and Family Policy. This office is directly responsible for programs and policies that establish and support community quality of life programs on military installations for service members and their families worldwide. This office also serves as the focal point for coordination of the broad range of quality-of-life issues within the Department of Defense.

Military Assistance Program. The Military Assistance Program (MAP) is sponsored by the Deputy Assistant Secretary for Military Community and Family Policy. This program offers information and tools for military members and their families in family support areas such as relocation, employment, and financial management. The program also provides a database to locate your nearest family support center.

Military Community Programs. Family support is an integral part of the department's strategy to maintain a ready force. Studies show family satisfaction with military life is a major determiner of retention. Often, family support is the lifeline for families in an unstable environment during deployments, frequent moves, and long work hours. These resources provide information on the DoD's programs for family support.

Defense Finance and Accounting Service. The Defense Finance and Accounting Service (DFAS) provides information on military entitlements, as well as general information on pay rates, per diem, taxes, and so on.

DoD Special Report—It's Your Move. This special report provides information on service member entitlements and responsibilities concerning shipment of household goods, unaccompanied baggage, boats, pets, POVs, and so forth.

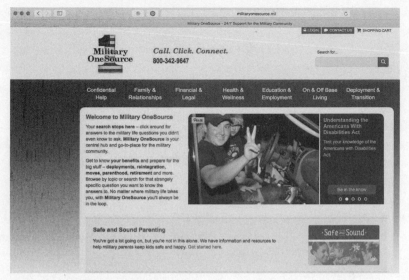

Figure 1.1.   Military OneSource.
Source: militaryonesource.mil

Additional Tips

Military OneSource is a 24-hour, 7-day-a-week resource for military and their families. Whether preparing for any type of deployment, seeking mental health services, or needing assistance with the service person or the family, counselors and researchers are available to help with most problems in one phone call. We encourage you to call any time you antici-pate a change such as a separation or relocation, and ask what resources are available to you for your particular situation.

Chapter Two

Being Apart but Staying Together

INTERVIEW SUMMARIES

The military wives that were represented in a couple of the interviews came from a Middle Eastern country and a Central American country. The Middle Eastern military wife had grown up in a high-conflict environment and then married a military member who continued working with military via another form of government service. One of the issues with this wife's experience, as indicated by her spouse, was her instinct to suppress anything that was stressful. This coping mechanism, the result of being raised in a country with a history of conflict, impacted the marriage. There was a recognition that what is brought into the environment, emotionally speaking, affects how well an individual or family may or may not be prepared to deal with these situations; and proper consideration needs to be given to any family history and any cultures that already have conflict issues.

The military wife originally from Central America talked about how she would have panic attacks and severe stress responses to attempting to raise multiple children and the stressors of raising children with educational, family, and other personal challenges and needs at home. Her husband, a colonel said, "It was important to me, but it wasn't important to me right then when I was in a war zone with other things that had to be important to me at that moment." He was clearly empathetic of her situation, and she of his, but they had to acknowledge the inability to be supportive of one another. She went on to add about how she was fighting battles with the schools and the districts attempting to ensure appropriate educational services for children with their own unique needs as he was off fighting battles for the nation. I asked her about whether or not she had requested any kind of mental health or other support for the family issues and she indicated they had; but the experience seemed to be a military process of "checking the boxes" rather than actually providing meaningful services that translated into improvement for the family. She said that filling out the paperwork and going through the questions they asked was more helpful to her in terms of being able to self-identify problems rather than actually receiving appropriate therapeutic intervention through the system. She indicated the system had been ineffective at providing remedy to the family and that they ultimately just worked through it the rest of the way on their own.

All the families commented about how "Joint" operations were very different deployments than some of the deployments that may be single-branch-of-military-specific, such as being on a Navy ship for a period of time, or a "rotation" abroad, and how those were different from being a "geographical bachelor."

GOOD COMMUNICATIONS

The secret to a successful marriage is good communications—being able to talk freely about any subject; able to share secrets, fears and fantasies; and able to offer advice if asked and discuss problems when they arise as partners.

It takes effort to be a good listener. It is not hiding behind your newspaper eating your breakfast as your spouse speaks and you mumble "yes dear." A good listener will put down the smartphone, look his or her spouse in the eye, and focus on what he or she is saying. What sort of message does it send if your partner is talking and you walk away and turn on the television?

With busy lives to lead, it is important that couples make time to talk to each other. If you are together, you can do this whenever you want. If your partner is deployed, the time you have to communicate is even more precious and limited.

Keeping this communication going during deployment may be difficult, but you can keep in touch through precious phone calls, texts, e-mails, and various Internet communication-friendly technologies such as Skype, Google Chat, Tango, and Facetime. There are always good old-fashioned letters and love notes.

Good communication is also part of the intimacy of marriage and of a loving relationship. Saying "I love you" to your partner every day is part of that. It is such an easy thing to say and takes only a moment; but so often, it doesn't get said enough. It doesn't matter how long you have been together, there are still little things you can do to communicate with your partner how much you still love them and how important they are to you. You can send e-mail messages (where appropriate), leave love notes for your partner to find, send flowers with a loving message, and just be encouraging and supportive at all times.

Good communication keeps togetherness and intimacy alive. It is when we stop communicating with each other that relationships tend to drift apart. If couples are not speaking to each other in ways that offer encouragement and positive reinforcement, other emotions can fill that void— anger, resentment, indifference—all negatives that can lead to strain and eventually a breakup.

It is as important to be a good communicator as it is to be a good listener. The good communicator will consider carefully what he or she says so as not to hurt or offend his or her partner. If there is an issue it is better to say, "What can we do?" rather than "Why did you let this happen?" When you start a sentence with "You . . . ," it sounds as if you are attacking that person. Pointing fingers is never a good way to start a conversation. You need to spell out the problem and concentrate on ways of resolving it. Collaboration on problem solving goes farther than blame ever will in any communication.

Start instead with "I think . . ." or "I am concerned about . . ." because this immediately tells your partner that these are your feelings and opens the door for them to respond with how they feel. Once you both know how the other feels you are better able to work out a solution that suits both. Remember that you are both entitled to your opinion, and you must respect your partner's right to hold it. Ongoing mutual respect and reciprocity should be a priority in healthy communication at all times. Sometimes it is better to agree not to agree—but always do it with love and a hug, and strive to show respect for differences whenever possible. There can be two perspectives with equal credibility; one does not have to be "right" and the other "wrong" in all cases. Sometimes two individuals in an exchange can both be "right," and be different, based upon their own belief system and experience.

A good communicator will be clear and to the point so there is little chance for misunderstanding. Arguments often result from misunderstandings—you said something and your partner totally misunderstood it.

How you say it is also important. If you are discussing something intimate or difficult take hold of your partner's hand to show that you are in this together and that care for them. Even if the subject matter is very serious it doesn't hurt to smile at your partner every now and then. It is a reassuring gesture that says "I love you. We are in this together, and we will work it out together."

The good listener will focus on what is being said and then consider an answer mindfully before replying. As you are listening, you are not thinking about what time the game starts or what you are doing tomorrow. Your partner deserves your full attention—and should get it.

Body language is every bit as important as the words you say. The wrong body language can send strong, antipathetic signals. If your arms are folded or you are leaning away from your partner you are building a barrier between you and distancing yourself from them. Leaning toward them as they speak demonstrates genuine interest in what they are saying and a desire to be close to them. Eye contact is critical because it creates a bond. If your eyes start to wander it shows you are not concentrating. Even eye movements can convey subtle messages. You should always break eye contact by looking down. Turning your eyes upwards might convey impatience (e.g., that was a stupid thing to say), whereas looking down can signal thoughtfulness and nonaggression. If your eyes flicker to the left and right it indicates you are uncomfortable, that is, looking for a way to get out of there.

Set aside a time during the day to talk to each other—face-to-face and eye-to-eye. It can be over breakfast or dinner or just before you go to sleep. Several studies show that the more a couple speaks to each other, the stronger their relationship/marriage is likely to be; while conversely, couples that hardly speak at all are likely to break up.

If you have a particularly difficult subject to discuss, set aside a special time for it and limit or eliminate distractions entirely. Don't try to have the conversation while you are cooking dinner or trying to put the children to bed. Find a time when you can sit down quietly and devote all your attention to the matter in hand and each other.

There may be times when your partner may not want to (or be ready to) communicate. They may have returned from a particularly harrowing deployment. You may be having an issue at work.

If you have a strong relationship, don't assume that the lack of communication is because you have done something wrong. By soothing and sympathetic words such as "I'm always here for you if you want to talk," or "Is there anything I can do to help," your partner should eventually open to you and your relationship should be right back on track. If not, suggest that counseling may help. Your Family Support Center can offer advice and recommend counselors.

Counseling, such as couples counseling, sometimes carries the stigma that something is "wrong" with someone in the relationship, and the other is going to get you "fixed" to see things "their way." Someone often feels threatened by counseling. There are fears that the counselor may be there to take sides and tell one side that they are "right" and the other side that they are "wrong" in terms of their thinking or behavior. Some of the benefits of couples counseling can include the following:

- Discovering positive communication strategies
- Obtaining assistance communicating through challenges and difficulties
- Opening a dialogue about perspectives, experiences, and exercises that can improve two-way communication
- Identifying new coping and adaptive techniques
- Strengthening bonds through professional coaching

It is important to remember that you and your loved one(s) are not the only ones to have ever had a particular type of problem before, and couples counseling can provide you new opportunities and techniques for communications strategies in your relationship(s) as well as obtaining the benefits of years of experience and wisdom of trained, qualified, mental health professionals.

If one individual is particularly resistant to couples counseling or assistance, it's important to ask why and understand any objections. Has there been a bad experience? Are they afraid of something? Do they associate such counseling with a stigma? In these types of instances, objections might be overcome by working together to identify a professional acceptable to both parties and/or teaming up to seek an alternative approach that remediates the anxiety or trepidation.

PREPARING TO LEAVE

Pre-deployment Essentials—Documents

Taking the time to gather and prepare the proper documents in advance of a separation allows service members to choose people to act on their behalf, to make their wishes known to their loved ones, and if they wish, to give legally binding instructions. While it may be uncomfortable to talk about certain possibilities, doing so in advance may help avoid conflict and allow for quick and decisive action in the event of an emergency. It is important to consider and plan for this in any type of a separation. For instance, an emergency may not only be associated with a wartime risk or injury; sometimes emergencies involving family members or financial matters may occur (for instance) and having something in place such as a durable power of attorney, an emergency fund, or other documents can be imperative. We recommend leveraging your access as an active duty service person or dependent to Military OneSource as an essential step of pre-planning for separations or similar significant life events. Asking for checklists, resources, kits, or information that helps families prepare for life events such as these types of separations are quite helpful as resources.

Service members and their relatives should gather identification documents such as birth certificates, marriage certificates, and any other similar documents that can verify family relationships. If you anticipate that a military ID card or other essential identification (such as a child's passport) would expire during the time of a separation, verify expiration dates and proactively make preparations for the active duty service person to provide appropriate signatures on requisite forms or obtain a durable power of attorney through military legal services for renewing that identification during the absence. Work with a spouse or partner to obtain state identification for minor children (such as through a Department of Motor Vehicles [DMV]) prior to an absence so that a back-up form of government identification is available to a child while one parent will be away.

These documents may become important when dealing with insurance companies, financial institutions, and government agencies. It is a good idea to keep the originals of these documents in a safe place together with other important documents and to keep copies in a second, easily accessible place in case the service member or a relative needs access to them at any point. In addition, certain documents empowering others to act on a service member's behalf, such as a financial or durable power of attorney, a health care advance directive, or a living will, should be made available in case the service member becomes unable to make decisions or to communicate his or her wishes to others.

Finally, all service members should make sure they have a legally valid will and should review the beneficiary designation forms for any life insurance policies they have to make sure they are current and accurate.

We recommend familiarizing the family with death benefits—such as those from the military, the Department of Veterans Affairs, and the Social Security Administration—and printing out any relevant information on any available benefits. Such information should be stored with copies of wills and life insurance as well as a copy of any documented, dated, signed final wishes for any family member—to include burial options, terms for resuscitation, or life support, and organ donor preferences.

Aging with Dignity is a private, nonprofit organization with a mission to safeguard the human dignity of people as they age or face serious illness. Today it is the most trusted resource for people who want to plan for care in advance of a health crisis. Its Five Wishes document is the most widely used advance directive or living will in America. It is often called the "living will with a heart and soul" because it includes the things that matter the most. Unlike most other advance directives, it is easy to use and

A "Base" legal department will often have templates for these types of documents. Military Onesource may also be able to provide access to free or low-cost resources to assist you with planning. Some of these documents may require a notary and/or witness signatures, so having access to friends or family who may be able to sign as witnesses will be helpful. Some banks will provide free notary services for their clients, as will a "Base legal" office. Your bank or credit union may also offer access to free or low-cost safety deposit boxes as a means for securely storing original documents.

> Wills, life insurance policies, and military benefit assignment policies
> should be compared annually or prior to any separation in order to be sure
> designations are consistent to avoid contest or probate.

understand. Caring for people with a serious illness involves more than
providing the best medical care. It means helping them to maintain their
human dignity. For more information, go to https://agingwithdignity.org.

"Five Wishes" is legally binding in multiple states. It is a wonderful
resource that very simplistically presents the user with important considerations that a family would need in the event of a tragedy such as a severe
illness, injury, or loss of life. By completing a copy of "Five Wishes" for
every family member and storing those copies with other important documents, the family will be more comprehensively prepared to deal with an
emergency situation while mitigating as many severe stressors as possible.

A financial power of attorney is a legal document by which one person
gives another person the authority to act in his or her place regarding financial affairs. For example, a financial power of attorney empowers one person
to sign a binding contract on behalf of another person. The person who signs
the power of attorney is called the principal or grantor, and the person who
gains rights to act under the power of attorney is called the attorney-in-fact.
Service members are often encouraged to grant powers of attorney prior to
deployment to enable a spouse or other family member to manage their affairs while they are away. Specific clauses can be incorporated by the grantor
to limit the scope or duration of the power of attorney. A Limited Power of
Attorney only enables the person to conduct a specific act—for example, to
sell your home—while General Power of Attorney grants the person broad
powers to act on your behalf, but there must be a specific list of the types of
activities he or she is authorized to perform. A Durable Power of Attorney
remains in force even if the principal becomes incapacitated.

A financial power of attorney can be general—giving the attorney-in-fact
unlimited authority over the principal's affairs—or limited to specific actions, such as filing tax returns or signing insurance forms. Powers of attorney may be limited to a specific period of time or may extend until the death
of the principal or until revocation. A power of attorney must be "durable,"
however, in order to remain valid if the principal becomes incapacitated.

Creating these documents often involves making difficult personal decisions and also requires legal expertise. Service members who wish to create a will or sign a power of attorney, health care advance directive or living will should consult a qualified legal professional. Planning in these situations requires positive, healthy communication skills and may require counseling or coaching from qualified professionals. It is perfectly acceptable to obtain the skills of a professional counselor to help facilitate difficult discussions and keep the family "on track" to achieving desired goals and outcomes, particularly by articulating those goals or desires at the beginning of a planning effort. The ultimate goal is to protect the best interests of all involved and to limit future risks, such as a potential conflict or misunderstanding. This also mitigates any risk involved in assuming someone's wishes without being able to ask them.

Terry Schiavo (1963–2005)

The Terri Schiavo case was a legal struggle over end-of-life care in the United States from 1990 to 2005, involving Theresa Marie "Terri" Schiavo, a woman in an irreversible persistent vegetative state. She was a wife and mother who was placed on life support in Pinellas County, Florida, without an advanced directive. Her story became famous in light of the conflict that occurred within her family in the absence of pre-need plans and disagreements between her husband and her parents as to what she would have wanted. The case became high-profile, and is an example of the worst that can happen when wishes are not properly documented.

Waiting for a loved one to deploy is hard on children as well as spouses. Children may not understand why a parent must leave and may fear the parent is leaving forever. Because children are not very good at expressing their worries verbally, they tend to express them behaviorally. Be sure your children have many chances to express how they are feeling. The following ideas may help your family prepare for and get through a period of separation due to deployment:

- Use your own words to help children find theirs. For example, "I don't want Daddy to leave, and waiting for him to leave makes me feel sort of sad and worried. Do you ever feel that way?"

- Explain that although many things will be different, many things will be the same.
- If the child plays imaginary games with dolls or animals, try to introduce the idea of one member of the doll family leaving. Let the other dolls say how they feel about this.
- Use a map or a globe to show where his or her parent will be.
- Use a calendar to show children when the deployment will take place, as they may not understand how long three weeks is. Some families cross a day off the calendar, others count with buttons, marbles, or coins from a jar.

Be sure that the departing parent has time with each child before deploying. Hug often. Take photos of each child with the departing parent. Sometimes a parent will go to "Build a Bear" and get a recording of their voice installed in the paw, so the child can squeeze it and hear a short, loving message from the parent. Others video-record stories, loving messages, and songs for their children to hear while they are away. Photos can also be placed on everything from mugs, to t-shirts and blankets, to pillowcases, which can help children have something to enjoy and share as a keepsake during the absence.

The departing parent might schedule a trip to the child's school to meet with the teacher. The point of this trip is to be sure the teacher knows about the change in the family dynamics. Let the child show you around his or her school world and perhaps hear you tell the teacher how proud you are of him or her. You will be able to ask better questions about your child's day if you are familiar with his or her school. If asked and if preplanned, many schools are willing to Skype, i-Chat, or otherwise virtually assist the deployed parent who wishes to participate in IEP (Individualized Education Program) meetings and school communications.

Have a family meeting about ways to keep in touch during the deployment. Letters, pictures, tapes, and movies are all good ways to stay connected. If possible, communications and "care packages" should also come from the child to the parent, so they remain engaged and involved.

Remember to occasionally send children their own letters, e-mails, or messages. Children enjoy few things more than receiving their own mail! A letter to the family pet will also bring a smile to a child's face.

Find the best way for the child to mark the end of the deployment. This may be making Xs on the calendar or assembling then removing links off a paper chain.

Remember that just because a child doesn't express his or her feelings, it doesn't mean they are not troubled. If a child is acting out, it may be the result of unexpressed emotions. Help the child name these feelings. Military OneSource can provide and assist with counseling services to help children receive additional support, ranging from mental and behavioral health services to free online tutoring services. Some theme parks offer free passes for military families with proper identification. These types of resources can help the children have special activities and support in the absence or presence of their full military family.

If an adult assesses that the child may or has become a danger to himself/herself or others, consider learning more about the Baker Act and the protocols for your state and/or military installation for calling in a Baker Act emergency so that immediate intervention and mental health services can be urgently engaged.

It is fine and even healthy for children to see you have sad feelings too, but if you are really about to fall apart, try to do this away from your kids. Strong emotions in a parent can be scary to a child.

Eliminating processed foods, artificial ingredients, refined sugars, grains, alcohols, and stimulants have been positively correlated with a reduction in certain behavioral challenges in both children and adults. Physical movement/activity, sunlight, access to guided meditation, Emotional Freedom Technique (EFT) or tapping, hand positioning (mudra), and deep breathing exercises have all been shown to immediately benefit an individual experiencing severe anxiety, anger, and panic symptoms. New Kadampa Tradition (NKT) Buddhist meditation centers are located throughout the United States and offer access to meditation assistance regardless of religious affiliation or denomination; both within the centers and online.

There are a variety of online, free resources that offer access to guided meditations, tapping instructions, mudra positions for particular health concerns, and breathing exercises. Janelle is particularly fond of Nicole Lewis Keeber Coaching for Nicole's EFT/ tapping instructions, free videos, Facebook page, and virtual services, as well as Gesha Kelsang's

YouTube videos explaining many facets of improving the condition of the state of one's mind.

Remind children that they are still safe and that a deployed parent is still a member of the family. Do not minimize the child's grief. To a child it may feel like a parent is lost forever. Grief without understanding is difficult to work through.

Children may often punish the present parent for the disappearance of the absent parent; and often the deployed parent is not aware of major behavioral changes that occur after their departure. Parents must be prepared for the potential of "acting-out" behavior because of anger, frustration, sadness, and confusion.

Taking the time to gather and prepare the proper documents in advance allows service members to choose people to act on their behalf, to make their wishes known to their loved ones, and if they wish, to give legally binding instructions. While it may be uncomfortable to talk about certain possibilities, doing so in advance may help avoid conflict and allow for quick and decisive action in the event of an emergency.

The emotional cycle of an extended deployment, six months or greater, is readily divided into five distinct stages. These stages are comprised as follows: pre-deployment, deployment, sustainment, re-deployment and post-deployment. Each stage is characterized both by a time frame and specific emotional challenges, which must be dealt with and mastered by each of the family members. Failure to adequately negotiate these challenges can lead to significant strife—both for family members and the deployed service member. Providing information early about what to expect, especially for families who have not endured a lengthy separation before, can go a long way toward "normalizing" and coping positively with the deployment experience.

Furthermore, promoting understanding of the stages of deployment helps to avert crises, minimize the need for command intervention or mental health counseling, and can even reduce suicidal threats.

Stage 1: Pre-deployment

Countdown

The onset of this stage begins with the warning order for deployment. This stage ends when the service person actually departs from home station.

The pre-deployment timeframe is extremely variable from several weeks to more than a year, and potentially comes with a significant amount of anxiety and anticipation for everyone involved.

The pre-deployment stage is characterized alternately by denial and anticipation of loss. As the departure date gets closer, spouses often ask, "You don't really have to go, do you?" Eventually, the increased field training, preparation, and long hours away from home herald the extended separation that is to come. Serving members energetically talk more and more about the upcoming mission and their unit. This "bonding" to fellow serving members is essential to unit cohesion that is necessary for a safe and successful deployment. Yet, it also creates an increasing sense of emotional and physical distance for military spouses. In their frustration, many spouses complain, "I wish you were gone already." It is as if their loved ones are already "psychologically deployed."

Some people cope with this through "compartmentalization," an unconscious psychological defense mechanism used to suppress their emotional discomfort and anxiety. Issues or behaviors that hurt emotionally are "compartmentalized" and then suppressed. While outwardly at first the person seems to be coping, it can lead to issues. The two personas—the outer and inner persons—can lead to borderline personality disorders. Serving members in war zones often compartmentalize by suppressing thoughts of family and loved ones as they prepare to go into action and then trying to suppress the images of the action, especially if comrades were severely wounded or killed.

As the reality of the deployment finally sinks in, the serving member and family try to get their affairs in order while simultaneously trying to process and accept what's coming. Long "honey-do" lists are generated dealing with all manner of issues including home repairs, security (door and window locks, burglar alarms, etc.), car maintenance, finances, tax preparation, child care plans, and wills, just to name a few. At the same time, many couples strive for increased intimacy. Plans are made for the "best" Christmas, the "perfect" vacation, or the "most" romantic anniversary. In contrast, there may be some ambivalence about sexual relations: "this is it for six months, but I do not want to be that close." Fears about fidelity or marital integrity are raised or may go unspoken. There is a term in the military called "geographical bachelors" that some associate with a mentality that "what happens on tour stays on tour," whether it happens on a Navy ship or in a war zone—and it somewhat endorses the stigma of military infidelity during absences. Other frequently voiced concerns may include, "How will the children handle the separation? Can I cope without him/her? Will my marriage survive?" In this very busy and tumultuous time, resolving all these issues, completing the multitude of tasks, or fulfilling high expectations often falls short. If you or your family members are not particularly technically savvy, ask a computer literate friend to help set up a solution for you to help you connect to your loved one while away. Apple Stores are located across the United States and internationally. They can assist you or your loved ones with technology solutions that include applications (apps) like FaceTime, and family sharing, so that even the self-described technologically illiterate individuals can get an easy solution to communicate over long distances simply with wireless Internet access. They do periodically run discounts for students. Military Exchanges often sell technology products at reasonable prices sans tax, to include special discounts on software licenses.

A common occurrence, just prior to deployment, is for serving members and their spouses to have a significant argument. For couples with a long history, this argument is readily attributed to the ebb and flow of marital life and therefore not taken too seriously. For younger couples, especially those experiencing an extended separation for the first time, such an argument can take on "catastrophic" proportions. Fears that the relationship is over can lead to tremendous anxiety for both serving member and spouse. In retrospect, these arguments are most likely caused by the stress of the pending separation. From a psychological perspective, it is easier to be angry than confront the pain and loss of saying goodbye for six months or more.

However, the impact of unresolved family concerns can have potentially devastating consequences. From a command perspective, a worried, preoccupied serving member is easily distracted and unable to focus on essential tasks during the critical movement of heavy military equipment. In the worst-case scenario, this can lead to a serious accident or the development of a serving member stress casualty who is mission-ineffective. It is essential to support our servicemen and women so they can be focused and mindful of their roles and responsibilities at all times. On the home front, significant spousal distress interferes with completing basic routines, concentrating at work, and attending to the needs of children. At worst, this can exacerbate children's fears that the parents are unable to adequately care for them or even that the serving member will not return.

Adverse reactions by children can include inconsolable crying, apathy, tantrums, and other regressive behaviors. In response, a downward spiral can develop—if not quickly checked—in which both serving member and spouse become even more upset at the prospect of separating.

Although easier said than done, it is often helpful for military couples— in the pre-deployment stage—to discuss in detail their expectations of each other during the deployment. These expectations can include a variety of issues: freedom to make independent decisions, contact with the opposite sex (fidelity), going out with friends, budgeting, child-rearing, and even how often letters or care packages will be sent. Failure to accurately communicate these and other expectations is frequently a source of misperception, distortion, and hurt later on in the deployment. It is difficult at best to resolve major marital disagreements when face-to-face, let alone over six thousand miles apart.

Pre-Deployment Checklist

Have you discussed your feelings on the deployment and your spouse's return?

Have the children been included in discussions on where you are going, when you are coming home, why you are leaving?

Have you reached an agreement on frequency of communication to include letter writing/phone calls?

Do you have current family snapshots or access to applications like Facebook or Instagram?

Have you recorded your children's favorite bedtime stories/songs?

Have you recorded your children's voices and saved them in an accessible way for the departing parent?

Do both the deploying member and remaining parent or guardian understand what the Airman and Family Readiness Center, Family Services, Air Force Aid Society, American Red Cross, Chaplain, and so on, can do for you and how to contact them?

Security

Has the home been given a security check?
Do all window locks work?
Do the windows open or are they painted shut?

Do all door locks work properly?

Do you have keys for all doors or combinations for all padlocks?

Do the smoke alarms function and do you know how to test them (or replace the batteries in them)? Do you have extra batteries on hand for smoke alarms?

Are all emergency numbers posted where they can easily be referred to?

Is there an appropriate message on the voicemail? (Having a strong, confident voice—sans children or animals in a noisy background—sometimes discourages crank phone calls.)

Do you need to change your phone number to an unlisted number?

Medical

Do you know and understand how to use the medical facilities?

Do you know who your children's pediatrician is and what his or her phone number is?

Do you know your children's dentist/orthodontist and their schedule?

Do you have access to all pertinent medical records?

(AlwaysMed [www.alwaysmed.com] is a fee-for-service portal that securely allows you to collect, manage, and maintain all of your own medical records in a central repository that you control for an annual fee.)

Financial

Have you determined who will pay the bills?

Do you have a spending plan?

Do you both understand the spending plan?

Does your spending plan consider the following?

- Rent/Mortgage
- Utilities
- Food
- Automobile Maintenance
- Insurance
- Loan Payments
- Emergencies
- Long Distance Phone Calls

- Postage
- Travel (Leave)
- Entertainment
- Presents
- Savings

Has an allotment been established?
Will the allotment be in effect in time?
Is there a "backup" plan if the allotment is late?
Do you both have signing powers for bank accounts?
Have you decided upon a procedure for income taxes?

Legal

Do you know your spouse's social security number?
Have you provided for Power of Attorney?
Do you have current wills?
Have guardians for the children been named in the will?
Does everyone who qualifies have a government identification (ID) card?
Will any ID cards need renewing?
If ID needs renewing, has Form DD 1172 been completed?
Is military member's record of emergency data on record and current?
Do you know the process for moving your household goods?

Important Papers

Are the following important papers current and in an accessible safety deposit box?

- Power of Attorney
- Wills
- "Five Wishes" Document (https://agingwithdignity.org/five-wishes/about-five-wishes)
- Insurance Policies
- Real Estate (Deeds, Titles, Mortgages, Leases)
- Bank Account Numbers
- Charge Account Numbers

- Savings Bonds
- Birth Certificates/Passports
- Marriage Certificates
- Naturalization Papers
- Citizenship Papers
- Family Social Security Numbers
- Inventory of Household Goods
- Car Title(s)
- Websites, Usernames, Log-ins for Account Management

Does each of you have the following phone numbers?

- Police
- Fire
- Medical (Hospital/Doctor)
- Service Member's Contact Number
- Service Member's Unit in Local Area
- Spouses in Unit/Squadron
- Reliable Neighbors
- Relatives
- Children's School
- Spouse's Workplace
- Utilities
- Repair Shops
- Insurance Company
- Airman & Family Readiness Center
- American Red Cross

Household Maintenance

Do you know who to call if something breaks?
Do you know how to operate the furnace?
Does the furnace have clean filters?
Does the furnace need periodic supplies of oil/gas?
Is the hot water heater operating properly?
Any pipes or faucets leaking?
Toilets operate correctly?

All drains operate correctly?
Are the following appliances operating correctly?

* Stove
* Refrigerator
* Freezer
* Dishwasher
* Clothes Washer
* Clothes Dryer
* Television
* Air Conditioner

Does everyone know where the fuse box is?
Are the switches of the fuse box labeled?
Are there extra fuses?
Is there adequate outside lighting?
Is there a list of repair persons?
Are there tools in the house?
Is the lawn mower tuned?
Is there an adequate amount of firewood?
Is it known how to turn off the water to the house if there is a major leak or breakage?

DURING THE ABSENCE

Stage 2: Deployment

This stage is the period from the serving member's departure from home through the first month of the deployment.

A roller coaster of mixed emotions is common during the deployment stage. Some military spouses report feeling disoriented and overwhelmed. Others may feel relieved that they no longer have to appear brave and strong. There may be residual anger at tasks left undone. The serving member's departure creates a "hole," which can lead to feelings of numbness, sadness, being alone, or abandonment. It is common to have difficulty sleeping and anxiety about coping. Worries about security issues may ensue, including

"What if there is a pay problem? Is the house safe? How will I manage if my child gets sick? What if the car breaks down?" For many, the deployment stage is an unpleasant, disorganizing experience.

On the positive side, the ability to communicate home is a great morale boost. The Defense Satellite Network (DSN) provides serving members the ability to call home at no cost, although usually for a fifteen-minute time limit. For some serving members, who are unwilling to wait in line, using commercial phone lines is an option. Unfortunately, it is common for huge phone bills to result, which can further add to familial stress. Another potential source of anxiety for families is that several weeks may pass before serving members are able to make their first call home.

For most military spouses, reconnecting with their loved ones is a stabilizing experience. For those, who have "bad" phone calls, this contact can markedly exacerbate the stress of the deployment stage and may result in the need for counseling.

One technique for balanced communication is to have a goal to talk about the high *and* the low of the day, or the last week, or the absence

One interviewed military spouse had a very young child and the marriage was still very new when the active-duty spouse began rotating to the Middle East to a high-conflict area. She shared that her upbringing was Jewish and his upbringing was Christian. She emphasized her hardships as a mother raising a very young child in a city where she had never lived before, with no close relatives, and no family. She seemed entirely focused on herself and her issues. I asked her, "What about what your husband was going through and where he was," and her response was "What about me? What about my needs? What about my family's needs?" She indicated that only one other military wife had invited them to dinner and actually inquired about whether or not she had a kosher diet. She seemed to take the position that his command was concerned with the active duty service person, and no one was concerned about her or her needs or her son's needs, and while there were some other military families trying to support one another, she struggled without proximity to her family and her religious community. She felt so overwhelmed with a young child and a deployed husband that she did not feel she had enough resources left to engage the community from which she needed support, to identify and build those new ties.

INTERVIEW SUMMARIES

A female Navy sailor (enlisted) said that ship deployments were like how she imagined living in the general population in prisons might be. She felt that she and other female sailors did not receive or benefit from equal treatment, and the medical care offered for stress symptoms equated to "drugging." She alleged that many of the military personnel on the ship were on Zoloft, a powerful pharmaceutical antidepressant.

She described chronic verbal abuse from her leadership and found herself compared to male leadership's wives at home rather than her professional peers. She described that despite her stellar on-ship performance at her assigned role, she was never afforded the respect of her male peers. She described how difficult it became for her to function as she developed a sleep disorder and chronic terrifying nightmares. She said that after her tour(s), the stress that had developed during her deployment experience led her to be placed into therapy groups as treatment for her disorder with "wives who were upset that their husbands were away."

She indicated that girls as young as seventeen (with waivers signed by their parents) would end up on ship, naive, and within a few months pregnant (by married Marines and sailors). She said the environment was ripe for this type of advantage to be taken of young women who didn't know any better and had no advocacy. She went on to say that the night terror disorder that she developed was directly attributed to the deployments during her Naval career, for which they basically tried to "medicate her to the point she was a zombie"; and she indicated that as she proceeded through the medical care for this, she was heavily medicated on three drugs that should not have been combined. She described a situation where more medications were added and her health deteriorated to the point where she was not functional.

She said that she was drugged by the Navy medical health care system to the point that eventually the Navy deemed her unfit to continue for duty—directly due to the medication load and her inability to continue to function in her job. The Navy separated/discharged her. She said after that she spent the following year or more of her life living in her mother's basement because she had no foreseeable future beyond her prior Navy career. She said she had become so dysfunctional she could not think clearly enough to even look into her GI Bill or think about any kind of a future.

When asked how she ended up completely off all her medications and how she went about getting healthy again, she indicated that it all started when she came home with another prescription and her mother intervened. She said that her mother dumped all her medications into the toilet and flushed them. Her mother then began providing herbalist approaches and working to detoxify her. She began engaging in meditation, working with reiki healing, yoga, Pilates, and fitness. She described how she began developing mental clarity and was able to then begin researching and embracing a lifestyle supported by raw healing foods, which helped her make even more significant healing and recovery strides. These changes, she said, convinced her that there needed to be life changes. She said that for her, these approaches allowed her to recover.

Presently she is leveraging her GI Bill and earning a degree in alternative medicine and healing arts. She was so sad and angry as she described her visits to Veterans Administration (VA) clinics where she observed overmedicated patients unable to maintain continence of their bowels and bladders. She shared a story about how she was mistaken for a medical professional because her physical appearance hid her medical disability. She indicated her desire to support military and veterans' programs that helped wounded warriors and those with mental health and trauma injuries using modalities such as chair yoga, meditation, and dietary intervention. Her belief is that these approaches can accomplish far more for patients like the one she had been than the traditional military system processes and procedures for treatment that were provided to her without any discussion of alternatives during her active-duty career or transition to the VA. In her new career she hopes to advocate for those who may not be aware of alternative medicine and modalities for health and healing.

so that attention can be given to the positive experiences as well as the challenges. It is unrealistic to expect a positive outcome to a call if the exchange is focused on only the negative, stressful aspects of the relationship. The exchanges should not always be focused on problem solving and troubleshooting. They should be for sharing love, admiration, and pride for what the other is contributing to the family and the service.

One possible disadvantage of easy phone access is the immediacy and proximity to unsettling events at home or in the theater. It is virtually impossible to disguise negative feelings of hurt, anger, frustration, and loss on the phone. For example, a spouse may be having significant difficulty (children acting out, car breaking down, finances, etc.) or a serving member may not initially get along with peers or a supervisor. Spouse and serving member may feel helpless and unable to support each other in their time of need. Likewise, there may be jealousy toward the individual(s) on whom the spouse or serving member relies or confides in during the deployment. These situations can add to the stress and uncertainty surrounding the deployment. Yet, military families have come to expect phone (and video) contact as technology advances. However, most report that the ability to stay in close touch—especially during key milestones (birthdays, anniversaries, etc.)—greatly helps them to cope with the separation.

APPROACHES TO PASSING TIME WITH FAMILY AND COMMUNITY

There are many things you can do to keep occupied while your loved one is away, while at the same time keeping your emotional bonds alive and strong.

Journaling is a great way to record what is happening to you and your family. You can use journaling to build a scrapbook with details of events and pictures that will last as a treasured keepsake. Make it a family project and let your children contribute. More importantly, you can use a journal to record your personal feelings. Focusing on your emotions and feelings and writing them down can, in itself, be a valuable therapy. If you are writing a personal journal you want to set aside some quiet time dedicated to it. Put on your favorite relaxing music, light a scented candle, have a glass of wine, or do whatever else that will allow you to focus on yourself and how you are feeling. The important thing is to record your feelings candidly. This allows you to look back and maybe learn that slowly, over the last few weeks, your mood has changed. This should sound warning bells that perhaps help is needed.

Support groups are found in all branches of the military and are there to help you. If you are having problems caused by loneliness, depression, children acting up, and so on, rest assured that there are thousands of other military families out there who have been there, done that—and are willing to help you overcome your issues. Don't try and go it alone. Let them help you.

Community is very special in the military, and there is a bond that few outsiders can appreciate. You are part of one huge family and by and large, everyone looks out for everyone else. Become active in your community, go to events and fun activities, grow your circle of friends and seek out groups that share your interests and understand your issues. As with all things, the more you put in, the more you will get out.

Assistance is available on all bases from family support groups to spiritual counseling. Again, do not convince yourself that the problems you are facing are unique to your special set of circumstances—they are not. The only reason these groups and services exist is to support people just like you.

Limited communication can be one of the most frustrating elements of separation. Being able to talk to your loved one thousands of miles away allows you to be together for a short time. This allows you to maintain that emotional connection that is so important for sustaining the relationship. When your channels of communication are disrupted—which is inevitable at times—it can be very distressing, especially if there was some important news—or a problem—you wanted to share. If you can't establish voice or video contact, use backups. Send e-mails, text messages, make short family videos or audio tapes, and leave voice mails. A good tip if you are writing letters is to number them. Because of many factors your mail may be delayed and your serving member could receive four letters on the same day. If they are numbered, they will know which one to read first. Remember, however, that if you are e-mailing, texting, or leaving voice messages, these are covered by your phone and Internet provider. You don't want unexpected high phone or cable bills. Many phone companies offer discounts for people calling military overseas.

Care packages are another great way of showing your service member that you care and are thinking of them. You must follow the special posting instructions to ensure they will get delivered and don't include anything too perishable because delivery can sometimes be long delayed with extreme temperature fluctuations. Include notes from the children, photos, homemade cookies, and any other little items that will boost the serving member's morale.

Countdowns help you focus on your serving member's impending return home. Don't start the countdown until you are sure that orders have been issued for their return because you don't want to raise false hopes especially if young children are involved. You can make a countdown calendar; crossing off each day can become a family ritual. It will also keep you posted on how much time you have left to do all the things that have to be done before the return.

Volunteerism and activism are both good ways to help pass the time, keep your mind occupied, and give back to your community. There are thousands of volunteer opportunities so you are bound to find something that you will get satisfaction from doing. It could be volunteering at a local library helping children and adults to read, working at a local animal shelter, or helping out at a local state park. If you are passionate about certain issues, become active in local groups supporting them.

Professional development is another excellent way of effectively utilizing your time. Learning new skills, going back to college, and expanding your knowledge base can all increase your eligibility in the jobs market, get you a promotion, and boost your own self-esteem.

Physical fitness challenges are growing in popularity for deployed families who use fitness and health routine strategies to compare progress, share interim progress pictures, support one another, and encourage one another's progress. It's also an outstanding way to relieve stress and anxiety.

Stage 3: Sustainment

The sustainment stage lasts from the first month through the fifth (penultimate) month of deployment. Sustainment is a time of establishing new sources of support and new routines. Many rely on the Family Readiness Group (FRG), which serves as a closed network that meets on a regular basis to handle problems and disseminate the latest information. Others are more comfortable with family, friends, church, or other religious institution as their main means of emotional support. As challenges come up, most spouses learn that they are able to cope with crises and make important decisions on their own. They report feeling more confident and in control. During the sustainment stage, it is common to hear military spouses say, "I can do this!"

One challenge during this stage is the rapid speed of information provided by widespread phone and e-mail access. In the near future, one can even expect that individual serving members will have the ability to call home with personal cellular phones. Over long distances and without face-to-face contact, communications between marital partners are much more vulnerable to distortion or misperception. Given this limitation, discussing "hot topics" in a marriage can be problematic and are probably best left on hold until after the deployment when they can be resolved more fully. Obvious exceptions to this rule include a family emergency (e.g., the critical illness of a loved one) or a joyful event (e.g., the birth of a child). In these situations, the ideal route of communication is through the Red Cross so that the serving member's command is able to coordinate emergency leave if required.

On a related note, many spouses report significant frustration because phone contact is unidirectional and must be initiated by the serving member. Some even report feeling "trapped" at home for fear that they will miss a call. Likewise, serving members may feel forgotten if they call—especially after waiting a long time in line to get to a phone—and no one is home. This can lead to anger and resentment, especially if an expectation regarding the frequency of calls is unmet. Now that Internet and e-mail are widely available, spouses report feeling much more in control as they can initiate communication and do not have to stay waiting by the phone. Another advantage of e-mail, for both serving member and spouse, is the ability to be more thoughtful about what is said and to "filter out" intense emotions that may be unnecessarily disturbing.

This is not to say that military couples should "lie" to protect each other, but rather it helps to recognize that the direct support available from one's partner is limited during the deployment.

Furthermore, rapid communication can lead to unanticipated rumors, which then circulate unchecked within the Family Readiness Group. The most damning rumor involves an allegation of infidelity that is difficult to prove true or false. Other troubling rumors may include handling the deployment poorly, accidents or injuries, changes in the date of return, disciplinary actions, or even who calls home the most. Needless to say, such rumors can be very hurtful to serving member and spouse. At its worst, unit cohesion and even mission success can suffer. Limiting the negative impact of such rumors is a constant challenge for unit leaders and chaplains. It is extremely important to keep serving members and family members fully informed and to dispel rumors quickly. In fact, rumors lose their destructive power once the "secret" is exposed.

The response of children to the extended deployment of a parent is very individualized and also depends on their developmental age: infants, toddlers, preschool, school age, and teenagers. It is reasonable to assume that a sudden negative change in a child's behavior or mood is a predictable response to the stress of having a deployed parent.

Unfortunately, some children may have great difficulty adapting to the stress of a deployed parent. If they are unable to return to at least some part of their normal routine or display serious problems over several weeks, a visit to the family doctor or mental health counselor is indicated. Children of deployed parents are also more vulnerable to psychiatric hospitalization—especially in single-parent and blended families. Despite all these obstacles, the vast majority of spouses and family members successfully negotiate the sustainment stage and begin to look forward to their loved ones coming home.

Stage 4. Re-deployment

The re-deployment stage is essentially defined as the month before the serving member is scheduled to return home. The re-deployment stage is generally one of intense anticipation. Like the deployment stage, there can be a surge of conflicting emotions. On the one hand, there is excitement that the serving member is coming home; on the other, there is some apprehension. Some concerns include "Will he (she) agree with the changes that I have made? Will I have to give up my independence? Will we get along?" Ironically, even though the separation is almost over, there can be renewed difficulty in making decisions. This is due, in part, to increased attention to choices that the returning serving member might make. Many spouses also experience a burst of energy during this stage. There is often a rush to complete "to-do" lists before their mate returns—especially around the home. It is almost inevitable that expectations will be high.

Lessons Learned

There are many challenges for military families to overcome during the five stages of deployment. Anticipating these challenges is important to minimize the emotional trauma caused by extended deployment. It is important not to overinterpret arguments that are often caused by the pain and loss of separation. Resolving marital issues that precede deployment is very difficult to accomplish over long distances and is probably best left until the serving member's return. Dates of departure and return often "slip" forward and backward.

Establishing or maintaining a support network helps families cope. Rumors are hurtful and are best not repeated. If they cannot be resolved, then contact the chain of command to find out the truth or put a stop to them. Breaking up the time is a useful technique to prevent being overwhelmed. This can include weekly get-togethers with other families, monthly outings for the children (a favorite restaurant, the park, a picnic, etc.), and a visit to, or from, parents and in-laws around mid-deployment, just to name a few.

In order to maintain their sanity, parents—now "single" because of the deployment—will need time without their children. Scheduling a regular "Mommy's (Daddy's) day out" can be achieved by daycare or sharing sitting with someone you trust. Overspending or increased alcohol use may provide short-term relief, but in the long-term, they will only exacerbate the stress of deployment. Lastly, and most importantly, serving member, spouse, and children will change and grow during the deployment. It is critical to go slow, be patient, and allow several months to reestablish family bonds.

Case Study

Being a senior Personnel NCO married to a Ranger, Sgt. Maj. Jennifer Pearson knows a thing or two about deployments and separations. She spent a year in Bosnia. Her husband, Sgt. Maj. James Pearson, was in Afghanistan at the beginning of Operation Enduring Freedom.

"We've probably been separated more than we've been together," she said.

Despite that, Pearson, who at that time was a student in the Sergeants Major Course Class 54 at the U.S. Army Sergeants Major Academy (USASMA), Fort Bliss, Texas, said that being a member of a dual-military couple is a great experience.

"I believe it's been very positive. The deployments are small stuff," she said. "Sure we're away from each other a lot, but we have a good relationship and our strengths complement each other's weaknesses."

INTERVIEW SUMMARIES

This particular interview featured a retired lieutenant colonel who had left active duty in the USAF to go to the National Guard. He had made this decision in order to be closer to his family. He explained that his career, which he described as "formerly fast track," was essentially "frozen" when he moved to the Guard. He was accused by military peers of "taking the easy way out" or "trying to get out of conflict," though he chose a job that he described as "actually more conflict-engaging." He stated that it had required him to take extreme shift work in order to have some physical presence and proximity to his family. He accepted prescriptions for sleep deprivation and described "living on prescriptions" and shift work in order to try to support the dysfunctional dynamics that had developed in his family.

He shared that the toll repeated deployments had taken on his marriage and family had led to extreme behavioral issues with his then-teenage daughter, which included diagnosis and medications for depression and similar disorders. He indicated that he and his former wife "had nearly divorced at the ten-year mark." He indicated that counseling through their church family had kept the marriage together for a time and that their religious foundation had ultimately been what had held the marriage and family together as long as it did. Eventually the military marriage led to divorce. He indicated he stayed married to her for "20" so that he could be sure she had long-term health care entitlements and partial pension for the rest of her life.

Another interview concerned a military spouse (who was on her second military marriage). She was able to speak to her history having had two military spouses as well as a social work background working with Wounded Warriors. Her prior enlisted spouse had been described as a functioning alcoholic over the span of multiple deployments and separations, and the marriage had ended in an abusive fashion involving law enforcement.

She alleged her two prior husbands were both caught in affairs. The enlisted former spouse had represented himself to her as on a deployment while he was allegedly engaged in an affair with another woman. She revealed that the former enlisted spouse allegedly kidnapped the woman he was having the extramarital affair with and held her at gunpoint. She claims that this took place during a time that the former enlisted spouse was also supposedly under supervision for substance abuse, which his command was aware of and was allegedly covering up. She indicated that he served some type of incarceration for this.

During that time she became pregnant and sought an abortion because she did not want to have another child with this individual, who was apparently quite unstable. The counseling or supervision this former spouse was allegedly receiving was clearly inadequate, and the family continued to be placed at risk despite diligent communication with his command regarding his conduct. Despite all her efforts to be sure that she and the children were protected, she indicated that his command shielded him, participated in covering up criminal behavior, and left her family exposed to his dangerous and unstable behavior.

Her comments were unfavorable to the military "system"; it was not protecting her or her family's interests, being singularly concerned with the active-duty spouse and his work duties. She alleged that she was not afforded therapeutic care or proper intervention. She also made comments about the Wounded Warriors she had worked with and how many of them, after several deployments, were self-medicating, their injuries merely exacerbated. She also brought to light what was broken inside many others who otherwise did not have a discernible injury befitting the label.

Being a member of a dual-military couple presents a unique set of challenges, still, many choose to endure the hardships, finding a balance between their marriages and their careers. More than 20,000 dual-military couples currently serve in the U.S. Army. The majority of these couples—79 percent—enjoy joint domicile assignments, but that doesn't mean they won't endure long separations and domestic difficulties.

For serving members contemplating trying to combine matrimony and the military, veteran dual-military couples stationed throughout the Army have plenty of advice to share on the subject.

"Being in the military has strengthened our relationship because every day is a test," said Pearson whose husband, she added, also a Class 54 student, has been a valuable resource for training and motivation. Being a Ranger, he's been able to help keep her tactical skills up to speed. She, in turn, has been able to provide him with personnel and finance information.

"We're a team," she said. "He'll use me in a heartbeat, just like I'll use him. We're both professional soldiers and we believe the Army is where we should be."

"You don't have to make a choice whether you want to stay in the military or stay together with your family," said Master Sgt. Yolanda Choates, Public Affairs chief for the U.S. Army Maneuver Support Center, Fort Leonard Wood, Missouri. Her husband, Sgt. 1st Class Meco Choates, is the Protective Services Training Branch course manager for Company A, 701st Military Police Battalion. "It's possible to do both; it's challenging. It's not easy, but anything worth striving for is never easy."

Doing both, keeping a family together while accomplishing the missions set forth by the Army, is something many dual-military couples face. One way to meet the challenge is by enrolling in the Married Army Couples Program (MACP). Established in August 1983, the MACP is a program designed to help ensure soldiers married to other soldiers are considered for joint domicile assignments.

"The hardships associated with maintaining a family while being a soldier are compounded in a married Army couple," said Lt. Col. Patrick Sedlack, chief of Plans, Procedures and Operations Branch, Army Human Resources Command. "The MACP was established to help alleviate some of the problems by trying, when possible, to assign married couples at the same location. The goal of the program is to ensure that MACP Soldiers are considered for assignment together as often as possible."

To enroll in the MACP, married couples need to submit a Department of the Army Form 4187, Request for Personnel Action, to their local military personnel office. The personnel office will then process the information and enroll the soldiers. If the soldiers are assigned to separate duty stations, each soldier must submit a DA Form 4187 to his or her personnel office.

"The Married Army Couples Program works, but it doesn't guarantee you will be assigned together," said Staff Sgt. William Herold, a paralegal assigned to Headquarters and Headquarters Company, 173rd Airborne Brigade, Vicenza, Italy. His wife, Sgt. Antoinette Herold, is a paralegal assigned to Headquarters Support Company, Southern European Task Force, Vicenza, Italy.

There are a number of things that can make it difficult for the MACP to station a couple together, said Sedlak. If two soldiers have the same low-density MOS (military occupational specialty), they may be more difficult to station together, he explained. Or if a soldier has an MOS in which most available assignments are outside the continental United States (CONUS), for example, a soldier who is a Korean linguist is married to a soldier with an MOS in which most available assignments are in CONUS, it may be difficult to station them together.

MACP also applies to soldiers married to members of other services or to Army Reserve or National Guard Soldiers, but it is more difficult for assignments managers to station them together, Sedlack said. In addition to the difficulties inherent in stationing soldiers from different career fields together, there are also problems stationing soldiers together when they volunteer for special duty.

"There are no specific restrictions on the MACP, but some programs and situations are much more difficult to accommodate a (joint domicile) assignment," said Sedlack. For assignments such as Drill Sergeant and Recruiter, selectees enrolled in MACP are required to provide a written statement saying he or she understands a joint-domicile assignment may not be possible due to restrictions pertaining to the duty.

"The assignments managers will still consider (joint domicile) for those couples, but want to make sure the soldiers understand that it is very difficult to provide (it) due to the demands and locations of those assignments," said Sedlack.

"If it meant being separated for a long period of time, I don't think either one of us could (provide) such a (written statement)," said Herold. "Our branch manager has worked very hard to ensure we stay together and I think signing a (written statement) wouldn't stop our branch from working just as hard to keep our family together."

While some, like Herold, place a lot of faith in their branch managers, others recommend that couples take a more proactive hand in their careers.

"You have to plan properly and manage your own career," said Sgt. Maj. Henry Garrett. Garrett is the Human Resources sergeant major for Fort Bliss, Texas. His wife, Sgt. Maj. Shirley Garrett, is a student in Sergeants Major Course Class 54 at USASMA.

For example, Garrett said when he knew he was due for an assignment outside CONUS, he volunteered for duty in Korea with the hope that his wife would be able to follow.

When Shirley became the tactical NCO (noncommissioned officer) at the U.S. Military Academy at West Point, New York, Henry called his branch manager to find out what was available for him at the same location.

The Choates's have made similar sacrifices. "When we moved here from the [Washington] D.C. area, [Yolanda] had only one position available here," said Sgt. 1st Class Choates. "If she had to choose a position, this probably wouldn't be it, but she made that choice for the family."

"I would rather have been a first sergeant in Korea, but that's not what was best for my family," said Master Sgt. Choates. "We do these things because, being in the Army, you don't always have a choice."

Unfortunately, this strategy also has some drawbacks.

"We had to decline appointments to command sergeant major for the last five years because as command sergeants major it would be harder to station us together," Garrett said. He added, the key to a successful dual-military marriage is consideration for each other's career goals.

"I really didn't want to go to West Point, but I knew Shirley needed something that would help her stand apart from her peers," he said.

"If a couple is not in the same career management field, I recommend they learn as much as they can so they know what it takes to advance each other's careers."

Communication, said the Choates, is another important factor in maintaining a successful dual military marriage.

"You have to communicate," said Sgt. 1st Class Choates. "If you don't let each other know what's going on or how you feel, you're not going to succeed."

"You have to talk about schedule requirements and needs," added Master Sgt. Choates. She said it is important to coordinate things like picking up children from school, parent/teacher conferences, and medical and dental appointments.

Another challenge dual-military couples must tackle are family care plans—written instructions for the care of family members in the event of deployments, temporary duty, or field exercises. Dual-military couples have thirty days after arriving at a new unit to produce a valid family care plan, which includes naming both a short-term and long-term care provider.

In some cases, finding a short-term care provider at a new duty station can be difficult.

"[Early in our careers,] we didn't really know anybody at our next duty stations. We had thirty days to find someone we'd trust enough to take care of our kids, who was willing to do it," said Master Sgt. Choates.

"Now that we're older and we've been in a while, we know people at most of our duty stations when we get there."

Master Sgt. Choates added that those who haven't been in the Army long enough to know someone at every duty station should look amongst their coworkers for short-term care providers, because the people a soldier works with on a daily basis are the ones they get to know first.

"Family readiness groups are another good source of information," said Sgt. 1st Class Choates. "But you have to go to the FRG meetings. They won't come to you."

Many serving members married to other serving members agree that being a member of a dual-military couple involves a lot of sacrifice. Some, however, find the sacrifice to be too much. Being a soldier is something Staff Sgt. Alison Kempke enjoys. A technical engineer assigned to Company A, 94th Engineer Battalion, Hohenfels, Germany, she was deployed in Iraq while her husband and two children waited for her in Germany. Kempke said she found her job both rewarding and challenging, but she ended her military career after only eight years.

"I love the military and I'd love to stay in, but the separations are hard," she said. "I'd also like to be around to raise my kids."

Support during Distances

Some Ways to Nurture Your Love through the Ups and Downs of Deployment

Talk about your upcoming separation. Set aside some quiet time to talk about your feelings and plan how each of you will manage during your time apart.

Discuss how you will stay in touch. Explore the available options, such as e-mail, phone calls, and regular mail.

Keep busy and stay active if you are the at-home spouse. The more fulfilled you feel, the better you will handle separations and difficult times. (Of course, if you have children you won't have concerns about not being busy.)

Share daily happenings from home. Hearing about your life (even the everyday routine) will help your deployed spouse feel closer to you.

Learn about your spouse's job and other interests. Learning what your spouse's life is like will help you better understand his or her experiences while you are apart.

Send care packages. Be sure to include special treats, funny notes, and items that have special meaning for the two of you.

Record your thoughts in a journal to share with your spouse. You may want to keep an online journal with pictures for your spouse to access over the Internet.

Record a tape or CD with songs that remind you of your spouse. Make a copy for each of you.

Send handmade coupons to your deployed spouse. Your coupons might be for a special dinner or hour-long backrub when your partner returns home.

Be realistic about communication. Keep in mind that your deployed spouse may be in an area with limited mail or e-mail service, or too busy to respond right away.

Consider making commitments to personal, emotional, educational, spiritual, and physical improvement—select some individual and family or couple goals and work together to decide how you will support and encourage each other to reach the goals while apart. Goals should be SMART: Specific, Measurable, Achievable, Results-Focused, and Time-bound.

Specific—Know what you want to achieve, specific goals are easier to achieve than general ones. "I want to be healthy" is too general. "I am going to eat a healthy diet and exercise three times a week" is better. Write down your goals and the reasons for them. If you lack motivation after a week or two, read your notes to remind you why you set out on this road.

Measureable—Choose goals that are measurable. If you want to lose weight, how much? If you want to lower your blood pressure, what is your target level? Don't set expectations so high that you doom yourself to failure. Success can also be measured by reaching a target: competing in—and finishing—a 5K race or getting into your favorite jeans that you haven't been able to wear for years.

Achievable—Be realistic. Don't expect to lose fifty pounds in the next four weeks! Decide on losing one to two pounds a week for the next six months. Maybe target to lose ten pounds in the first month because that will fuel your desire to carry on with your weight-loss program. Also, there is nothing wrong with revising your goal along the way. The important thing is not to abandon it. Revising your goal may mean it takes longer to achieve it, but at least you will have achieved it.

Relevant or Results-Focused—You have set your goal and written down the reason for it. It is important to keep reminding yourself that what you are doing is going to have a beneficial impact on your life. If your goal is not achieving the results you hoped for, or worse, starts to have a detrimental effect, reevaluate your goal.

Timebound—Establish a time target for achieving your goal and, if possible, mini targets along the way that you can celebrate to keep you motivated.

Above all, get SMART and achieve your own personal goals.

Stage 5: Post-deployment

See next chapter.

Chapter Three

Preparing to Return Home

POST-DEPLOYMENT

The post-deployment stage begins with the arrival to home station. Like the pre-deployment stage, the timeframe for this stage is also variable depending on the particular family. Typically, this stage lasts from three to six months and starts with the "homecoming."

This can be a wonderfully joyous occasion with children rushing to the returning parent followed by the warm embrace and kiss of the reunited couple. The unit then comes to attention for one last time, followed by words of praise from the senior commander present. Lastly, weapons are turned in and duffle bags retrieved and the family goes home. Homecoming can also be an extremely frustrating and upsetting experience. The date of return may change repeatedly or units may travel home piecemeal over several days. Despite best intentions, the spouse at home may not be able to meet the returning warrior (short notice, the children might be sick, sitters cannot be found in the middle of the night, unable to get off work, etc.). Returning service personnel may expect to be received as "heroes" and "heroines," only to find that they have to make their own way home.

Typically, a "honeymoon" period follows in which couples reunite physically, but not necessarily emotionally. Some spouses express a sense of awkwardness in addition to excitement: "Who is this stranger in my bed?" For others, however, the desire for sexual intimacy may require time in order to reconnect emotionally first.

Eventually, serving members will want to reassert their role as a member of the family, which can lead to tension. This is an essential task, which requires considerable patience to accomplish successfully. Serving members may feel pressure to make up for lost time and missed milestones. Serving members may want to take back all the responsibilities they had before.

However, some things will have changed in their absence: spouses are more autonomous, children have grown, and individual personal priorities in life may be different. It is not realistic to return home and expect everything to be the same as before the deployment. During this period, spouses may report a lost sense of independence. There may be resentment at having been "abandoned" for six months or more. Reunion with children can also be a challenge.

Spouses may consider themselves to be the true heroes (watching the house, children, paying bills, etc.) while serving members cared only for themselves.

At least one study (Zeff et al., 1997) suggests that the stay-at-home parent is more likely to report distress than the deployed serving member. Spouses will also have to adapt to changes. Spouses may find that they are more irritable with their partners underfoot. They may desire their "own" space. Basic household chores and routines need to be renegotiated. The role played by the spouse in the marriage must be reestablished.

Reunion with children can also be a challenge. Their feelings tend to depend on their age and understanding of why the serving member was gone. Babies less than one year old may not know the serving member and cry when held. Toddlers (1–3 years) may be slow to warm up. Pre-schoolers (3–6 years) may feel guilty and scared over the separation. School age children (6–12 years) may want a lot of attention. Teenagers (13–18 years) may be moody and may not appear to care. In addition, children are often loyal to the parent that remains behind and do not respond to discipline from the returning serving member. They may also fear the serving member's return: "Wait till Mommy/Daddy gets home!" Some children may display significant anxiety up to a year later ("anniversary reaction"), triggered by the possibility of separation. In addition, the serving member may not approve of privileges granted to children by the non-deployed parent. However, it is probably best for the serving member not to try to make changes right away and to take time renegotiating family rules and norms. Not heeding this advice, the serving member risks invalidating the efforts of his or her mate and alienating the children. Serving members may feel hurt in response to such a lukewarm reception. Clearly going slow and letting the child(ren) set the pace goes a long way toward a successful reunion.

Post-deployment is probably the most important stage for both serving member and spouse. Patient communication, going slow, lowering expectations, and taking time to get to know each other again is critical to the task of successful reintegration of the serving member back into the family. Counseling may be required in the event that the serving member is injured or returns as a stress casualty. On the other hand, the separation of deployment—unlike civilian couples—provides serving member and spouse a chance to evaluate changes within themselves and to contemplate what direction they want their marriage to take. Although a difficult as well as joyful stage, many military couples have reported that their relationship is much stronger as a result.

INTERVIEW SUMMARIES

An active-duty officer's wife noted the instability that gradually developed over multiple deployments with her then-spouse. It was clear to her that he was developing signs of severe PTSD, and she observed behaviors ranging from road rage to night terrors and fitful sleep. She and a mall food court of eye witnesses saw him pick up a rented child "buggy" and hurl it in a spontaneous angry rage, knocking over tables and chairs and drawing the attention of onlookers and security. She observed changes in behavioral drinking and unhealthy eating; she noticed he had become a neglectful and emotionally abusive spouse and parent who was frequently withdrawn. She indicated that she had contacted Military OneSource and requested a therapist who was trained to address specific issues with behavior in the child as well as some educational challenges the child was having.

She indicated that the provision and arrangements for therapy through MCCS (Marine Corps Community Service) were rapid, and they were very responsive to her. The therapist they put her in touch with was a fantastic advocate, but when the therapist told her about her husband's disorders, she then attempted to seek therapeutic intervention for her spouse, despite his insistence that it would risk his career and subsequently their long-term health care and benefits. He agreed to one session on base under assurance it would not be held against him. He was told, "It's not if you develop PTSD, it's when. Whether it takes one deployment or seventeen, everybody gets it."

Her spouse was not required to continue sessions nor was he evaluated in a way that would lead him to be medicated or otherwise treated. He refused further treatment since he was not under order to do so and indicated he believed the "female Air Force Major wasn't qualified to treat him because she wasn't a Marine and had never seen a day of combat," despite this individual's assignment at a Special Operations Command (SOCOM). The wife also believed he refused treatment because the professional was a woman. She indicated her nightmare continued because the Marine officer either directly injured her child in her absence or neglected the child and the child ended up severely injured. She left with the child and filed for divorce.

The father pled for his parental rights and the child continues to be returned frequently showing signs of mental, emotional, and physical abuse. She indicated that the courts, military, and Department of Family Services systems have minimized, if not completely disregarded, domestic violence injunctions and steps to ensure her and her child's safety, despite eyewitness accounts and affidavits of his behavior. She indicated she has now been fighting nearly seven years to protect herself and her child without any appropriate assistance from the military or the courts, and that at no time has the military required him to have any type of psychological assessment.

In addition, when his attorney pled to the court that psychological findings could have an adverse impact on his career, the courts intervened and did not order psychological intervention or appropriate therapy that would have forced him to receive treatment. She claims she and her child continue to be victims of his dangerous and unstable behavior, and that it has progressively worsened over time. Her now twelve-year-old child begs to be kept away from him, yet she is court ordered and forced to timeshare regardless of the documentation.

RETURNING FROM DEPLOYMENT

It is normal to feel nervous and anxious about the homecoming. You may wonder whether your spouse will "Like the way I look?" "Like what I've done with the house?" "Be proud of me for how I've handled things?" "Still need me?" "Still love me?"

Plan for homecoming day. After homecoming, make an agreement with your spouse on the schedule for the next few days or weeks. Where do the children, parents, extended family members, or friends fit in?

Realize the day of homecoming is very stressful. You and your spouse may not have slept much and may be worn out from preparations. Take time to get used to each other again. Reestablishing sexual intimacy will take patience, time, and good communication—some people need to be courted again.

COMMUNICATE!! Tell your spouse how you feel—nervous, scared, happy, that you love and missed them. Listen to your spouse in return. The best way to get through the reacquaintance jitters, regain closeness, and renegotiate your roles in the family is by talking and actively listening. You've both been used to doing what you wanted during personal time. Feeling like you need some space is normal.

Remember . . .

- Your fantasies and expectations about how life will be upon return may be just fantasies.
- Be prepared to be flexible.
- You and/or your spouse may be facing a change in job assignment or a move. Readjustment and job transition cause stress. This may be especially true for demobilizing Guard/Reservists who are transitioning back to civilian life.

Be calm and assertive, not defensive, when discussing decisions you have made, new family activities and customs, or methods of disciplining the children. Your spouse may need to hear that it wasn't the same doing these things alone, that you're glad he or she is back, and that you'd like to discuss problems and criticisms calmly.

Reassure your spouse that they are needed, even though you have coped during the deployment. Talk about keeping some of the independence you have developed. It's best not to "dump" all the chores—or only the ones you dislike—back on your spouse.

Your spouse may have seen or experienced some things that were very upsetting. Some normal reactions to these stressful situations are fear, nervousness, irritability, fatigue, sleep disturbances, startle reactions, moodiness, trouble concentrating, feelings of numbness, and frequent thoughts of the event. Talking with others and/or counselors trained in crisis stress reactions is very important.

REUNION

The reunion of a family after a separation can be just as stressful as the separation itself. If your family has experienced some strain or tension during a reunion, you are not alone. You may have wondered why an occasion that is "supposed" to be so romantic and exciting should turn out less than perfect.

From the moment you are separated from the person you care about, you may begin to build up an image of that person in your mind. You may fantasize about how wonderful everything will be when you are together again.

You may remember the members of your family as they appear in the photograph in your wallet—the picture-perfect all-American family. A similar process is happening with the spouse and children. The missing member may be placed on a pedestal as the warrior out defending the country. Memories of everyday life such as making ends meet, occasional disagreements, and disciplining the children, begin to fade from everyone's mind. The reunion is seen as the solution to all problems. "Once we are together again, everything will be perfect." However, reality rarely has a chance to live up to the high expectations you have set in your minds.

This is not meant to be a forecast of "doom and gloom." Homecomings can be very happy occasions as long as all family members make an effort to be as realistic as possible. If the tendency to not pick up after oneself around the house occurred before the separation, that habit probably has not miraculously disappeared. If a weight problem existed prior to the separation, do not expect a fifty-pound loss to have occurred during the separation. If one of the children was experiencing problems at school, do not expect the problem to disappear at reunion time.

Talking to one another and working through the everyday challenges that family life presents is what is important. This does not all have to be accomplished on the day of the family reunion. Give yourselves some time to enjoy one another. Everyone needs to get reacquainted before problem solving begins.

Resist the temptation to go on a spending spree to celebrate the reunion. The extra money saved during deployment may be needed later for unexpected household expenses. Stick to your household budget. Show you care through your time and effort.

WHAT TO EXPECT FROM YOUR CHILDREN

Children may be feeling the same confusing things you and your spouse feel—worry, fear, stress, happiness, and excitement. Depending on their age, they may not understand how your spouse could leave them if he or she really loved them. They may be unsure of what to expect from your spouse. They may feel uncomfortable or think of him or her as a stranger.

It's hard for children to control their excitement. Let them give and get the attention they need from the returning parent before you try to have quiet time alone with your spouse. Children's reactions to the returning parent will differ according to their ages. Here are some normal reactions you can expect:

- Infants
  - Cry, fuss, pull away from the returning parent, cling to you or the caregiver
- Toddlers
  - Be shy, clingy, not recognize the returning parent, cry, have temper tantrums, return to behaviors they had outgrown (no longer toilet trained)
- Preschoolers
  - Feel guilty for making parent go away, need time to warm up to returning parent, intense anger, act out to get attention, be demanding

- School Age
  - Excitement, joy, talk constantly to bring the returning parent up to date, boast about the returning parent, guilt about not doing enough or being good enough
- Teenagers
  - Excitement, guilt about not living up to standards, concern about rules and responsibilities, feel too old or unwilling to change plans to meet or spend extended time with the returning parent

Prepare children for homecoming with activities, photographs, participating in preparations, talking about dad or mom. Children are excited and tend to act out. Accept and discuss these physical, attitudinal, mental, and emotional changes.

- Plan time as a couple and as a family with the children.
- Stay involved with your children's school and social activities.
- Take time for yourself.
- Look into ways to manage stress—diet, exercise, recreation—and definitely take care of yourself!
- Make time to rest.
- Negotiate the number of social events you and your family will attend.
- Limit your use of alcohol. Remember, alcohol was restricted during your spouse's deployment and tolerance is lowered.
- Go slowly in getting back into the swing of things. Depend on family, your spouse's unit, and friends for support.

Remember . . .

- Go slowly—don't try to make up for lost time.
- Accept that your partner may be different.
- Take time to get reacquainted.
- Seek help for family members, if needed.
- If you feel like you are having trouble coping with adjustment, it is healthy to ask for help.

Many normal, healthy people occasionally need help to handle tough challenges in their lives. Contact a counseling agency or a minister, a

Military Family Center, military chaplain, the Veterans Administration, or one of your community support groups that has been established in your area.

If a child is demonstrating resistance, it is important to go at the child's pace; not the adult's pace. Behavioral intervention services and counseling are available through an MTF (Medical Treatment Facility) referral and/ or MCCS OneSource call requesting support. It is imperative not to force anyone to adapt to an adult's singular emotional needs without the consideration of the needs of all family members and their emotional health.

FOR THE RETURNING MILITARY

Even if you've been through a mobilization/deployment before, this one has been different because of the increased stressors of the time. Regardless of your experience and assignment, you will have a natural period of adjustment.

Ease yourself back into the family gradually. If you come on like a "Sherman tank" and try to bulldoze your way back into your family's life, feelings of resentment will surface. See yourself as a "special guest" for a while. Allow everyone to adjust in their own time and their own way(s).

Take some time to observe how the family has been running in your absence. You might be tempted to jump right in with "Now that I am home, there are going to be a few changes around here." You will see that some things will change naturally as a result of your presence in the family. If you disagree about the way other things have been handled, wait a few days and discuss it openly with your spouse.

Do not try to take over the finances immediately. A complete interrogation regarding the state of the checkbook as soon as you walk through the door is bound to create hostility. Set aside some time when things have calmed down to review the financial situation with your spouse.

Take it easy with the children in terms of discipline. For a while, stick with the rules your spouse has established during your absence. Immediately playing the "heavy" will not open up opportunities for you and the children to get to know one another again. It is not difficult to understand why some children are afraid of the returning parent if all they have to look forward to is "a changing of the guard."

On the other hand, sometimes it is easy to spoil your children. If you have not seen them for a long period of time, or you are home for only short periods of time, you may find yourself not wanting to discipline them. You are probably eager to make up for the time you were unable to spend with them. This is certainly understandable. But do not put your spouse in the position of constantly playing the "heavy" while you have all the fun with the children.

Do not be surprised if your spouse is a little envious of your travels. Your life may look very exciting compared to the job of "keeping the home fires burning." Surprise your spouse with a gift when you return from a new place. This way they can show off their "treasures" from different states or countries and cultures and share in your experiences.

Expect your spouse to have changed. Neither of you is the same person you were a few months ago, or even a few weeks ago. The main adjustment for military families after a separation is the change in roles. Your spouse has learned to cope alone as a matter of survival. Out of necessity, some of your roles have been taken over in order to compensate for your absence. Try not to be threatened if you find an independent person when you return home. The fact that your spouse can cope without you does not necessarily mean that he or she cares about you any less.

REUNITING WITH YOUR SPOUSE

- It is normal to feel nervous and anxious about homecoming. Often service members wonder whether my spouse will still "Be proud of me?" "Love me and need me?" "Expect things from me?"
- Plan for homecoming day. After homecoming, make an agreement with your spouse on the schedule for the next few days or weeks. Where do the children, extended family members or friends fit in?
- Realize the day of homecoming is very stressful. You and your spouse may not have slept much and may be worn out from preparations.
- Don't be surprised if your spouse is a bit resentful of your mobilization/deployment. Others often think of the deployment as more fun and exciting than staying at home—even if you know otherwise.
- Take time to get used to each other again. Reestablishing sexual intimacy will take patience, time and good communication—some people

need to be courted again. Set aside "date" nights where you can do the things you did when you were courting and go to the places that have a special meaning for you both. Remember the rules about building strong relationships and stoke up that fire.

- Communicate. Tell your spouse how you feel—nervous, scared, happy, that you love and missed them. Listen to your spouse in return. The best way to get through the reacquaintance jitters, regain closeness, and renegotiate your role in the family is by talking and actively listening.
- You've both been used to doing what you wanted during personal time. Feeling like you need some space is normal.
- Your fantasies and expectations about how life will be upon return may be just fantasies.
- Be prepared to be flexible.
- You and/or your spouse may be facing a change in job assignment or a move. Readjustment and job transition cause stress. This may be especially true for demobilizing Guard/Reservists who are transitioning back to civilian life.
- Resist the temptation to go on a spending spree to celebrate the reunion. The extra money saved during deployment may be needed later for unexpected household expenses. Stick to your budget. Show you care through your time and effort.

INTERVIEW SUMMARY

The couple interviewed within this segment was a same-sex couple, both officers on active duty. They indicated that they had not had any dealings with the military health care system. They have been together for ten years; dating back to when "Don't Ask, Don't Tell" was in effect. They had a three-and-a-half year long-term separation, but they could not be open in their relationship early on. In 2014, they were facing another international three-year separation, but they describe it as currently very different, as now they are legally married, and they have nothing but positive things to contribute to their overall military experience. They have "seen both sides of it": when they had to conceal their relationship and when they were able to be open.

According to both, it was a big struggle when it wasn't legal, because they didn't have a military family; it was really only the two of them, and there was no preparation back then as to how separations were going to affect them. After three-and-a-half years, they had built a strong bond through communication, FaceTime, and seeing each other by traveling every quarter—all described as a big struggle. As a commander in Kurdistan, having that foundation and relationship during those professional pressures was helpful.

They made it ten years and are facing another three-year separation, but they feel more prepared. They figure it's part of their lives now and they've acclimated to it. There were times in their relationship when they were apart more than together. The biggest issue now—they wonder if they can be together full time when the military spouse retirement draws near for them both, because that is a foreign concept to them.

There have been many technological advancements during the span of their careers and duties apart. The technology to help people has evolved far beyond "mail." Leveraging technology, syncing calendar events, communicating, and planning time together is easily accomplished.

Being highly organized helped them. When they were together, they scheduled the next visit so they could plan it and look forward to it. They were goal oriented about sharing time together, sticking to hard dates on the calendar. With the deployments—they had a nine-month total separation at the longest stint—that was really hard, but they made sure they scheduled calls and tried to have at least a weekly call.

Even back during "Don't Ask, Don't Tell," trusted communities where they knew they would be accepted became their chosen military friends and families, their "under the radar" support system. Friends were willing to accept the risk of being "fired" for knowing and supporting them: "You just didn't talk about it." They have always had really supportive friends: "I think everybody knew, and we've never had any issues; we never threw it in anyone's face. They knew it and didn't care. They cared that we wanted to serve our country and that we were good people."

"Even the most homophobic people don't realize they actually have gay people in their lives. They have had friends who were investigated and kicked out of the military, and they agree that success depends on who they trust and how they conducted their personal lives."

These individuals were in the academies and they are pilots—they were typically the only females in their classes and/or the only females in the squadron. They never had any issues with any men in the cockpit. They brought professionalism and capability to their jobs, and they were treated with respect. They look at it as having thick skin, being focused on doing the best job they possibly can, and as part of the thick skin, "if people dish it out, you dish it back, you draw the line quickly"—just to convey the message that the job is important.

Maturity is important too; you don't back down when someone behaves inappropriately. They established boundaries and enforced them. Sometimes conflict teaches where and how to define your boundaries. Sometimes it's not always a flaw in the process; it can be a flaw with the individual within the process. The military can ensure they hire the appropriate professionals in the field, and they could do a better job of that. They can recognize the symptoms of a bad situation and turn it around by focusing individuals on the job. There are things that get in the way of the job, so meet the system halfway. People need to be accountable and responsible for their actions, know limits and boundaries, and focus on the job.

When it became legal to be gay in the military in 2011, it was like any other day at work. They felt that shows how professional their colleagues were. Being married wasn't much different except for the change in their tax bracket, according to their comments. They didn't experience any real issues with it. "The military has been at the leading edge at times with social change."

Once you know the problem: What are you going to do about it?

One challenge they feel is real is that the people in the process aren't fully informed of the services and how to do their jobs, and this doesn't just apply to processes for help in terms of stresses or counseling based upon deployments and difficult separations, it applies to all aspects of the jobs. There are processes, but they discern that processes and the people involved in those processes are two different things, and there's room for improvement in the people part of things.

Some people were able to find the support and care they needed and others are facing a process that is dysfunctional, with people who may or may not have the proper training.

They are both colonels. They have a unique support system because they are both in the service, unlike many couples where one is a military member and the other is a dependent/spouse/family member who may or may not have direct military experience. In other words, because both are in the military, they get it, and that goes a long way in supporting and understanding the other. When one individual is having the active duty experience, the other, never having walked in those shoes, may not wholly understand it—though they may be able to intellectually grasp the concept; both are in very different places in the relationship.

For this couple, the dynamics of the relationship and the success of maintaining the relationship, in whatever form, during deployments and separations, wasn't all that different from investing in a non-military relationship. A good relationship is a lot about personality. It's the little things that you do to support the other; it's how you respect someone else, how you find something positive in someone else and communicate it. For example, this couple chooses to focus on things that make them giggle— finding joy in the mundane.

"The Mason Jar": They write things down that make them smile, or giggle, or feel special. They write them down, save them, and add them to the mason jar. On December 31, they open all the notes from the year and read them. This reminds them to value and respect and cherish one another each year. Respect applies to all relationships, all friendships; acknowledge and value the people you have in your life. What are you doing to be invested in the relationship, whether you are near, far, gay, straight, whatever color? It's about quality; it's about making the investment in people.

Another tool they have used in their relationship applied because one personality was more stoic, the other more emotional. To address this, they created "Role Reversal Time" to illustrate the following: "How you say things and how they are perceived are two different things." In these exercises, they switch roles from giver to receiver of information; this helps those who may be "over or under" sensitive. They said their family loves to watch them fight because people find each other's examples really funny.

Their branch is the U.S. Air Force (USAF): "Service before Self." Sometimes we fail to take care of ourselves because we are focused on putting others before ourselves. Caregivers can suffer more than the patient in some of these types of relationships; their own health suffers. They also talked about how many times the caregivers burn out in the family because they put their all into the care position, at their own expense, and how important it is to have the ability to take care and recharge.

SINGLE SERVICE MEMBERS/SINGLE PARENTS— REUNITING WITH PARENTS, EXTENDED FAMILY MEMBERS, CHILDREN, AND FRIENDS

- You have certainly missed your family and friends, and they have missed you. Let them be a part of the reunion but balance your needs with those you love and care about. You will have a period of readjustment when you return home.
- If you are single or live with your parent(s), family, or a friend, many of the above tips for a reuniting with spouses and children may apply. Changes in the house or routine may be stressful. Go slowly in trying to make the adjustment to being home again.
- Some things will have changed at home while you were gone—marriage in your family or with friends, new babies born, new neighbors, and changes in relationships.
- Some things will change with the people you have lived and worked with prior to deployment. Married friends will be involved with their families. Others may return to their old friends and you may feel left out.
- Your parents and family have been very worried about you over the past months. Give them time and special attention.
- You may be facing a change in job assignment, a move, trying to meet new people, or looking for a new relationship. All these things cause stress.

Take Time for Yourself:

- You may have seen or experienced some things that were very upsetting. Some normal reactions to these abnormal situations are fear, nervousness, irritability, fatigue, sleep disturbances, startle reactions, moodiness, trouble concentrating, feelings of numbness, and frequent thoughts of the event. Talking with others who were there and/or counselors trained in crisis stress reactions is very important.
- Look into ways to manage stress—diet, exercise, recreation—and definitely take care of yourself!
- Make time to rest. Negotiate the number of social events you will attend.

- Limit your use of alcohol. Remember alcohol was restricted during your deployment and your tolerance is lowered.
- Depend on family, your unit, and friends for support.

Remember . . .

- Go slowly—don't try to make up for lost time.
- Accept that your partner and loved ones may be different.
- Take time to get reacquainted.
- Seek help, if needed.

BECOMING A COUPLE AGAIN

How to Create a Shared Sense of Purpose after Deployment

Coming together as a couple after war deployment isn't always easy or something that happens naturally. It requires effort, and an understanding that each person has grown and changed during the separation. A positive way to think about this is that both of you, service person and spouse, have developed your own sense of purpose coping with new experiences while apart. What's important now is to come together and create a "shared sense of purpose" that is essential for your well-being as a couple, as parents, and as members of your community. This won't happen overnight; it will take time, mutual compassion, and a desire to do so. Here are four steps to help you create a "shared sense of purpose."

Understand Each Other's Sense of Purpose during Separation

The returning service member's sense of purpose has been shaped by his or her deployment experiences:

- Traumatic events that can be difficult to process and talk about
- Identification and closeness with their military unit and comrades who have shared similar experiences
- Regimentation in the form of highly structured and efficient routines
- Heightened sensory experiences including sights, sounds, and smells
- Expanded self-importance and identity shaped by war

The spouse's sense of purpose has also been shaped by new experiences:

- Different roles and responsibilities. Many spouses have assumed new or more taxing employment, oversight of finances, and child rearing.
- Community support trade-offs. Some spouses and children left the military base to stay with parents and in-laws for various reasons; they will have experienced loss of connection with their military community, its familiarity and support.
- Emotional changes. Some spouses may have experienced growing independence and thrived on it; others may have found this a difficult time leading to depression, anxiety, increased alcohol or substance use and abuse, and other symptoms of stress.

Recognize that the following concerns upon return are common, often shared or felt indirectly, and will require mutual adjustments and time:

Home. Life at home does not have the edge and adrenaline associated with wartime duty, which often leads to letdown, disappointment, and difficulty shifting gears.

Children. Reconnecting with one's children is an anticipated event by service member and spouse. Children react differently depending upon their age, and can be shy, angry, or jealous as new bonds are reestablished. Discipline will now be shared, often resulting in conflicting opinions and styles.

Relationship. Concern about having grown apart, growing close again without giving up individual growth and viewpoints, issues of fidelity, and being able to discuss these issues without raising more anxiety or anger challenge many couples.

Public. While there has been widespread support of the service member, the public has mixed views of the war. Protracted deployment and an upcoming election may polarize the public, promoting media coverage that can undermine the pride and purpose military families feel about their involvement.

Relationship Breakers

Most couples argue about three things: sex, money, and children. Understanding the potential of these issues to divide rather than unite is key to reestablishing a shared sense of purpose. These issues involve the following:

Intimacy. Intimacy is a combination of emotional and physical togetherness. It is not easily reestablished after stressful separations creating an emotional disconnect.

Partners may also experience high or low sexual interest causing disappointment, friction, or a sense of rejection. In due time, this may pass, but present concerns may include hoping one is still loved, dealing with rumors or concern about faithfulness, concern about medications that can affect desire and performance, and expected fatigue and alterations in sleep cycles.

Finances. During the deployment, most service members and families received additional income from tax breaks and combat duty pay, as much as $1,000 extra a month. Some families may have been able to set aside appreciable savings; other families may have spent some or all of the money on justifiable expenses and adjusted family budgets. This may create disagreement that can hamper the important work of building shared trust and financial planning as a couple that is essential to moving forward.

Children. Children have grown and changed during deployment. Some returning soldiers will see children for the first time. It is important to build upon the positive changes in your children, and work as a couple to address issues of concern that need improvement or attention. Discipline of children will now be shared and should be viewed as something that can be built together rather than criticized or ignored.

Relationship Makers

Here are some thoughts and tips for building a shared sense of purpose and a stronger family.

Expectations. Remember that fatigue, confusion, and worry, common during this transition, often lead to short tempers. In that frame of mind, it is easy to revert to the relationship breaker issues listed above. If this happens, suggest taking time out and return to discussions when both parties feel more relaxed.

Enjoy life. Find and do activities that are pleasurable such as a movie, a family picnic, bowling, or shopping. Create time in your weekly schedule to do something as a couple and as a family. Plan one-on-one activities that are shared between the returning service member and his or her child or children.

Give thanks. Together, thank those people, family, friends, coworkers, and new service member buddies, who have helped you and your family during this deployment. Showing appreciation through writing notes together, calling people, or visiting them will bring a sense of fulfillment that reunites each other's experiences.

Communicate. Talking together builds a shared sense of purpose. Desire to communicate is more important than details. Service members often prefer to discuss war stories with military buddies to protect their spouse and family from traumatic memories. Spouses should not be offended. Other ways to communicate involve physical activity. Take walks, work out together, or engage in a sport. Healthy communication involves processing feelings, new information, and relieving stress. Read, draw, paint, dance, sing, play an instrument, volunteer at church or in the community to keep a sense of perspective

Let time be your friend. Time may not mend everything, but it is often one of the most important factors in healing and solving problems.

Be positive. A positive attitude is one of the most important gifts you can bring to each other and your family during this time. Appreciating what one has gives strength and energy to a family and a couple. Special circumstances such as physical injury and psychological problems are not addressed in this fact sheet and require additional support, information, and resources.

Know when to seek help. Both service member and spouse have endured a level of stress, uncertainty, worry, and lonesomeness that can affect one's health—both physically and mentally. If either spouse or service member suspects they may be suffering from a health or mental health problem, it is essential to seek help. Many service members do not want to seek help for mental health problems from the military for fear of damaging their career. However, the consequences of letting a problem linger untreated can be much more damaging. There are excellent treatments including medications that can help people reclaim their lives and enjoy their families, as they should. You owe it to yourself and your family to be in good health.

IMPACT ON CHILDREN

The response of children to the extended deployment of a parent is very individualized and also depends on their developmental age: infants, toddlers, preschool, school age, and teenagers. It is reasonable to assume that a sudden negative change in a child's behavior or mood is a predictable response to the stress of having a deployed parent.

Infants (< 1 year) must be held and actively nurtured in order to thrive. If a primary caregiver becomes significantly depressed, then the infant will be at risk for apathy, refusal to eat, and even weight loss. Early intervention becomes critical to prevent undue harm or neglect. Pediatricians can perform serial exams to ensure growth continues as expected on height/weight charts. Army Community Services and Social Work can assist with parenting skills and eliciting family or community support. Lastly, the primary caregiver may also benefit from individual counseling. Babies less than one year old may not recognize the returning warrior and may at first cry when held.

Toddlers (1–3 years) will generally take their cue from the primary caregiver. One issue is whether it is the mother or father who is leaving—especially when children are very young. If the "non-deploying" parent is coping well, they will tend to do well. The converse is also true. If the primary caregiver is not coping well, then toddlers may become sullen, tearful, throw tantrums, or develop sleep disturbances. They will usually respond to increased attention, hugs, and holding hands. The "non-deploying" parent may also benefit from sharing their day-to-day experiences with other parents facing similar challenges. In particular, it is important for the primary caregiver to balance the demands of caring for children alone with their own needs for time for self. It may take time for toddlers to warm up again to the returning warrior.

Preschoolers (3–6 years) may regress in their skills (e.g., difficulty with potty training, "baby talk," thumb sucking, refusal to sleep alone) and seem more "clingy." They may be irritable, depressed, aggressive, prone to somatic complaints, and have fears about parents or others leaving. Caregivers will need to reassure them with extra attention and physical closeness (e.g., hugs, holding hands). In addition, it is important to avoid changing family routines such as sleeping in their own bed, unless they are "very" scared. Answers to questions about the deployment should be brief, matter-of-fact, and to the point. This will help to contain the free-floating anxiety of an overactive imagination. They may feel guilty and scared over the separation.

School age children (6–12 years) may whine, complain, become aggressive, or otherwise "act out" their feelings. They may focus on the soldier-parent missing a key event, for example: "Will you (the soldier) be here for my birthday?" Depressive symptoms may include sleep disturbances and loss of interest in school, eating, or even playing with their friends. They will need to talk about their feelings and will need more physical attention than usual. Expectations regarding school performance may need to be a little lower, but keeping routines as close to normal as possible is best for them. On the warrior's return they are likely to want a lot of attention.

Teenagers (13–18 years) may be irritable, rebellious, fight, or participate in other attention-getting behavior. They may show a lack of interest in school, peers, and school activities. In addition, they are at greater risk for promiscuity, alcohol, and drug use. Although they may deny problems and worries, it is extremely important for caregivers to stay engaged and be available to talk out their concerns. At first, lowering academic expectations may be helpful; however, return to their usual school performance should be supported. Sports and social activities should be encouraged to give normal structure to their life. Likewise, additional responsibility in the family, commensurate with their emotional maturity, will make them feel important and needed. On the warrior's return it is not uncommon for the teenager to be moody and appear not to care and to seem to be more loyal to the spouse that remained behind.

Keep in mind that children of deployed parents are more vulnerable to psychiatric hospitalization—especially in single-parent and blended families.

Despite all these obstacles, the vast majority of spouses and family members successfully negotiate the sustainment stage and begin to look forward to their loved ones coming home.

Remember . . .

• Go slowly—don't try to make up for lost time.
• Accept that your partner may be different.

- Take time to get reacquainted.
- Seek help for family members, if needed.
- If you feel like you are having trouble coping with adjustment, it is healthy to ask for help.

Many normal, healthy people occasionally need help to handle tough challenges in their lives. Contact a counseling agency or a minister, a Military Family Center, military chaplain, the Veterans Administration, or one of your community support groups that has been established in your area.

One huge advantage of being married to someone in the military is the wealth of resources available to you through your new extended family and this is especially true when you have children. There are family support services, spouses' clubs, mentoring organizations, child care facilities, "respite care" for wounded families, volunteer networks, and many other licensed and professional services all aimed at providing you and your family with the support you need, particularly if you have wounded love ones or children with special needs. All the branches have dedicated, trained, and professional family support advisors who are available to help you. In the USMC, for instance, these advisers are known as Family Readiness Officers and work with Marine Corps Community Services. Your Family Support Center can put you in touch with the right people. You should never feel alone or helpless. There is always someone to turn to for help.

Remember, each branch of the military has its own name for Family Support Centers and their own programs for new spouses. These are as follows:

- Army Community Service Center—Family Team Building
- Airman and Family Readiness Center—Heartlink
- Marine Corps Community Services Center—LINKS (Lifestyle, Insights, Networking, Knowledge, and Skills)
- Navy Fleet and Family Support Center—COMPASS

Chapter Four

Physical, Mental, and
Spiritual Care

It is important to take care of yourself—both outwardly and inwardly. Physical and spiritual well-being are equally as important.

GETTING HELP

If there is one lesson above all else that you can get from this book it is this—if you need help, get it.

There are more than 9,000 social workers employed by the Department of Veterans Affairs (VA). They are assigned to the fifty-seven VA facilities located in all fifty states, the District of Columbia, and six territories. VA social workers work as case managers, clinicians, and administrators in hospitals and community-based outreach programs throughout the United States. They are there to help you.

Every person going through treatment, therapy, or counseling should know how to ask to be assigned a social worker to help them with resources via military treatment and VA resources. From the time you begin medical treatment, ask "Who is my social worker?," and keep asking until you are assigned one.

Outreach

Recognizing the stresses military life and multiple deployments put on families, the services have also stepped up their efforts to help members strengthen their family relationships and avoid the divorce courts. A full range of outreach programs—from support groups for spouses of deployed troops to weekend retreats for military couples—aims to help military families endure the hardships that military life often imposes.

According to Department of Defense statistics published in February 2015, the military's divorce rate continues to drop and is now at its lowest level since 2005. The divorce rate among both officers and enlisted men and women over 2014 was 3.1 percent, Pentagon officials said—only slightly higher than the 2005 rate of 3 percent. The statistics show how the rate has steadily declined since 2011, when it reached a high water-mark of 3.7 percent. The rate in 2001, at the start of the wars in Iraq and Afghanistan, was 2.6 percent.

"The health and well-being of service members and their families is a priority," said Lt. Cmdr. Nate Christensen, a Pentagon spokesman. "Strong relationships are important to our readiness."

The declining rate is largely due to a major drop in the divorce rate among married female troops. The divorce rate among male service members dropped only 0.3 percent over last year and only 0.5 percent since 2011.

But the rate among females has seen a major, steady decline over that period. Since 2011 the female divorce rate has moved steadily downward from 8 percent among both officer and enlisted to 6.5 percent last year.

"The latest data confirm and continue some general trends that we have been seeing for some time. Across all branches, divorce rates for males have been relatively flat," said Benjamin Karney, a researcher with the RAND Corp. who has studied military divorce. "Something else is going on for females, however. Across all branches, divorce rates for female service members have been declining substantially. . . . We see it among enlisted and officers."

The biggest rate of decline has been among married female Marines. In 2011, 9.5 percent of female enlisted and officer Marines got divorced, compared to 6.2 percent last year.

The civilian divorce rate stands at about 3.6 percent as of 2011, according to the most recent data. Military and civilian divorce rates cannot be accurately compared because of differences in tracking methodology.

While the divorce rate in the military is based on personnel data used to distribute benefits, the civilian rate is calculated on a per-one-thousand-person basis by the Centers for Disease Control and Prevention. The CDC's calculation, however, only accounts for forty-four states and the

District of Columbia because several states, including California, do not track or report their rates.

These statistics reflect a general trend in American society, according to Army Chaplain (Col.) Glen Bloomstrom, director of ministry initiatives for the Army's Office of the Chief of Chaplains. Forty-five percent to 50 percent of all first marriages end in divorce nationwide, he said, and the failure rate is even higher for second marriages: a whopping 60 percent to 70 percent.

Divorce rates run even higher in specific occupations, particularly those that expose people to traumatic events and danger, as well as heavy responsibilities and public scrutiny, Army officials noted. Military police officers, for example, face divorce rates averaging between 66 percent and 75 percent, they said.

Despite the nationwide trends, Bloomstrom was quick to point out that the numbers represent far more than just statistics. "These are people we're talking about," he said. "When a marriage ends, it's the end of a dream."

The toll goes beyond the human side, and affects military operations as well, he said. Service members in happy marriages tend to be more focused on their jobs and less likely to become disciplinary problems, Bloomstrom said. They are also more likely to remain in the military.

To help reverse the statistics, the services have introduced new programs and pumped up existing ones, offered through their family support, chaplain, and mental-health counseling networks.

For example, the Army's offerings include

- the new Deployment Cycle Support Program, which includes briefings for soldiers on how their absence and return may affect their family relationships and how they can cope with the inevitable changes;
- a family support group system that provides both practical and emotional support for spouses of deployed soldiers;
- the Building Strong and Ready Families Program, a two-day program that helps couples develop better communication skills, reinforced by a weekend retreat;
- the Strong Bonds marriage education program that focuses specifically on issues that affect Reserve and National Guard couples; and
- the Pick a Partner program that helps single soldiers make wise decisions when they choose mates.

The Army is not alone in offering programs to help its families survive the rigors of deployments and strengthen their relationships in the process.

The Marine Corps' Prevention and Relationship Enhancement Program is a two-day workshop that teaches couples how to manage conflict, solve problems, communicate effectively and preserve and enhance their commitment and friendship, Marine officials said.

Participants begin the program by taking a marriage survey, developed by a retired Navy chaplain, to help them evaluate their relationship and identify problems before they become serious. The four top problems generally involve communication, children and parenting, money, and sexual intimacy, according to a Navy chaplain involved in the program.

The Marine Corps program focused on what the chaplain calls "the mother lode of all issues" that can affect marriages: communication. "If you don't have good communication skills, you can't talk about the rest of the issues," he said.

The Navy has a similar program in its Marriage Enrichment Retreat. This weekend getaway is designed to give Navy couples the tools they need to help strengthen their marriages, according to Rachelle Logan, public affairs director for Navy Installations Command.

Participants begin the weekend session by getting a profile of their personalities, then attending sessions on marital communication, personality and family dynamics, and problems associated with military separation, Logan said.

While the Air Force does not have service-wide marital support programs, Air Force officials said individual bases offer a wide variety of programs to support military families and help them through separations, deployments, and the stresses relating to them.

Bloomstrom said he is optimistic about the emphasis the military services are putting on programs for married service members. The goal, he said, is to help couples recognize and address danger signs before they escalate. Another objective is to help military couples get more satisfaction out of their marriages by injecting a healthy dose of "fun and friendship" that he said builds up their "emotional bank account."

"We're talking about investing in the relationship in the good times," he said. "That way, when you have to make a withdrawal—as you do during a deployment—you still have enough left in the bank to cover it."

SPIRITUAL CARE FOR ONESELF

While often overlooked, spiritual well-being is essential for overall wellness. It provides the ability to deal with problems rationally and calmly. It gives an inner peace, especially during times of great stress, and there is an overwhelming body of research that shows that spiritual health helps block or fight many physical health problems.

There are many ways to achieve spiritual well-being—from meditation and yoga to prayer and deep relaxation. Spiritualism does not necessarily mean getting in touch with your god, if you have one, although if you are a religious person, spiritual well-being can give you a much deeper awareness of your spirituality. Just being able to communicate with your own inner self can bring you inner peace, harmony, and balance.

Deep relaxation is hard to achieve so you have to work at it. There are so many distractions nowadays—cell phones, laptops, and the like—that it is hard to unwind and completely relax. There are, however, various techniques you can use to relax. Once you have learned them, you will feel more confident in yourself because pressures and stresses will be put into better perspective, you will be able to sleep better, and you should see improvements in your overall physical health. One advantage of deep relaxation is that it lowers blood pressure and decreases muscle tension.

Regular relaxation techniques often include movement such as walking, jogging, and swimming. These can help you unwind, as can massages and aromatherapy or listening to your favorite relaxing music—not hard rock!

Deep relaxation involves stillness—either sitting in a chair or lying on the floor in a darkened room with all electrical appliances turned off. The aim is to achieve a therapeutic level of inner calm. This is best done by controlling your deep breathing and focusing only on it as you drive all other thoughts out of your mind. Even five minutes of deep-breathing techniques has been shown to lower stress levels. The advantage of deep relaxation is that once mastered, it can be practiced anywhere and as already stated, even if a few minutes can be very beneficial.

Meditation is deep relaxation taken to the next level. You can meditate sitting in a chair or sitting on the floor. The aim is to attain a state of inner calm, clarity, and focused concentration.

In order to do this, you need to find a quiet area where you will not be disturbed for fifteen minutes or so. Sit down on the floor in a comfortable position with your hands resting in your lap. It is important that your back is straight. Close your eyes and take slow, deep natural breaths—breathing in through your nose and out through your mouth. As you continue your breaths will become deeper and it will take longer to inhale and exhale but it is important not to rush the process. Focus all your attention on your breathing. If you start to think of something else, refocus on your breathing. Ultimately—and it does take time to perfect this—you will be focused throughout only on your breathing with no distractions. As you breathe deeply you will find your body relaxing and destressing. When you are ready to end your meditation open your eyes, stand up slowly, and stretch. New Kadampa Tradition centers offer meditation instruction, courses, books, and similar offerings, and are open to the general public: http://kadampa.org/centers

Faith and prayer combined can be another powerful ally. Believing in a higher being gives special meaning to your existence, and how you conduct yourself and being part of a spiritual community means you also have another large, extended family out there to support you. Church members tend to do more social networking and reach out when one of their own needs help. There are also studies that show that people who regularly attend religious services enjoy a boost in their happiness.

Prayer is an important element of faith—appealing to a higher power that can influence your life and the lives of others. Praying doesn't have to be ritualized—first thing in the morning or last thing before going to bed—it can and should be spontaneous.

For those who do not find themselves affiliated with a religious or spiritual persuasion, author Gregg Braden offers instruction on the Lost Mode of Prayer, teaching the technology of prayer in a manner separate from religious practices.

PHYSICAL CARE OF ONESELF—DIET, EXERCISE

Resilience

Resilience is the ability to cope and recover from stress and life-changing events. It helps us adjust to a normal life after deployment and it provides the strength to overcome adversities and illness, especially when there is an accompanying strong and loving support group.

With homecoming, you may need to relearn how to feel safe, comfortable, and trusting with your family. Developing resilience will help you do this and make you a stronger person in the process.

You must get to know one another again. Good communication with your partner, children, parents, siblings, friends, coworkers, and others is the key. Give each other the chance to understand what you have been through. When talking as a family, be careful to listen to one another. Families work best when there is respect for one another and a willingness to be open and consider alternatives.

Tips for Feeling Better

It's fine for you to spend some time alone. But if you spend too much time alone or avoid social gatherings, you will be isolated from family and friends. You need the support of these people for a healthy adjustment. You can help yourself to feel better by doing the following:

- Getting back to regular patterns of sleep and exercise
- Pursuing hobbies and creative activities
- Planning sufficient R&R (rest and relaxation) and intimate time
- Trying relaxation techniques (e.g., meditation, breathing exercises) to reduce stress
- Learning problems to watch out for and how to cope with them
- Striking a balance between staying connected with former war buddies and spending individual time with your partner, kids, other family members, and friends
- Communicating more than the ''need-to-know'' bare facts
- Talking about your war zone experiences at a time and pace that feels right to you
- Not drinking to excess, or when you're feeling depressed or to avoid disturbing memories; drink responsibly, or don't drink
- Creating realistic workloads for home, school, and work

Steps to Assuming Normal Routines

Soon after your return, plan to have an open and honest discussion with your family about responsibilities. You all need to decide how they should be split up now that you're home. It's usually best to take on a few tasks at first and then more as you grow accustomed to being home. Be willing to compromise so that both you and your family members feel that needs are understood and respected.

Try to reestablish a normal sleep routine as quickly as possible. Go to bed and get up at the same time every day. Do not drink to help yourself sleep. You might try learning some relaxation techniques, such as deep breathing, yoga, or meditation.

Important Points to Remember

- Readjusting to civilian life takes time—don't worry that you are experiencing some challenges. Find solutions to these problems. Don't avoid.
- Take your time adding responsibilities and activities back into your life.
- Reconnect with your social supports. This may be the last thing you feel like doing, but do it anyway. Social support is critical to successful reintegration.
- Review Battlemind (training program to help transition from combat to home) to understand where some of your automatic behaviors come from.
- Remind your loved ones that you love them.
- Realize that you need to talk about the experiences you had during deployment.
- If you can't talk to family or friends, be sure to talk to a chaplain or counselor.

Red Flags

You now know the reactions that are normal following deployment to war. But sometimes the behaviors that kept you alive in the war zone get you on the wrong track at home. You may not be able to shut them down after you have returned home safely. Some problems may need outside assistance to solve. Even serious post-deployment psychological problems can be treated successfully and cured. Being able to admit you have a problem can be tough:

- You might think you should cope on your own.
- You think others can't help you.

- You believe the problem(s) will go away on their own.
- You are embarrassed to talk to someone about it.

If your reactions are causing significant distress or interfering with how you function, you will need outside assistance. Here are some things to watch out for:

- Relationship troubles—frequent and intense conflicts, poor communication, inability to meet responsibilities
- Work, school, or other community dysfunction—frequent absences, conflicts, inability to meet deadlines or concentrate, poor performance
- Thoughts of hurting someone, or yourself
- If you get assistance early, you can prevent more serious problems from developing. If you delay seeking help because of avoidance or stigma, your problems may actually cause you to lose your job, your relationships, and your happiness. Mental and emotional problems can be managed or treated, and early detection is essential.

---

10 WAYS TO BUILD RESILIENCE

Make connections. Good relationships with close family members, friends, or others are important. Accepting help and support from those who care about you and will listen to you strengthens resilience. Some people find that being active in civic groups, faith-based organizations, or other local groups provides social support and can help with reclaiming hope. Assisting others in their time of need also can benefit the helper.

Avoid seeing crises as insurmountable problems. You can't change the fact that highly stressful events happen, but you can change how you interpret and respond to these events. Try looking beyond the present to how future circumstances may be a little better. Note any subtle ways in which you might already feel somewhat better as you deal with difficult situations.

Accept that change is a part of living. Certain goals may no longer be attainable as a result of adverse situations. Accepting circumstances that cannot be changed can help you focus on circumstances that you can alter.

Move toward your goals. Develop some realistic goals. Do something regularly—even if it seems like a small accomplishment—that enables you to move toward your goals. Instead of focusing on tasks that seem un-achievable, ask yourself, "What's one thing I know I can accomplish today that helps me move in the direction I want to go?"

Take decisive actions. Act on adverse situations as much as you can. Take decisive actions, rather than detaching completely from problems and stresses and wishing they would just go away.

Look for opportunities for self-discovery. People often learn some-thing about themselves and may find that they have grown in some respect as a result of their struggle with loss. Many people who have experienced tragedies and hardship have reported better relationships, greater sense of strength even while feeling vulnerable, increased sense of self-worth, a more developed spirituality, and heightened appreciation for life.

Nurture a positive view of yourself. Developing confidence in your ability to solve problems and trusting your instincts helps build resilience.

Keep things in perspective. Even when facing very painful events, try to consider the stressful situation in a broader context and keep a long-term perspective. Avoid blowing the event out of proportion.

Maintain a hopeful outlook. An optimistic outlook enables you to expect that good things will happen in your life. Try visualizing what you want, rather than worrying about what you fear.

Take care of yourself. Pay attention to your own needs and feelings. Engage in activities that you enjoy and find relaxing. Exercise regularly. Taking care of yourself helps to keep your mind and body primed to deal with situations that require resilience.

Additional ways of strengthening resilience may be helpful. For ex-ample, some people write about their deepest thoughts and feelings related to trauma or other stressful events in their life. Meditation and spiritual practices help some people build connections and restore hope.

The key is to identify ways that are likely to work well for you as part of your own personal strategy for fostering resilience.

Source: American Psychological Association Help Center

Getting help when you need it is crucial in building your resilience. Beyond caring family members and friends, people often find it helpful to turn to the following:

Self-help and support groups. Such community groups can aid people struggling with hardships such as the death of a loved one. By sharing information, ideas, and emotions, group participants can assist one another and find comfort in knowing that they are not alone in experiencing difficulty.

Books and other publications. Find books and other publications by people who have successfully managed adverse situations, such as surviving cancer. These stories can motivate readers to find a strategy that might work for them personally.

Online resources. Information on the web can be a helpful source of ideas, though the quality of information varies among sources.

For many people, using their own resources and the kinds of help listed above may be sufficient for building resilience. At times, however, an individual might get stuck or have difficulty making progress on the road to resilience.

A licensed mental health professional such as a psychologist can assist people in developing an appropriate strategy for moving forward. It is important to get professional help if you feel like you are unable to function or perform basic activities of daily living as a result of a traumatic or other stressful life experience.

Different people tend to be comfortable with somewhat different styles of interaction. A person should feel at ease and have good rapport in working with a mental health professional or participating in a support group.

HEALTH AND WELLNESS

Wellness is a proactive approach to being healthy. It encompasses what you eat and drink, how you exercise and how you manage stress. It usually involves lifestyle changes but the bottom line is a healthier, longer, and happier (stress-free) life—and that has got to be something worth going for.

Self-help

Wellness research shows that Americans who take care of themselves and manage their lifestyles are healthier, more productive, have fewer absences from work, and make fewer demands for medical services. An article published in the *Journal of the American Medical Association* indicated that, in one study, the "wellness" approach resulted in a 17 percent decline in total medical visits and a 35 percent decline in medical visits for minor illness.

Eat sensibly, exercise properly and manage stress and you will achieve physical, emotional and psychological wellness.

Sensible Eating

Eating well, eating regularly and staying hydrated are standard "sensible eating" recommendations. The latest dietary trends show that adjusted dietary lifestyles such as veganism, Paleo, and Paleo AutoImmune Protocol offer nutritional approaches that tend to expedite healing and wellness protocols and may help mitigate depression, anxiety, weight challenges, and a variety of disorders. Consult your doctor or a nutrition expert.

EXERCISE

Be as physically active as possible. For health benefits, adults should do at least two-and-a-half hours a week of moderate-intensity or one-and-a-quarter hours a week of vigorous intensity aerobic physical activity or an equal combination of both. You'll see a difference in your weight and your health.

Lifestyle changes that include healthy eating, regular physical activity, and maintaining a healthy weight are the keys to good health. If you need to lose weight, losing even a little will help. Losing as little as 5 percent to 10 percent of your current body weight can lower your risks for many diseases.

A reasonable and safe weight loss is one to two pounds per week. It might take six months to reach your ultimate goal, but making gradual lifestyle changes can help you maintain a healthier weight for life.

Benefits of Regular Physical Activity

Regular physical activity has many benefits:

- Helps you manage your weight
- Reduces your risk of coronary heart disease
- Reduces your risk of stroke
- Decreases blood pressure
- Reduces your risk of colon cancer

- Helps prevent and control diabetes
- May decrease "bad" (LDL) cholesterol and raise "good" (HDL) cholesterol
- Helps you sleep better
- Strengthens bones and helps prevent injury
- Increases muscular strength and endurance
- Increases flexibility and range of motion
- Improves your mood
- Helps with stress and depression
- Improves self-esteem
- Makes you feel better

Exercise should be FUN

So you don't like physical activity? There are lots of ways to be physically active without doing what you might consider "a workout" or "exercise." MWR facilities—Morale, Welfare and Recreation—provide exercise opportunities for those near military bases with appropriate military or veteran identification. There are a variety of online sources for MWR facilities by base, branch of service, and programs. There are lots of other options too:

- Go walking with others.
- Dance.
- Get the whole family involved in some physical activity like walking in a park.
- Find a beginner's exercise class that you might enjoy.
- Do housework to music.
- Try out a new sport or activity.
- Go bicycling with family or friends.
- Check out your local community center for upcoming events.
- Play golf—carry your clubs to burn more calories or use a pull cart.

Exercise on a Budget

Sometimes cost can be a barrier to being more physically active. There are lots of activities that involve little or no cost.

- Walking is free.
- Churches and community centers often have free events.

- Build strength using household items for weights (canned foods, small bottles of water, etc.).
- Simple stretches can improve flexibility and range of motion.
- Find a local trail.
- Buy a bicycle from a secondhand shop or at a yard sale.
- Try a new sport that doesn't require expensive equipment.
- Look at senior centers, the YMCA, and local recreational centers for free or reduced-cost activities.
- Physical activities that you build into your daily routine like taking the stairs or parking farther away and walking are free!
- Most military installations offer access to physical fitness centers and offer free or low-cost programs.

Indoor Physical Activities

If the weather is bad or you prefer the indoors, there are still lots of physical activities you can do.

- Put on some music and dance.
- Do strength exercises at home using items such as water bottles and canned foods as dumbbells.
- Walk around the mall (most open early for walkers).
- Do chair stretches (ask your MOVE! Weight Management Program team for a sample handout; MOVE! is specifically designed to improve the lives of veterans).
- Exercise to a TV program.
- Borrow an exercise video from the library or a friend (examples include chair dancing, step walking, and beginner aerobics).
- Go to a gym or recreation center (join the YMCA).
- Get involved with fitness activities at a local community center or senior center.
- Too hot outside? Go for a swim at an indoor pool.
- Take a water aerobics class.
- Look for sales or visit secondhand stores for used exercise equipment.
- Do indoor activities such as racquetball, tennis, roller skating, bowling, and so on, at a sports center/gym.

Planned Physical Activities

There are lots of activities to consider if you are trying to become more active. For fitness and variety, choose activities from all three categories. Start slowly and choose activities you enjoy.

- Aerobic activities
  - Walking
  - Stair climbing
  - Gardening
  - Dancing—any type
  - Sports
  - Jogging or running
  - Aerobic classes
  - Roller or ice skating
  - Snow skiing
  - Exercise machines (treadmill, stair climber)
  - Non-weight-bearing and low-impact activities. (These are good for everyone but particularly beneficial for those with arthritis.)
  - Swimming
  - Bicycling
  - Water walking or water aerobics
  - Some exercise machines (stationary bike, row machine, ski machine, elliptical trainer)
- Strength activities
  - Free weights (dumbbells, plastic bottles of water, cans of food)
  - Elastic bands (available from prosthetics)
  - Conditioning exercises (e.g., sit-ups, push-ups, and pull-ups)
  - Pilates
  - Circuit machines
  - Medicine (weighted) and balance balls
- Flexibility activities
  - Stretching
  - Chair exercises
  - Yoga
  - Tai Chi

Physical Activity and Your Safety

If you are diabetic or have heart or lung disease, check with your primary care team before beginning a physical activity program.

General Safety Tips

- Carry identification, emergency contact information, and illness information.
- Drink water before, during, and after exercise.
- Let someone know where you are going and how long you'll be gone.
- Carry a cell phone if you have one.
- Prepare for the weather.
- Wear comfortable, good fitting socks and shoes suitable for physical activity.
- Dress to be seen. Wear bright colored clothing. In poor light, wear safety reflective materials designed for improving your visibility to drivers.
- Use a familiar route.
- Be active in public places.
- Avoid isolated trails, paths, and poorly lit areas.
- When approaching another walker or jogger from behind, give a verbal warning before passing them.

When to Stop Exercising

Physical activity is usually safe. Stop exercising right away if you have any of these symptoms:

- Pain, tightness, pressure, or discomfort in your chest, neck, shoulder, arm, back, or jaw
- Severe shortness of breath
- Cold sweats
- Severe nausea or vomiting
- Muscle cramps
- Trouble swallowing, talking, or seeing
- Severe headache, dizziness, or lightheadedness
- Joint pain

If symptoms don't go away after a few minutes, call 911 or go to the nearest emergency room. If the symptoms go away but return each time you exercise, see your primary care provider.

Increasing Physical Activity for Veterans with Physical or Medical Limitations

Do I need to see my healthcare provider before beginning a program of physical activity?

Many veterans can begin a program of mild or moderate activity *safely* without having a check-up from their primary care provider. Your MOVE! healthcare team can tell you whether or not you should have a check-up before starting.

In general, the following veterans should always see their provider before starting an exercise program:

* Veterans with heart and/or lung conditions
* Veterans planning a program of "vigorous" activity

What is the difference between "mild," "moderate," and "vigorous" levels of activity?

* Mild activities should feel like slow walking/rolling. They should not cause much of a sweat or cause you to have trouble catching your breath.
* Moderate activities are like fast walking/rolling. These activities will make your heart beat a little bit faster. This may cause light sweating but should never cause you to be "out of breath" or exhausted.
* Vigorous activities will cause the heart to beat very fast. With these activities, you will sweat heavily and have some difficulty breathing.

Are there certain activities I should avoid?

Regardless of your limitations, very few activities are "off limits." See the MOVE! handout "Activity Limitations for Certain Medical Conditions."

Will I make my condition worse by exercising?

Physical activity almost always helps improve medical conditions. It is wise to avoid or reduce physical activity during times when your condition worsens or causes distress.

Will my medicines affect my ability to be physically active?

Physical activity is compatible with all medications. However, some medications require a close watch. Refer to the MOVE! handout "Physical Activity and Medications."

What if I'm in too much pain to be physically active?

Regular physical activity often improves chronic pain conditions. It can sometimes take several weeks to begin to see a benefit. See your health care provider to discuss options if you feel your current pain is at a level that will keep you from even getting started with physical activity.

Staying Motivated with Physical Activity

Make physical activity part of your daily routine. Here are some ways to help you keep on track with your physical activity program.

- Set realistic and achievable goals.
- Schedule activity by making it part of your regular routine.
- Have a support system—friends, family, group exercise.
- Log your progress.
- Consider a trainer.
- Use music and TV fitness programs.
- Use a pedometer/odometer.
- Variety is key.
- Even small amounts of movement throughout the day add up.
- Check your progress regularly.
- Choose a convenient time of the day.
- Stay encouraged.
- Join a gym or club.
- HAVE FUN!

STOP SMOKING

Don't Give Up on Quitting! No matter how long you've smoked or how many times you've tried to quit, you can be smoke-free. Smoking is the leading preventable cause of premature death and a leading cause of illness and mortality.

Smoking and tobacco use cessation persists as one of the VA's biggest public health challenges. Many veterans began using tobacco while in the military. The rate of smoking among veterans in the VA health care system is higher than among the U.S. population.

Approximately 70 percent of all smokers say they want to quit, but even the most motivated may try to quit five or six times before they are able to quit. Over 3 million Americans successfully quit smoking every year.

To help veterans quit smoking and tobacco use, the VA offers

* screening for tobacco use during primary care visits;
* individual counseling;
* prescriptions for nicotine replacement therapy, such as a nicotine patch or gum, or other medications; and
* participation in evidence-based smoking cessation programs.

HOW CAN FAMILY AND FRIENDS ASSIST

Make it a family goal to achieve wellness together. Be honest with each other—are you fit, are you healthy, do you eat wisely? Resolve together to adopt a wellness program that will encompass healthier eating, more exercise, and having fun. Healthier eating does not mean boring food. On the contrary, you can make wonderful meals from healthy foods. You can have fun exercising too—go for long walks, especially along the beach if you are near the coast. Adopt a rescue dog—it will provide companionship and force you to take it on walks. Take up a sport or join a club that has lots of outdoor activities. There are many ways of becoming healthier. Choose the ones that are right for you and stick to them.

RESOURCES

Aim for a Healthy Weight. National Heart Lung and Blood Institute: www.nhlbi.nih.gov

National Center for Complementary and Alternative Medicine: http://nccam.nih.gov/health

National Institutes of Health: www.nih.gov

NIH Senior Health: http://nihseniorhealth.gov/

Noise Reduction: www.noisyplanet.nidcd.nih.gov/Pages/Default.aspx

Office of Dietary Supplement: http://ods.od.nih.gov

Quit Smoking: Smokefree.gov

Rethinking Drinking: http://rethinkingdrinking.niaaa.nih.gov

Weight Control. Weight-Control Information Network: http://win.niddk.nih.gov

Indtai's Military Community Compass Resources focus on Individual and Family Wellness for the Military Community: www.MCAeX.net to learn about education opportunities; www.MCSFeX.net to find scholarship and financial aid opportunities; www.MCJeX.net to explore job opportunities; and www.MCInfoEx.net to access a one-stop knowledge base and the latest news.

MARRIAGE COUNSELING

Love and marriage have become more complex in the past few decades as the pressures of daily living take their toll on relationships. The military lifestyle creates additional pressures on couples who may already be struggling with communication and intimacy.

When couples have difficulty resolving these relationship problems, they often turn to family and friends for guidance. If that doesn't work, the next step is to see a marriage counselor. Many military couples seek free and confidential counseling through their Family Support Centers.

Of course, there has to be a commitment on both sides to try to make this work. If one partner doesn't want to go or goes very reluctantly the counseling is not likely to work. And, don't expect it to be a speedy process. It could have taken many years for your marriage to deteriorate to the level where you need this sort of help, so it may take many sessions, some of them emotionally very painful, before you both understand where things have been going wrong and hopefully, what needs to be done to make things right again.

Counseling only works if you are honest. You both have to speak from the heart, and some of the things said may be hurtful, but if it helps in the healing process it is all for the good. The sessions alone won't mend your marriage. You both have to put into practice the things you have learned at the sessions and work really hard.

Relationship counseling is the process of counseling the parties of a relationship in an effort to recognize and to better manage or reconcile troublesome differences and repeating patterns of distress. The relationship involved may be between members of a family or a couple (see also family therapy), employees or employers in a workplace, or between a professional and a client.

Couple therapy (or relationship therapy) is a related and different process. It may differ from relationship counseling in duration. Short-term counseling may be between one to three sessions whereas long-term couples' therapy may be between twelve and twenty-four sessions. An exception is brief or solution-focused couples' therapy.

In addition, counseling tends to be more "here and now" with new coping strategies the outcome. Couples therapy is more about seemingly intractable problems with a relationship history, where emotions are the target and the agent of change. Marriage counseling or marital therapy can refer to either or some combination of the above.

Counselors can help couples clarify obstacles and develop solutions to their marital problems. By using some of the tips listed here and using other available resources, many couples have strengthened the quality of their relationships.

Communicate clearly and specifically with each other about expectations, needs, and feelings. Check out assumptions and ask questions to clarify. Many arguments occur as a result of simple misunderstandings that can easily be avoided with clear communication.

Build a strong sense of commitment, trust, honesty, and openness. Keep your promises and be able to count on each other. Be loyal to one another to create a sense of safety and security in the relationship.

Accept that conflict is normal. Work toward resolution with a spirit of teamwork rather than as a battle to be won. Respect your partner's right to have a different opinion and agree to disagree when necessary. Negotiation, compromise, and give-and-take can help create a win-win situation.

Make a point of saying or doing something supportive or affirming for your partner daily. Often the little things are taken for granted over time but are helpful in maintaining a happy relationship. Always be respectful and courteous. Good manners still apply when you are married. Don't interrupt or dominate the discussion. Say "please" and "thank you."

Anger is normal and how it is expressed is important. Don't attack your partner. Stick to one issue at a time. Begin statements with "I feel . . ." rather than "You always . . ." or "You never . . ."

Make time for sharing and discussing. Maintain respect and give the discussion full attention. Turn off the TV or radio when discussing important issues.

Unconditional love and acceptance are important. Whereas some behaviors cannot be tolerated in a healthy marriage, learning to tolerate smaller faults or personality differences can help. Don't try to change your partner into someone they are not.

According to the American Association for Marriage and Family Therapy (AAMFT; www.aamft.org), almost every couple can, at times, benefit from some help with their marriage. Premarital preparation and marital enrichment programs such as the Prevention and Relationship Enhancement Program (PREP) and the Relationship Enhancement Program are available in many localities, and most people find them helpful regardless of how well their relationship is going. Many people seek couple counseling with a trained therapist to improve their marriages, even when their marriages are not unduly distressed. You don't need to be in a distressed marriage to be in marital therapy. Many people with very solid marriages choose this path to enhance their relationships.

Experiencing marital distress, however, represents a different state from the ups and downs of married life that most people experience. In distressed marriages, people feel fundamentally dissatisfied with their marriages. Disappointment in the relationship doesn't just come and go; it is a constant companion. Most frequently, couples with high levels of marital distress fight a good deal and their fights don't lead to resolution, but simply a sense of being worn out. Or they may not fight, but simply feel completely disconnected. People stop doing nice things for each other, they stop communicating, and things tend to go from bad to worse.

Frequent arguments that don't get resolved, loss of good feelings, and loss of friendship, sex, and vitality are other signs that a marriage is distressed. Other signs, such as contempt, withdrawal, violence, and a complete loss of connection signal that a marriage is in desperate trouble and that it is at high risk for divorce. And you need not be legally married to have "marital distress." Serious, long-term, committed relationships can experience these kinds of major problems, too.

Sometimes marital problems are purely about problems in the relationship such as communication, solving problems, arguing, intimacy, and sex. These kinds of problems often begin with partners simply not having a good sense of how to be married and how to communicate and provide support. Other times couples may do well for a while, particularly in the earliest stages of their romance, but they are not ready for the longer-term tasks in marriage. Studies of couples show that while the risks for marital distress and divorce are highest early in marriage, these risks also grow just after the transitions that occur when couples begin to have children and when the children reach adolescence.

Other times, marital problems are directly the result of individual problems, such as substance abuse. And marriages can even seem to be going well, but one shattering event like an extramarital affair will throw a marriage into distress.

Marital distress has powerful effects on partners, often leading to great sadness, worry, a high level of tension, and problems such as depression. If prolonged, it even has been shown to have a direct effect on physical health. The effect on families is also profound, especially when conflict is high. Children raised in high-conflict homes tend to have many more problems than other children. And once marriages are distressed, a progression begins that easily becomes a cascade downward, ultimately leading to the ending of a marriage.

Chapter Five

Health Issues

Our returning service members can face a myriad of physical and mental health issues. Understanding these issues and the options available for support and treatment is critical in overcoming them.

FREE MENTAL HEALTH SERVICES TO OUR NATION'S MILITARY AND VETERAN COMMUNITY

Barbara Van Dahlen, founder and president, of the Give an Hour nonprofit organization (www.linkedin.com/pub/barbara-van-dahlen/5/820/a29) has been involved in problems relating to deployment for over ten years.

Interview Summary

Deployments (whether during wartime or peacetime) are stressful experiences. Wartime is a whole other type of stress, challenging on both sides of the equation, although it was great to try to help the families. It's not about being unable to handle it or someone isn't strong enough; this is about what happens when humans handle stress, and helping them recognize the signs of stress. What can we do to help them get through that? To recover?

It's not just a military issue; families have to be taken care of as well. We must change our culture. We expect members of the military and their families to "raise their hand" and ask for help. Our culture doesn't support that. It's not a military or veteran issue; it's a human issue. They are choosing to serve their country, to put themselves into situations that create conditions that lead to understandable mental health consequences for themselves and their families. It's all about changing the conversation about mental health in general.

They've been living this experience. We see a generational experience through other wars. What we are doing right is that we are addressing it; we might not have all the answers but we have broken ground connecting with high-level officials to really connect about the impact of service. This current generation can help us lead our country, help our families and help them reintegrate, and have very understandable reactions. For too long, there's been an unfortunate distortion about PTSD and the real issues, but there are a lot of folks out there functioning, be it in their families and be it in their communities, while dealing with these challenges. We will get more comfortable and be more supportive with recognition.

Give an Hour is ten years old this year. As a clinical psychologist whose father served in World War II, Van Dahlen developed a healthy respect for service members serving our country. As a mental health professional, she wanted to find a way to help as the war unfolded after 9/11; she saw people coming home and struggling. She had heard of a veteran losing his family who was living out of a car; and she chose to ask mental health counselors to devote an hour a week to helping a vet. Give an Hour is an organization that provides direct mental health care to anyone who needs it. They define families very broadly and provide free care for as long as it's needed. They have providers in every state, with about 7,000 providers nationally who have given over 170,000 hours of care already. They are supported by other volunteers and helpers who give talks and provide in-services. The program has now grown so much within her professional community that it can be leveraged to find a local provider for both military and their families. They are now branching out into telehealth via HIPPA-secure access such as Skype and other platforms.

There was some concern because they were outside the military framework, but they have memorandums of understanding (MOUs) with some services to provide support outside the system. The serving member and family can have a provider in their community, outside of base, if they choose.

For families facing deployment, mental health issues are a risk. We do a really good job of preparing our men and women who serve our country (and our families) that they may be physically injured; they may lose their life. They sign on the line accepting that risk. We don't yet do a good job of preparing them on a psychological side. Even by explaining "here's what may happen"—you may come home with anxiety, depression, substance abuse, PTSD—might help them recognize the symptoms earlier and address it earlier. One size does not fit all; as humans, that isn't how we work. Sometimes traditional counseling is needed, combined with yoga, or community activity, or family counseling, or diet, or meditation, or exercise with medication—you have to look at a whole solution; just one thing may not be enough. All of the parts need to be treated and healed so that the person recovers.

The key is paying attention and addressing the needs, in communicating and looking at alternatives like Give an Hour. We work very closely with the community and the system. There are great opportunities to help service members heal.

How can we help families moving forward? We can help them be prepared by knowing what issues their loved one may come back with and that the strain is totally understandable—and ignoring it will more likely lead to longer-term and more serious issues in their families. It's just like physical issues, if you ignore a toothache, eventually you will need that tooth extracted. The sooner you address it and get help, the better. We need to ask, "How can I be part of the solution?" when someone is hurting.

The Campaign to Change Direction

Military and veteran communities are at a higher risk, but this isn't just about them. Certainly they have the conditions, but there can be other family or community indicators to really encourage all Americans to pay attention to their mental well-being and to recognize the signs of well-being or suffering and to step in. Since we launched the Campaign to Change Direction, we have reached over 15 million Americans, and we are just getting started. We have over 150 partner organizations that have joined the campaign and they all have their own spheres of influence—major organizations like MOAA (Military Officers Association of America); Easter Seals; Team Red, White and Blue; and so on. We have partners in the VA as well. All these different groups are helping us reach out. Everybody understands that it's time to tackle this and to help acknowledge when those who are struggling need help.

PTSD TREATMENT

In discussing treatment options for PTSD sufferers, it would be remiss not to mention a technique that's been scientifically proven effective in reducing the symptoms of PTSD—and it's completely free, legal, and immediately accessible.

The technique is EFT (Emotional Freedom Technique), a form of psychological acupressure that utilizes the same energy meridians used in traditional acupuncture for more than five thousand years, but without the invasiveness of needles. The best part is you can learn to do EFT for yourself, but please understand that self-administered EFT may not work, and you're far more likely to get benefit by seeing a skilled therapist.

A key aspect of PTSD is anxiety, and EFT is typically effective with many forms of anxiety. A large proportion of the scientific research about EFT has been done using populations of PTSD-diagnosed veterans—with stunning success. This ongoing study is part of the Veterans Stress Project. In a randomized controlled trial, veterans with moderate to severe PTSD received six sessions of EFT. Upon completion, 90 percent had such a profound decrease in symptoms that they no longer met the criteria for PTSD. Their levels of pain were also assessed, and even though pain was not the primary target of the study, it decreased by 41 percent.

If you would like to be considered for participation in the Veterans Stress Project, you can obtain information on their website at www.stressproject.org.

SUBSTANCE ABUSE

Dependence on alcohol and drugs is our most serious national public health problem. It is prevalent among rich and poor, in all regions of the country, and all ethnic and social groups.

Millions of Americans misuse or are dependent on alcohol or drugs. Most of them have families who suffer the consequences, often serious, of living with this illness. If there is alcohol or drug dependence in your family, remember you are not alone.

Most individuals who abuse alcohol or drugs have jobs and are productive members of society creating a false hope in the family that "it's not that bad."

The problem is that addiction tends to worsen over time, hurting both the addicted person and all the family members. It is especially damaging to young children and adolescents.

People with this illness really may believe that they drink normally or that "everyone" takes drugs. These false beliefs are called denial; this denial is a part of the illness. Drug or alcohol dependence disorders are medical conditions that can be effectively treated. Millions of Americans and their families are in healthy recovery from this disease. If someone close to you misuses alcohol or drugs, the first step is to be honest about the problem and to seek help for yourself, your family, and your loved one.

Treatment can occur in a variety of settings, in many different forms, and for different lengths of time. Stopping the alcohol or drug use is the first step to recovery, and most people need help to stop. Often a person with alcohol or drug dependence will need treatment provided by professionals just as with other diseases. Your doctor may be able to guide you.

Warning Signs

Not all drinking is harmful, and moderate drinking might even be good for you. However, at-risk or heavy drinkers can face serious risks unless they take action.

Injuries. Drinking too much increases your chances of being injured or even killed. Alcohol is a factor, for example, in about 60 percent of fatal burn injuries, drowning, and homicides; 50 percent of severe trauma injuries and sexual assaults; and 40 percent of fatal motor vehicle crashes, suicides, and fatal falls.

Health problems. Heavy drinkers have a greater risk of liver disease, heart disease, sleep disorders, depression, stroke, bleeding from the stomach, sexually transmitted infections from unsafe sex, and several types of cancer. They may also have problems managing diabetes, high blood pressure, and other conditions.

Birth defects. Drinking during pregnancy can cause brain damage and other serious problems in the baby. Because it is not yet known whether any amount of alcohol is safe for a developing baby, women who are pregnant or may become pregnant should not drink.

Alcohol use disorders. Generally known as alcoholism and alcohol abuse, alcohol use disorders are medical conditions that doctors can diagnose

SUBSTANCE ABUSE AND THE MILITARY

Substance abuse is a growing problem in the military because of the tremendous strains both on military personnel themselves and their families. Some have experienced devastating consequences, including family disintegration, mental health disorders, and even suicide. Research conducted by the RAND Corporation has shown that 25 to 30 percent of Iraq and Afghanistan war veterans have reported symptoms of a mental disorder or cognitive impairment. Post-traumatic stress disorder (PTSD) is the most common, and traumatic brain injury may be a causal factor in some reported symptoms. Although less common, substance use is also a large concern, with aggregated data from the Substance Abuse and Mental Health Services Administration's annual household survey revealing that from 2004 to 2006, 7.1 percent of veterans (an estimated 1.8 million persons eighteen years of age or older) met criteria for a past-year substance use disorder (SUD).

Problems with alcohol and nicotine abuse are the most prevalent and pose a significant risk to the health of veterans as well as to Reserve component and National Guard soldiers. At greatest risk are deployed personnel with combat exposures, as they are more apt to engage in new-onset heavy weekly drinking, binge drinking, and other alcohol-related problems, as well as smoking initiation and relapse. Within this group, Reserve and National Guard personnel and younger service members are particularly vulnerable to subsequent drinking problems. And although alcohol problems are frequently reported among veterans, few are referred to alcohol treatment.

The military today have a number of things working against them, causing them to return home addicted to drugs or alcohol, or suffering from mental illness. The military today regularly prescribes medication to help ease stress and anxiety, to help with physical pain, or to keep them alert when they need to be. These kinds of prescription drugs, while they might be necessary in a war situation, become addicting; and on their return to normal life, they can't do without them. Many other members of the military are self-medicating and becoming addicted in the process.

To gain a fuller understanding of these burgeoning issues, the Millennium Cohort Study—the largest prospective study in military history—is following a representative sample of U.S. military personnel from 2001 to 2022. Early findings highlight the importance of prevention in this group, given the long-term effects of combat-related problems and the ensuing difficulties experienced in seeking or being referred to treatment, likely because of stigma and other real and perceived barriers. To fill this need, a host of government agencies, researchers, public health entities and others are working together to adapt and test proven prevention interventions, as well as drug abuse treatments, for potential use with military and veteran populations and their families.

To address the social problems both caused by and contributing to drug use, the Department of Defense and partners are developing and testing novel treatment approaches with veterans. For example, Rosen's Money Management Intervention trains those in drug treatment to better manage their money by linking access to funds to treatment goal completion. For relapse prevention, McKay's telephone treatment approach delivers counseling at home for several months once a veteran has completed an initial face-to-face treatment episode.

While the National Institute on Drug Abuse (NIDA) is striving to expand its portfolio of research related to trauma, stress, and substance use and abuse among veterans and their families, a number of promising projects are already being funded. These include studies on smoking cessation and PTSD, behavioral interventions for the dually diagnosed, substance use, and HIV progression, and virtual reality treatment of PTSD and substance abuse. Additionally, NIDA's National Drug Abuse Treatment Clinical Trials Network (CTN) is developing, in conjunction with researchers from the Veterans Administration, a protocol concept on the treatment of PTSD/SUD in veteran populations.

Further, efforts are under way to make it easier for veterans to access treatments. Research on drug courts, for example, is now being applied to developing courts for veterans, the former having demonstrated their effectiveness in addressing nonviolent crimes by drug abusers and ushering them into needed treatment instead of prison. Because the criminal justice system is a frequent treatment referral source for veterans, such specialized courts may give them the opportunity to access the services and support they may not otherwise receive. While New York has the only court that exclusively handles nonviolent crimes committed by veterans, other states are considering establishing such courts.

when a patient's drinking causes distress or harm. In the United States, about 18 million people have an alcohol use disorder.

See if you recognize any of these symptoms in yourself or a loved one:

- In the past year, have you had times when you ended up drinking more, or longer, than you intended?
- More than once wanted to cut down or stop drinking, or tried to, but couldn't?
- More than once gotten into situations while or after drinking that increased your chances of getting hurt (such as driving, swimming, using machinery, walking in a dangerous area, or having unsafe sex)?
- Had to drink much more than you once did to get the effect you want? Or found that your usual number of drinks had much less effect than before?
- Continued to drink even though it was making you feel depressed or anxious or adding to another health problem? Or after having had a memory blackout?
- Spent a lot of time drinking?
- Or being sick or getting over other aftereffects?
- Continued to drink even though it was causing trouble with your family or friends?
- Found that drinking—or being sick from drinking—often interfered with taking care of your home or family?
- Or caused job troubles?
- Given up or cut back on activities that were important or interesting to you, or gave you pleasure, in order to drink?
- More than once gotten arrested, been held at a police station, or had other legal problems because of your drinking?
- Found that when the effects of alcohol were wearing off, you had withdrawal symptoms, such as trouble sleeping, shakiness, restlessness, nausea, sweating, a racing heart, or a seizure?
- Or sensed things that were not there?

If you or a loved one have any of these symptoms, then alcohol may already be a cause for concern. The more symptoms you have, the more urgent the need for change. A health professional can look at the number, pattern, and severity of symptoms to see whether an alcohol use disorder is present and help you decide the best course of action.

Alcoholism is chronic alcohol abuse that results in a physical dependence on alcohol and an inability to stop or limit drinking.

Family Intervention

Getting a loved one to agree to accept help and finding support services for all family members are the first steps toward healing for the addicted person and the entire family.

When an addicted person is reluctant to seek help, sometimes family members, friends, and associates come together out of concern and love, to confront the problem drinker. They strongly urge the person to enter treatment and list the serious consequences of not doing so, such as family breakup or job loss.

This is called "intervention." When carefully prepared and done with the guidance of a competent, trained specialist, the family, friends, and associates are usually able to convince their loved one—in a firm and loving manner—that the only choice is to accept help and begin the road to recovery. People with alcohol or drug dependence problems can and do recover. Intervention is often the first step.

Children in families experiencing alcohol or drug abuse need attention, guidance, and support. They may be growing up in homes in which the problems are either denied or covered up. These children need to have their experiences validated. They also need safe, reliable adults in whom to confide and who will support them, reassure them, and provide them with appropriate help for their age. They need to have fun and just be kids.

Families with alcohol and drug problems usually have high levels of stress and confusion. High stress family environments are a risk factor for early and dangerous substance use, as well as mental and physical health problems.

It is important to talk honestly with children about what is happening in the family and to help them express their concerns and feelings. Children need to trust the adults in their lives and to believe that they will support them.

Children living with alcohol or drug abuse in the family can benefit from participating in educational support groups in their school student assistance programs. Those aged eleven and older can join Alateen groups, which meet in community settings and provide healthy connections with others coping with similar issues. Being associated with the activities of a faith community can also help.

If you're considering changing your drinking, you'll need to decide whether to cut down or to quit. It's a good idea to discuss different options with a doctor, a friend, or someone else you trust. Quitting is strongly advised if you

- try cutting down but cannot stay within the limits you set;
- have had an alcohol use disorder or now have symptoms;
- have a physical or mental condition that is caused or worsened by drinking;
- are taking a medication that interacts with alcohol; or
- are or may become pregnant.

If you do not have any of these conditions, talk with your doctor to determine whether you should cut down or quit based on factors such as

- family history of alcohol problems;
- your age;
- whether you've had drinking-related injuries; or
- symptoms such as sleep disorders and sexual dysfunction.

There is help available on base and in your local community. Look in the Yellow Pages under Alcoholism for treatment programs and self-help groups. Call your county health department and ask for licensed treatment programs in your community. Keep trying until you find the right help for your loved one, yourself, and your family. Ask a family therapist for a referral to a trained interventionist or call the Intervention Resource Center at 1-888-421-4321.

Self-Help Groups

Al-Anon Family Groups: www.al-anon.org
Alateen: www.alateen.org
Alcoholics Anonymous: www.aa.org
Adult Children of Alcoholics: www.adultchildren.org

Quitting Techniques

Several proven treatment approaches are available; one size doesn't fit all, however. It's a good idea to do some homework on the Internet or at the library to find social and professional support options that appeal to you, as you are more likely to stick with them (see also Resources on the inside back cover). Chances are excellent that you'll pull together an approach that works for you.

Social Support

One potential challenge when people stop drinking is rebuilding a life without alcohol. It may be important to educate family and friends, develop new interests and social groups, find rewarding ways to spend your time that don't involve alcohol, and ask for help from others. When asking for support from friends or significant others, be specific. This could include not offering you alcohol, not using alcohol around you, giving words of support and withholding criticism, not asking you to take on new demands right now, and going to a group like Al-Anon.

Consider joining Alcoholics Anonymous or another mutual support group (see Resources). Recovering people who attend groups regularly do better than those who do not. Groups can vary widely, so shop around for one that's comfortable. You'll get more out of it if you become actively involved by having a sponsor and reaching out to other members for assistance.

Professional Support

Advances in the treatment of alcoholism mean that patients now have more choices and health professionals have more tools to help.

Medications to treat alcoholism. Newer medications can make it easier to quit drinking by offsetting changes in the brain caused by alcoholism. These options (naltrexone, topiramate, and acamprosate) don't make you sick if you drink, as does an older medication (disulfiram). None of these medications are addictive, so it's fine to combine them with support groups or alcohol counseling. A major clinical trial recently showed that patients can now receive effective alcohol treatment from their primary care doctors or mental health practitioners by combining the newer medications with a series of brief office visits for support. See Resources for more information.

Alcohol counseling. "Talk therapy" also works well. There are several counseling approaches that are about equally effective—12-step, cognitive-behavioral, motivational enhancement, or a combination. Getting help in itself appears to be more important than the particular approach used, as long as it offers empathy, avoids heavy confrontation, strengthens motivation, and provides concrete ways to change drinking behavior.

Specialized, intensive treatment programs. Some people will need more intensive programs. If you need a referral to a program, ask your doctor.

DRUGS

Each year, drug and alcohol abuse contributes to the death of more than 120,000 Americans. According to the Office of National Drug Control Policy, drugs and alcohol cost taxpayers more than $328 billion annually in preventable health care costs, extra law enforcement, auto crashes, crime, and lost productivity.

Drug abuse is the use of drugs to get "high." It is a voluntary act unlike drug addiction, which is involuntary. The addict is not able to stop using drugs unless there is intervention. Like alcoholism, drug addiction is a disease for which there is no cure.

Becoming addicted to drugs can occur extremely easily and very quickly leaving the addict suffering from the severe effects of the drugs, and strong withdrawal effects if they do not take the drug. In order to cease the addiction, a lot of support, help, and willpower is needed from both the addict and those around them.

The physical signs of a drug addiction can be quite varied depending on the drug used, the amount taken, and the environment in which it is taken. The early signs of a drug addiction can include mixed moods, sleepiness, or excessive or unusual tiredness during the day, agitation, and paranoia. As the dependency develops the signs can change to being frequently distracted, depression, mixed mental states, including psychosis, and a decrease in the ability to coordinate or perform tasks that are normally easy to complete. The degree of effect is variable between users and also on the substance of choice. Other very obvious signs are needle marks on the arms (though these can appear on other areas of the body once the veins in the arms have deteriorated and cannot be used any longer), but this only occurs in those who have been injecting the drugs. People who are normally non-smokers are likely to suffer from breathlessness or coughing if they have been smoking drugs for long periods. As the drug addiction develops the person is likely to become isolated from their usual family and friends and may get quite agitated when approached about this.

Although they are cheaper than they were a few decades ago, drugs are still an expensive commodity and most users struggle to keep up financially with the demand for their habit.

What happens to your brain when you take drugs?

Drugs are chemicals that tap into the brain's communication system and disrupt the way nerve cells normally send, receive, and process information. There are at least two ways that drugs are able to do this: (1) by imitating the brain's natural chemical messengers, and/or (2) by overstimulating the "reward circuit" of the brain.

Some drugs, such as heroin, have a similar structure to chemical messengers, called neurotransmitters, which are naturally produced by the brain. Because of this similarity, these drugs are able to "fool" the brain's receptors and activate nerve cells to send abnormal messages.

Other drugs, such as cocaine or methamphetamine, can cause the nerve cells to release abnormally large amounts of natural neurotransmitters, or prevent the normal recycling of these brain chemicals, which is needed to shut off the signal between neurons. This disruption produces a greatly amplified message that ultimately disrupts normal communication patterns. Nearly all drugs, directly or indirectly, target the brain's reward system by flooding the circuit with dopamine. Dopamine is a neurotransmitter present in regions of the brain that control movement, emotion, motivation, and feelings of pleasure. The overstimulation of this system, which normally responds to natural behaviors that are linked to survival (eating, spending time with loved ones, etc.), produces euphoric effects in response to the drugs. This reaction sets in motion a pattern that "teaches" people to repeat the behavior of abusing drugs.

As a person continues to abuse drugs, the brain adapts to the over-whelming surges in dopamine by producing less dopamine or by reduc-ing the number of dopamine receptors in the reward circuit. As a result, dopamine's impact on the reward circuit is lessened, reducing the abuser's ability to enjoy the drugs and the things that previously brought pleasure. This decrease compels those addicted to drugs to keep abusing drugs in order to attempt to bring their dopamine function back to normal. And they may now require larger amounts of the drug than they first did to achieve the same dopamine high—an effect known as tolerance.

Long-term abuse causes changes in other brain chemical systems and circuits as well. Glutamate is a neurotransmitter that influences the reward circuit and the ability to learn. When the optimal concentration of gluta-mate is altered by drug abuse, the brain attempts to compensate, which can impair cognitive function. Drugs of abuse facilitate nonconscious (conditioned) learning, which leads the user to experience uncontrollable cravings when they see a place or person they associate with the drug ex-perience, even when the drug itself is not available. Brain imaging studies of drug-addicted individuals show changes in areas of the brain that are critical to judgment, decision making, learning and memory, and behavior control. Together, these changes can drive an abuser to seek out and take drugs compulsively despite adverse consequences—in other words, to become addicted to drugs.

Why do some people become addicted, while others do not?

No single factor can predict whether or not a person will become ad-dicted to drugs. Risk for addiction is influenced by a person's biology, social environment, and age or stage of development. The more risk fac-tors an individual has, the greater the chance that taking drugs can lead to addiction. These factors may include the following:

Biology. The genes that people are born with—in combination with en-vironmental influences—account for about half of their addiction vulner-ability. Additionally, gender, ethnicity, and the presence of other mental disorders may influence risk for drug abuse and addiction.

Environment. A person's environment includes many different influences—from family and friends to socioeconomic status and qual-ity of life in general. Factors such as peer pressure, physical and sexual abuse, stress, and parental involvement can greatly influence the course of drug abuse and addiction in a person's life.

Development. Genetic and environmental factors interact with critical developmental stages in a person's life to affect addiction vulnerability, and adolescents experience a double challenge. Although taking drugs at any age can lead to addiction, the earlier that drug use begins, the more likely it is to progress to more serious abuse. And because adolescents' brains are still developing in the areas that govern decision making, judgment, and self-control, they are especially prone to risk-taking behaviors, including trying drugs of abuse.

Treatments

Before deciding on a program of drug treatment and support, the individual must be able to admit they have an addiction and actually want to overcome it. Positive thinking, willpower, and determination are fundamental to the success of following a drug treatment plan.

Consideration should be given to whether a support group, individual counseling, or a combination of both will be beneficial. These types of therapy are useful as the therapists know what addiction is about, will help you to determine the cause, and will have a vast amount of advice regarding craving control, managing withdrawal, and how to restructure life without the addiction.

Find out about help lines and when they can be accessed, who runs them, and what can be offered using them. Keep the list in close proximity at all times during the initial period of withdrawal and use these help lines when cravings are becoming too strong or anxieties are building up.

Allow for the "cold turkey" period. Warn family and close friends of what is happening and explain that it may cause distress to all those concerned. Exercise helps to ease symptoms of withdrawal so plan an exercise regime.

Overcoming an addiction is a very individual experience, and a wide variety of resources may be needed to help break the drug addiction.

COPING WITH STRESS

All marriages undergo stress from time to time. This can be a result of emotional strains, work or financial problems, children, and so on. For military families, there are many other situations that can be very stressful—coping with deployment and separation and frequent moves being at the top of the list.

When people are stressed they react differently. It is difficult for them to eat and sleep. They become irritable and short tempered. They may say things in the heat of the moment they would not otherwise say. As couples tend to react differently under stress, one partner may be affected far more than the other, and so the relationship gets out of kilter. The answer is to identify the source of stress and see what can be done about it. First you must accept that you are under stress and that this is causing problems in the relationship. Then sit down together and talk about the issues. That alone is often enough to relieve some of the stress. Whatever the cause of the stress, it is not likely to be resolved easily or quickly, but just recognizing it and having some sort of plan to tackle it is reassuring. Much more important, by sitting down with your partner and talking about it, you can work together to resolve it. There is a lot of truth in the saying "A problem shared is a problem halved."

Talking about the problem is half the battle; showing that you care is the other half. Be supportive and loving. Buy your partner something special; it doesn't have to be expensive. It will show that you are thinking of them and are there for them.

Stress is a response to signals called "stressors" that your brain interprets as a call to prepare for action. Adrenaline and stress hormones are released that activate your body (initiating the "fight or flight" response), and affect your actions, your thoughts, and your emotions. Stress helps to protect you, but it can be unhealthy if it continues for a long time. Too much stress can also interfere with your performance. Stress-related physical changes include the following:

- Increased blood pressure and heart rate
- Rapid breathing
- Sweating
- Stomach muscles contracting, causing "butterflies," cramps, diarrhea
- Muscle tension

Potential Long-Term Effects of Chronic Stress include the following:

- Hypertension (high blood pressure)
- Heart disease

- Immune system suppression
- Increased risk for infectious disease
- Gastrointestinal disorders such as colitis
- Asthma
- Mental health problems

Quick Stress-Reduction Techniques

When you feel stressed, your breathing becomes fast and shallow and your muscles get tense. You can interrupt the stress response with the following actions:

- Slow your breathing and take deep, slow breaths from your belly.
- Relax your muscles (e.g., by tensing and releasing muscles throughout your body).

Mental Reframing

Everyone has a stream of private thoughts running through their minds. This is called *self-talk*. These thoughts reflect your beliefs and attitudes about the world, other people, and yourself, and they may be adding to your stress. To interrupt the automatic thought process, become aware— monitor your thoughts and self-talk.

Recognize that thoughts cause feelings and motivate behavior. There is rarely a direct link between the stressful situation and your response. In fact, it's usually not the event or situation that leads to a stress reaction; *it's your interpretation of the event or situation* that causes you to respond in various ways.

The sequence of events that leads to feelings and behaviors in response to stressors is called the "ABCs":

You experience the *Activating* event.

Your *Beliefs* about the event lead to an interpretation of the event.

Your interpretation of the event either increases or decreases the stress you feel, the *Consequences*.

So: *A* (*A*ctivating event) + *B* (*B*eliefs) = *C* (*C*onsequences)

Check your thoughts and self-talk for these stress-promoting thinking patterns:

All-or-nothing thinking: judging things as being all good or all bad, usually based on a single factor.

Exaggeration: blowing the negative consequences of a situation or event way out of proportion.

Overgeneralization: drawing conclusions about your whole life based on the negative outcome of a single incident.

Mind-reading: believing you know what another person or group of people is thinking about you (usually bad) when you have no evidence.

Challenge your negative thoughts and self-talk by asking yourself whether there is evidence to support the way you are perceiving the situation.

Replace negative or stressful self-talk with more positive, useful, and realistic self-talk. For example, while on leave, you decide to take the bus to go visit your family and get stuck in traffic due to road construction. Change *negative self-talk* ("This will take forever. I will never get home. Why does this always happen to me?") to *positive and useful self-talk* ("I'm glad they are fixing this road. I can take this time to relax and listen to some music I enjoy.")

Controlling the Source of Stress by Solving Problems

Take action over stressors that you can control (your own habits, behavior, environment, relationships) by using the problem-solving process:

Step 1: Define the problem.
Step 2: Set a goal (for example, what would you like to see happen?).
Step 3: Brainstorm possible solutions.
Step 4: Evaluate the pros and cons of various possible solutions.
Step 5: Choose the best solution (weigh the pros and cons).
Step 6: Make a plan to implement the solution and try it!
Step 7: Assess how well it went.
Step 8: If the first solution doesn't work, try others.

If a Source of Stress Is Beyond Your Control

Try an activity to distract or soothe yourself:

• Listen to music.
• Get together with a friend.

- Read a good book or watch a movie.
- Engage in physical exercise.
- Consider spiritual activity such as prayer.
- Perform yoga.
- Use humor (jokes or funny movies).
- Meditate.
- Take a nap.
- Write in a journal or diary.
- Take a hot bath or shower.
- Help others in need.
- Express your stress creatively.
- Take a "mental holiday."

Plan for Future Stressful Events

Create a personalized "Stress Toolkit" by making a list of coping strategies that work for you when you're stressed, including deep breathing, muscle relaxation, and activities that you find soothing.

Visualize potential future stressful situations.

Determine if you will have some control in the situation.

Decide how you will use the problem-solving process to reduce stressors.

Plan to use various helpful activities to reduce the stress response.

Remember to include friends and family for support.

DEPRESSION

Service members and their families experience unique emotional challenges.

Deployment and redeployment, single parenting, and long absences of loved ones are a stressful part of military life. At times, these events can lead to sadness, feelings of hopelessness, and withdrawal from friends, families, and colleagues. Parenting can feel more a burden than a joy. We may feel irritable and even neglectful of our children's needs. When these feelings and behaviors appear, depression may be present. Seeking care for depression, for ourselves or loved ones, takes energy and courage.

Depression is one of the most common and treatable mental disorders. Delay in identifying depression often leads to needless suffering for the depressed individual and his or her family. Depression is not uncommon during or after the holiday season. Preparing for the holidays, the increased expectations of family and friends, the sadness of not having a loved one present, or having to say good-bye after a holiday reunion, can contribute to depression.

Courage to Care (http://helplinecenter.org/military-and-family-support/ courage-to-care/) provides information to help you talk more effectively about depression with health care providers, family, and friends. Depression is very treatable and can be a part of chronic fatigue or unexplained aches and pains. A primary care visit is an opportunity to explore concerns about the mental health of your spouse, yourself, or your children. The earlier depression is detected and treated, the less likely it is to develop into a more serious problem that can impact one's job, career, health, and relationships.

The following information might help you or someone you love identify and seek help for depression.

What Is Depression?

Depression is an illness that involves one's body, mood, and thoughts. It affects the way a person eats and sleeps, the way one feels about oneself, and the way one thinks about things. Individuals who are depressed often experience more difficulty in performing their job, caring for their children, and maintaining their personal relationships. Depression is not a passing blue mood, nor is it a sign of personal weakness. Depression is a *medical* illness and a *treatable* illness just like diabetes or heart disease.

A family history of depression and negative life experiences such as loss, trauma, serious illness, and stress can also contribute to the onset of depression. There are effective treatments today for depression including medications and therapy. Without treatment, symptoms can last for weeks, months, or years. Appropriate treatment, however, can help most people who suffer from depression.

The majority of people who are treated for depression will improve, even those with serious depression. Unfortunately, only one third of sufferers seek help, as they do not realize depression is a treatable illness.

Who Gets Depression?

Depression is one of the most common mental disorders. Women are at a higher risk and experience depression about twice as often as men. Many women are also particularly vulnerable after the birth of a baby. The hormonal and physical changes, as well as the added responsibility of a new life, can be factors that lead to postpartum depression. While the "blues" are common in new mothers and go away, a major depressive episode is not normal and requires active intervention.

Depression in men often shows up in the form of alcohol or drug use and working long hours. Men may act irritable, angry, and discouraged when they are depressed. Men are often less willing than women to seek help. Depression commonly affects people between the ages of thirty to forty-four. These are prime parenting years and prime working years.

Parenting is challenging in good health, but can be more so if one is depressed. As a parent, it is important to seek treatment for depression, as this condition affects everyone in your family.

In any given year, 9.5 percent of the population (about 18.8 million Americans) experience depression. The economic cost for this disorder is high, but the cost in human suffering cannot be estimated.

Factors That Contribute to Depression

Depression can seem to happen "out of the blue," with no specific cause. A person can get depressed even if everything seems to be going well. Many things can contribute to depression:

- Dwelling on negative automatic thoughts about oneself, the world, and the future (such as job loss, divorce, illness or injury, trauma)
- History of feeling bad about oneself
- Changes in brain chemicals
- Using alcohol and/or illegal drugs to avoid or cope with emotional pain
- Use of certain prescribed and over-the-counter drugs (it is best to discuss the possible side effects of medications with a physician)
- The important role of family history and genetics
- Medical conditions, such as hypothyroidism, diabetes, or brain injury
- Anxiety disorders or other psychological problems

Traumatic or stressful life events can bring on depression:

- Combat experience
- Threat of death
- Death of another person or other major loss
- Physical, sexual, and/or emotional abuse
- A long period of stress at home and/or work

- Relationship problems or divorce
- Money problems
- Job loss
- Natural or man-made disasters

  The good news is that no matter what causes or contributes to depression, depression can be resolved with appropriate treatment.

  Negative *thoughts* (for example, "I'm a failure" or "Things will never get better") often bring on depressed *feelings*. Feeling depressed in turn makes people less likely to do the things (*engage in behavior*) that might make them feel better. This leads to greater depression, which in turn leads to more negative thoughts resulting in doing even less things that feel good. Note: war injuries and/or chronic pain may keep a person from doing enjoyable things.

Signs and Symptoms of Depression

There are some common signs that might indicate depression, but getting a doctor's opinion is the first step to evaluation. Signs and symptoms include the following:

- **Symptoms of Adult Depression**
    - Persistent sad or empty mood
    - Loss of interest or pleasure in ordinary activities
    - Changes in appetite or sleep
    - Decreased energy or fatigue
    - Inability to concentrate or to make decisions
    - Feelings of guilt, hopelessness, or worthlessness
    - Thoughts of death or suicide
- **Symptoms of Adolescent Depression**
    - Loss of interest in school and regular activities; drop in school performance
    - Withdrawal from friends and family
    - Negative thoughts of self and future
    - Difficulty making decisions
- **Symptoms of Depression in Pre-adolescent Children**
    - Children with other psychiatric disorders (ADHD, conduct disorder, eating disorders, and anxiety disorders) and those with general medi-

cal conditions (diabetes, asthma, cancers, and other chronic illnesses) may be prone to depression. The prevalence may also be higher among children with developmental disorders and mental retardation.

- ○ Physical symptoms, like chronic headaches or stomachaches that cannot be attributed to a physical illness
- ○ Aggression and excessive crying
- ○ Irritability, withdrawal, isolative behavior, loss of interest, and/or pleasure in previously enjoyed activities
- ○ Sleep disturbances (reduced or increased sleep), changes in appetite (reduced or increased appetite), and reduced energy

- **Symptoms of Depression in the Elderly**
  - ○ Depression in older adults can be disabling and contribute to the inability to perform activities of daily living. Depression in the elderly is complex and difficult to diagnose due to other medical illnesses that may be present.
  - ○ Clinicians need to differentiate between depression and problems such as dementia, stroke, and other types of brain injuries and illnesses.

- **Other Signs of Depression**
  - ○ Decline in physical health
  - ○ Decreased energy, fatigue, or tiredness; feeling "slowed down" or sluggish
  - ○ Physical problems that don't get better with treatment, such as headaches, stomach problems, and chronic pain
  - ○ Losing or gaining weight due to an unhealthy diet or lack of exercise
  - ○ Thoughts of death or suicide; past suicide attempts
  - ○ Hopelessness, excessive pessimism, negativity
  - ○ Thoughts of guilt, worthlessness, helplessness
  - ○ Negative thoughts about oneself, about the world, and about the future
  - ○ Problems paying attention and focusing
  - ○ Memory problems
  - ○ Negative thoughts that keep playing over and over again
  - ○ Being confused, finding it hard to make everyday decisions
  - ○ Poor judgment
  - ○ Racing thoughts that are difficult to slow down
  - ○ Thinking, "I'm a loser," or harsh self-criticism

- **Behaviors**
  - ○ Loss of interest or pleasure in hobbies and activities that were previously enjoyed

o Loss of interest or pleasure in sex
o Having a hard time getting started with activities
o Pulling away or isolating from others, or wanting to be alone
o Increased use of tobacco, alcohol, drugs, and/or caffeine
o Taking dangerous risks
o Laughing or crying at odd moments
o Sleeping too much or too little
o Eating more or less
o Always feeling sad, anxious, or "empty"
o Feeling restless, annoyed, or nervous
o Feeling anger, guilt, or regret

An actual depression may exist when some or several of the signs listed above occur together, for example, decreased energy, decreased appetite, sleep difficulty, and poor concentration.

Symptoms may

• last longer than two weeks;
• be very bothersome or cause a lot of distress; and
• get in the way of social, work, and family duties, or other important areas or activities.

When this is the case, it is best to seek out professional consultation with a primary care physician or mental health professional.

General Health Tips for the Holidays

The following health tips are important for managing mild depression and for optimizing one's health, especially during the holiday season:

• Manage your diet
• Get adequate rest
• Avoid alcohol
• Participate in regular exercise
• Surround yourself with people who are important to you
• Communicate your feelings to someone you trust
• Join a social support group in your military community or in your local area

Behavior and Depression

Negative Action, Negative Mood

People with the blues usually feel "down," tired, sad, and hopeless. The natural instinct when feeling down is to just go with the feelings. A person who is depressed might exhibit the following behavior:

- Not do things that take energy or effort
- Decide that they will put things they don't want to do off until later when they feel better
- Keep to oneself and not spend time with family or friends
- Sleep a lot or spend a lot of time trying to sleep
- Misuse alcohol and other substances (such as drugs, nicotine, or caffeine)
- Overeat, or not eat enough or nutritiously
- Avoid feelings or others by keeping busy with habit-forming activities such as watching television or video-gaming

Here's an interesting point about depression: when a person just goes with depressed feelings, and stays away from activities, it is those very activities that are being avoided that may help a person to feel better. Not doing things only makes the depression worse because avoiding activities

- keeps a person from having fun and living a full life;
- puts off facing and solving problems;
- keeps a person from dealing with important feelings and issues (for example, grief when a loved one dies);
- makes it harder to cope with painful feelings in the future; and
- makes it more likely that the problems will get worse.

Overall, when Bob is not doing things that are fun and rewarding, he is more likely to feel depressed. When Bob feels depressed, he doesn't enjoy, or feels less satisfied, doing things, and so he stops doing them. This creates the downward spiral. The less Bob does, the more depressed he feels, and the more depressed Bob becomes, the less he does.

Finding Your Depress TRAPS

To get out of the downward spiral, it's first necessary to figure out the behavior that's making the problem worse. One way to do this is to look for depression *TRAP*s. A *TRAP* is a shorthand way to help determine the behavior or behaviors that might be making the depression worse. Usually a *situation* or *thought* brings on a *feeling*, like sadness, which then makes it more likely that the situation will be avoided. This is a problem because it means that a person may then avoid things that could help him or her feel better. *TRAP* stands for

> **T** = **T**rigger (situation or thought)
> **R** = **R**esponse (usually a feeling)
> **AP** = **A**voidance **P**attern (avoidance behavior)

> **EXAMPLE:**
> **T** = *John's friends ask him to watch a football game with them. John thinks to himself, "I don't feel like it. It's pointless; I won't have fun anyway."*
> **R** = *John feels irritated, tired, and more depressed.*
> **AP** = *John decides to stay home and doesn't go out with his friends.*

It can be difficult to figure out what behavior is causing the problem to worsen or not improve. In depression, often it's *avoidance* that causes problems.

Avoidance: Avoidance can be defined as a person doing or not doing something to get out of tough situations or to stop themselves from feeling bad. Another example of avoidance is thinking, "I'm not in the mood," and then putting off doing things that should be done. Avoidance ends up making depression worse in the long run. For example, sleeping isn't avoidance behavior when it's during a set time period and needed rest is being obtained. On the other hand, feeling down and taking a long nap in the middle of the day when adequate rest was gotten the night before would probably be an avoidance behavior. Over the long run, using sleep to avoid activities means not getting the benefits that those activities might provide.

POSITIVE ACTION, POSITIVE MOOD

Once the depression *TRAP*s have been determined, the behaviors that are contributing to the low mood will be better understood. When the behaviors that are *not* helpful are known, it becomes possible to choose to do something to pull out of the negative spiral.

Exactly what should a person do when they are feeling depressed? The key to finding the way out of depression is to *move toward what's important. Do things that are in line with individual goals and values even if there isn't a lot of motivation at first.*

Taking Positive Action during a Depression

At this point, it's common to think that taking action toward goals is a lot easier said than done. If it were that easy to move toward goals when fatigue and feeling "down" have set in, then feeling better would be easy. But even though feeling better may be difficult at times, it's important to make the effort.

It's common to think that feeling better should come before taking positive action, but this is not a good idea. It's also common to think, "I have to *feel* like doing something positive before I do it." These ways of thinking are myths. Feelings shouldn't determine actions! In fact, acting in line with life values and goals is possible *even when there isn't much motivation.*

While feelings do influence decision making, *feelings don't cause behavior.* Here's an example:

Instead of going out with friends, John decides to stay home. Walking in to the kitchen, he notices that the sink is full of dirty dishes. He considers washing the dishes, but then realizes that he feels tired and depressed. He chooses to take a nap, thinking, "I'll wash the dishes later, when I feel like it."

In this example it seems like John's choice to take a nap was caused by feeling tired and depressed, but this isn't really the case. While John's feelings *influenced* his choice to take a nap, those feelings didn't *cause* him to take a nap. Here's another example:

As John is walking to his bedroom to take a nap, his roommate says, "Hey John, I have a date coming over tonight. I'll pay you $100 to wash

Consider individual goals in these terms: where would you like to be and what would you like to be doing in one month, one year, five years? When you know where you would like to be and what you would like to be doing, think about some small, doable steps that you can take to reach these goals. Taking small steps toward your goals can help lift your depression.

*the dishes before she gets here." Even though John still feels tired and he
doesn't want to wash the dishes, he decides to wash them before he takes
a nap because he could really use the extra money.*

In this example, while John's feelings of depression and tiredness made
him *want* to take a nap he still *chose* to wash the dishes when offered
$100. His feelings didn't cause his actions. Remember: feelings don't
control actions or behaviors.

So, what causes and controls behaviors? *Thoughts* affect feelings and
actions. A person can think it's a good idea to work toward life values and
goals, and choose to do so even if there isn't much motivation to follow
through.

Moving toward Goals

Here are some ways to work toward personal goals even when there isn't
much motivation to do so:

Set small goals that are realistic and achievable. For example, rather
than deciding to get a better paying job by next week, a more achievable
goal would be to start looking at job postings and update resumes and
cover letters over the next week.

Break big goals into smaller steps and set priorities. For example,
instead of planning to clean the whole house, planning to clean for ten
minutes at a time is probably more realistic.

Create a to-do list with big tasks broken down into smaller tasks. This
will help the big tasks seem less overwhelming. For example:

- Pay bills:
  o Gather all bills.
  o Write checks.
  o Put checks in envelopes and seal.
  o Place stamps on envelopes.
  o Put in mailbox.
- Go at a moderate pace. For example, clean for ten minutes a day for five
  days instead of trying to clean fifty minutes over the course of one day.
- Set up routines to get in the habit of taking positive action. For example,
  regularly walking the dog at eight o'clock every night will make a routine out of getting exercise.

Don't worry about doing things perfectly. Just doing them is the important thing. For example, rather than assuming it's not worth it to mail a resume that isn't perfectly written, it's more important to send the imperfect resume than not sending it at all.

A great idea is to reward oneself for taking steps toward reaching goals by doing things that are fun, such as laughing at a funny movie, relaxing, eating good meals, seeing beautiful scenery, or playing games.

Say yes to invitations to do things with friends and family or start doing the things that were once enjoyable (such as fishing, hiking, shopping, socializing, and so on) even if the motivation isn't there. Give the activity a serious try before deciding that it won't help.

Now that we have shown how behaviors affect depression, let's take a look at how thinking affects depression.

Thinking and Depression

People are always thinking, even if they are not aware of what they are thinking. As one thought passes, there is another one ready to take its place. Most of the thoughts people have are *automatic thoughts*—in other words, the thoughts pop up without a person even trying to think them. Automatic thoughts are usually about what's going on around a person. Automatic thoughts are often about what a person thinks about himself (or herself). Some automatic thoughts are negative. For example, "I'm not good enough." Or, "I shouldn't have made that mistake." Automatic thoughts can also be positive; however, it's the negative thoughts that contribute to depression.

Fortunately, automatic thoughts are changeable. This is because *thinking is learned,* much like doing is learned. Much of what a person thinks and believes comes from what they have learned from others and how others have related to the person. Influences in a person's life include parents, friends, the media, and society.

This means that even negative thoughts are learned and they may or may not be accurate or true. Since negative thinking can cause depression, some forms of depression can be thought of as a *learned thinking problem.* The good news is that because thoughts are learned, reducing depression is possible by learning new thoughts to take the place of unhelpful thoughts. It *is* possible to gain control over negative thoughts.

Remember: *thinking affects feelings and actions*. For example, if SPC Jones *thinks* that he will perform well on a mission, then he will probably feel excited about that mission and do a good job. If SPC Jones *thinks* that he won't do well, then he might feel upset or get distracted and not do such a great job. So, what SPC Jones thinks about his mission will affect how he feels about the mission and how he performs.

Often, people blame others or an event for making them feel a certain way, such as happy, sad, or angry. For example, "My roommate makes me so mad." But *people and events do not cause thoughts or feelings*. Remember: it's how a person *thinks and interprets* an event or situation that affects feelings and actions. Feelings and behaviors are influenced by thoughts, by belief systems, and by how situations are interpreted.

Depression tends to bring up thoughts that are negative and that focus more on the bad things that happened in the past or might happen in the future. Depressed people often have thoughts that they are worthless, helpless, and hopeless. It's important to realize that these negative thoughts are part of the depression and aren't necessarily true or useful.

During a depression, why do negative thoughts hold such sway?

- The thoughts are automatic, so the person doesn't stop to check if they're true.
- A depressed person doesn't choose to have negative thoughts and it's hard to make the thoughts just stop.
- The thoughts seem to be true, and the feelings connected with them are so strong and real that a depressed person doesn't even question or challenge them.
- Having negative thoughts over and over again makes them easier to believe and accept as the truth.

Negative thoughts often center on three ideas:

- "I am the cause of _____ (bad event)." For example, "I failed the training because I'm not good enough." Or, "I caused all the bad things in my life because I'm a bad person."
- One bad thing means everything is bad. For example, "I failed my training and so my whole life sucks" or "My girlfriend broke up with me so all women are losers."

• Things will always be bad. For example, "I failed my training so my future is hopeless" or "This is never going to get better."

Ten Common Types of Thinking Errors

Negative automatic thoughts often distort or twist the truth, making things seem worse than they really are. These kind of negative thoughts are called *thought distortions, negative thinking patterns*, or *thinking errors*. Let's use the term "thinking errors." Errors in thinking happen when thoughts don't really fit all the facts. Thinking errors can be grouped into at least ten common types.

All-or-Nothing Thinking: This is thinking in terms of either/or, black-and-white, good or bad, right or wrong. A healthier way to think is to look for a middle ground or look for the gray areas. Rarely in life is something all-or-nothing.

For example, because Mack couldn't do enough sit-ups during a physical training test, he automatically thinks, "I failed so I must be a loser." Mack can challenge this thinking error by thinking, "I did well in other areas of the PT test, so I'm not a complete failure, and I'm not a loser."

Exaggerating or Minimizing: Exaggerating means making too big of a deal out of a negative experience or making things much more negative than they really are. Exaggerated thinking is often associated with "making a mountain out of a molehill" or "blowing things way out of proportion." Minimizing means not giving oneself or others enough credit for doing something good. Too little is made out of something, such as a compliment or success.

A healthier way to think is to stop blowing things out of proportion and recognize and value successes. For example, Sheila completed her assigned mission faster and better than last time, but her commander told her that she had made some mistakes. Sheila made a big deal out of what her commander told her and thought that she had blown her chance for promotion. Sheila can challenge this thinking error by reminding herself that mistakes can happen to anyone who is in training, that she is continuing to improve, and if she acts on her commander's feedback, there's no reason why she wouldn't have a chance for promotion.

Overgeneralization: Overgeneralization involves thinking that something that happened once or twice will keep happening again and again, especially if it is something bad.

A healthier way to think is to recognize that just because something happened once or twice does not necessarily mean it will always happen. For example, because SPC Wynne lost her ID yesterday she thinks to herself, "I'm always doing stupid things like this! I'm never going to be organized!" Instead of this kind of overgeneralization, SPC Wynne could realize that just because she misplaced her ID once doesn't mean she always has or always will be disorganized.

Mental Filter: Using a mental filter means only seeing the bad and not the good side of things. The positive is forgotten or ignored, and only the bad things are considered.

A healthier way to think is to notice the good things and realize that they count as much if not more than the negative. For example, Regina gets an e-mail card from her friend on her birthday and thinks to herself, "My friend doesn't even care enough to send me an actual birthday card. I don't have any *real* friends." Regina can challenge this thinking error by thinking, "It was cool that my friend remembered and sent me birthday wishes."

Not Accepting the Positive: People with this thinking error reject anything positive, especially positive information about themselves.

A healthier way to think is to accept the positive without thinking that it doesn't count for anything. Positive actions that have been taken, talents or skills, and comments about strengths from others are important and are a real part of who a person is. It's important to ask oneself why it's so easy to believe negative comments and reject positive compliments. Is that fair?

For example, every time Marty's bosses praise him for doing a good job, he doesn't believe the praise. He thinks to himself, "They're just being nice. I really can't do anything right." Marty can challenge this thinking error by thinking, "My bosses really do believe I'm doing a good job, and I can be proud of my work."

Reasoning with Feelings Instead of Logic or Facts: Saying, "I feel like a loser, so I must be a loser," is an example of using feelings instead of facts as proof of truth.

A healthier way to think is to question the feelings that are being used to make conclusions or decisions. It's a good idea to use negative feelings as a *signal* that it's necessary to look for facts to disprove the negative thought.

For example, two of Joel's friends died after a bomb exploded as they drove under an overpass in Iraq. Ever since then, Joel feels nervous when he drives under an overpass. Now that he's back home he uses his nervous feelings as proof that it's not safe to drive under overpasses. Joel can challenge this thinking error by reminding himself that his feelings don't prove that overpasses at home are dangerous, and instead he needs to remember real facts about overpasses (such as they are safe to drive under). Once he realizes this, he will likely begin to feel less nervous and stop reasoning with his feelings about driving under overpasses.

Jumping to Conclusions: This type of thinking error happens when people think they know what will happen without first finding out the facts. Expecting something bad to happen usually goes along with this type of thinking. *Mind-reading* is another way of jumping to conclusions. An example of mind-reading is when a person thinks he knows what *others* are thinking, without finding out the truth first. Mind-reading often results in *incorrectly* believing what the other person is thinking.

A healthier way to think is to check all the facts before jumping to any conclusions. No one knows what will happen in the future, and no one knows how to read minds.

For example, Jimmy thought that two guys in his unit were talking about him because they were whispering when he walked into his tent. Jimmy can challenge this thinking error by asking the guys what they were talking about. It turned out that the guys were talking about a personal problem that they didn't want other people to hear. It had nothing to do with Jimmy.

Labeling: A person can label him- or herself, or label others, based on very little information or based on mistakes that were made. When people label themselves, they often do so harshly. This has the effect of making it harder to accept mistakes. And once the labels get "attached," they become difficult to remove.

When depressed, it is best not to attach labels, either to oneself or to others. It is preferable to find ways to accept mistakes and shortcomings and move on. For example, PVT Roberts forgot to pass on a message to her sergeant from the commander, so she labeled herself a "flake." PVT Roberts can challenge this label by accepting that she made the mistake, learning from it, forgiving herself, and moving on. She also can note that labeling only makes it worse because it brings up all the negative things associated with being a flake that aren't true for her.

"Should" Statements: "Should" statements are based on rules or standards that people set up for themselves and others to follow, but they are usually impossible to do all of the time. People sometimes set the standards so high that they set themselves and others up to fail, which only confirms the negative thoughts.

A healthier way for individuals to think is to avoid beating themselves up with "shoulds" or "shouldn'ts." Remember: it's not always possible to get things done *exactly* as planned or expected. For example, CPT Smith assigned SPC Gray to a duty that SPC Gray thinks is beneath him. He would rather be leading the team and thinks CPT Smith should have given him that job. As he thinks about it more, he gets angrier and angrier. SPC Gray can challenge his thinking error by telling himself that even though he would have *liked* CPT Smith to have given him the job, it is CPT Smith's job to make that decision. His job is to do what CPT Smith decides for him, not to decide what CPT Smith should do.

Taking It Personally: Taking things too personally involves the assumption that others do negative things on purpose. People who take things too personally may also tend to take responsibility for something that they are not responsible for.

A healthier way to think is to look at the facts; most likely it will turn out that negative things are not done as a personal attack. For example, SPC Gray might think that CPT Smith did not assign him the leader position because CPT Smith doesn't like him or that CPT Smith has something against him. SPC Gray gets angry thinking of reasons why CPT Smith doesn't like him. A healthier way to think is that CPT Smith has a lot of responsibilities and needs to get things done. It's nothing personal against SPC Gray.

Targeting Thoughts

Although everyone has negative thoughts at some point, negative thoughts become a problem when they happen on a regular basis, when they cause distress, and when they are disruptive. Challenging negative thoughts means taking control, which often can help with mood problems. Here are the best ways to challenge negative thoughts:

- Think about what's going on in the moment that may be setting off any negative thoughts and feelings.

- Play "devil's advocate" with negative thoughts. Challenge those thoughts by looking at the actual facts.
- Learn to change thinking errors; how a person feels and acts can also be changed.

No one is helpless to make some change—and it's not hopeless! There are plenty of tools people can use to help change their negative thinking. There is hope, because changing what and how we think allows us to get control over how we feel and act. Sometimes, though, life gets so tough that it's easy to think that there's no way to change thinking patterns. This is when some people may even start thinking about suicide.

SUICIDE

Suicide is when someone purposely takes his or her own life. Many people think about committing suicide at some time in their lives, especially in times of extreme stress or depression, but most don't follow through. Suicide, like depression, affects people of all ages and backgrounds.

Usually, people who commit suicide think their situation is totally hopeless. In this state of mind, death can seem like the only option. But **there are always other options and there is hope**. The quickest way to get help is to call one of the national suicide prevention hotlines available 24/7 at **1-800-273-TALK** (1-800-273-8255) or **1-800-SUICIDE** (1-800-784-2433). You can also seek help from your unit medic, corpsman, chaplain, or medical treatment facility.

Warning Signs of Suicide

While it's often hard to know who will commit suicide, there are warning signs that signal when a person is at high risk. These warning signs can include the following:

- Talking About and Planning One's Death:
  - Talking about dying and making plans to harm or kill oneself
  - Having the means to carry out the suicide plan, such as owning a gun or having potentially dangerous pills available

- ○ Having attempted suicide in the past
- ○ Feeling depressed: most people who commit suicide are depressed; however, a person doesn't have to show signs of depression to commit suicide
- No Hope for the Future
  - ○ Thinking that one is all alone in the world, that no one likes him or her, that no one would care if he or she were dead, and/or feeling that the future is hopeless
  - ○ Going through a very stressful time and feeling overwhelmed by problems in life
  - ○ Thinking that there are no other solutions to the problem except death
  - ○ Having suffered a loss (such as loss of a relationships, job, or death of a friend or family member)
- Combat Trauma
  - ○ Having combat-related guilt about acts carried out during times of war and/or upsetting thoughts about the war that feels overwhelming
- Changes in Personality
  - ○ Wanting to be alone all the time
  - ○ Feeling sad, tired, irritable, aggressive, anxious, and/or agitated
  - ○ Not interested in things that were once enjoyable or important in life
- Low Self-Esteem
  - ○ Feeling worthless, ashamed, guilty, and/or hating oneself.
  - ○ Thinking, "The world would be better off without me," or, "I'm a failure"
- Reckless or High-Risk Behavior
  - ○ Reckless driving, gambling, threatening others' lives, or putting one's life at risk
- Changes in Behavior
  - ○ Having no interest in work and other activities
  - ○ Having more problems than usual with one's leader, coworkers, family, and/or partner or spouse
  - ○ Sleeping more or less than usual and still feeling exhausted
  - ○ Loss of appetite or overeating, and changes in weight not due to a healthy diet
  - ○ Treating others poorly or rudely
  - ○ Having a hard time concentrating on and finishing routine, everyday tasks
  - ○ Giving away valued possessions

- Substance Abuse
  - Using alcohol and/or illegal drugs for a long period of time
  - Abusing prescribed medications as a way to deal with problems

Suicide hotlines are free and confidential, are staffed by trained counselors, and have information about support services that can be of assistance. Contact suicide hotlines when the following occurs:

- The sadness is overwhelming, or there are thoughts of hopelessness or suicide.
- There is concern about someone who may be experiencing these feelings.
- There is interest in suicide prevention, treatment, and service referrals.

What to Do If Someone Says They're Thinking about Suicide

When someone is at risk for suicide, take immediate action: Tell someone right away! Never promise to keep thoughts about suicide a secret.

If there is a serious risk of suicide, do the following:

- Take the person's concerns seriously, and listen without judging.
- Tell the person what will be done to help, such as not discussing the issue with coworkers unless it's on a need-to-know basis. A need-to-know basis might include command or someone else who can help.
- Limit the person's access to firearms or other lethal means of committing suicide (this may require getting additional assistance).

It may be necessary to involve others—military law enforcement, 911, friends, and family members can help.

Get the person to a health care professional. Give him or her the number to a mental health professional, chaplain, or a counselor in your installation, or to the national suicide prevention hotlines at **1-800-273-TALK** (1-800-273-8255), **1-800-SUICIDE**, or (1-800-784-2433). Military One-Source (1-800-342-9647; www.militaryonesource.com) is another resource. Stay with the person until he or she has contacted help.

If the person refuses to get help, don't keep their suicidal thoughts a secret. Tell a friend, family member, professional, or supportive leader who can find them the help they need.

Chapter Six

Life Goes On

After deployment the military family may be posted to another station, which means changing homes, finding new schools for the children, and a thousand and one other tasks. The serving member might even be transitioning out of the military and will have to decide on what new career to enter. The following looks at these issues and how to handle them.

CONTINUING EDUCATION

Service members leaving the military sometimes find a gap between the civilian careers they want and the specific education or training they need to achieve it. The following section will help you identify the resources available to assist you in getting the training and education needed to help close that gap.

Your Education Benefits: Montgomery GI Bill, Post-9/11 GI Bill, VEAP, and More

Several programs administered by the Department of Veterans Affairs (VA) provide financial assistance to veterans for education programs. This includes enrollment in degree programs, technical and vocational programs, correspondence courses, flight-training courses, and on-the-job training and apprenticeship programs. To be eligible programs must be approved, usually by a state-approving agency, for VA purposes before VA education program benefits are paid.

Two of these programs are the Post-Vietnam-era Veterans' Educational Assistance Program (VEAP) and the Montgomery GI Bill (MGIB). Both programs are intended to help you develop skills that will enhance your opportunities for employment. As a rule, the benefits under either of these programs must be used within ten years of separation from active duty.

Post-Vietnam-Era Veterans' Education Assistance Program (VEAP) Eligibility

With the exception of some people who signed delayed entry contracts before January 1, 1977, VEAP is for people who first entered active duty during the period January 1, 1977, through June 30, 1985, and who made a contribution to a VEAP account before April 1, 1987. If you participated in VEAP and withdrew your contribution, you may start a new allotment, or make a lump-sum contribution, at any time while you are on active duty.

Montgomery GI Bill (MGIB) Eligibility

MGIB eligibility is straightforward for most veterans, but it can be complex for others. If you have questions about MGIB eligibility, check with your Education Center, or call the VA toll-free education number, 1-888-GIBill-1 (1-888-442-4551). You may also get information at the VA Education Service website at www.gibill.va.gov.

With the exception of some officers who received a commission after December 31, 1976, as a result of graduating from a service academy or after completing a Reserve Officer Training Corps (ROTC) scholarship program, the MGIB is for people who first came on active duty on July 1, 1985, or later, and who did not decline—in writing—to participate in the MGIB program.

To be eligible for the full thirty-six months of MGIB benefits, veterans must normally meet the character of service and minimum length of service requirements. Some veterans who are separated from active duty early for the convenience of the government may also receive the full thirty-six months of MGIB benefits. Depending on the reason for separation, other veterans who are separated from active duty early may be eligible for prorated—that is, reduced—MGIB benefits; one month of benefits for each full month of active duty.

Some veterans who were eligible for the Vietnam Era GI Bill (VRA) have increased MGIB eligibility. They must have had some remaining VRA entitlement on December 31, 1989, when all benefits under the VRA expired. With some exceptions, they must have served on active duty from July 1, 1985, through June 30, 1988. For these veterans, the ten-year period of time in which they must use MGIB benefits is reduced by any time, from January 1, 1977, through June 30, 1985, that they were not on active duty.

Individuals who are involuntarily separated from the military and who were not originally eligible for the MGIB may have a second opportunity to receive MGIB benefits. This includes officers not normally eligible for the MGIB because they were commissioned after December 31, 1976, as a result of graduating from a service academy or after completing a ROTC scholarship, and people who declined to participate in the MGIB. Contact your Education Center or VA for details.

$600 Buy-up Program: You can get up to $150 per month added to your standard MGIB "payment rate." This could increase your total GI Bill benefit by up to $5,400. To take advantage you must be on active duty and elect to contribute up to $600 (in $20 increments) before you leave the service. Each $300 contributed earns an additional $75 a month in benefits. You can use form DD Form 2366-1, "Increased Benefit Contribution Program," to process your request through your local payroll or personnel office (www. dtic.mil/whs/directives/forms/eforms/dd2366-1.pdf).

GI Bill Apprenticeship and OJT Programs: The Department of Veterans Affairs On-the-Job Training (OJT) and Apprenticeship Program offers you an alternative way to use your Montgomery GI Bill education and training benefits.

When you are trained for a new job, you can receive monthly training benefits from the Department of Veterans Affairs (VA) in addition to your regular salary. If you are qualified for the Montgomery GI Bill or the Montgomery GI Bill for Selected Reserve and you have or are planning to start a new job or apprenticeship program, you should apply for this little known MGIB benefit. In some cases, the VA will even pay retroactively for OJT from the past twelve months.

Call 1-888-GIBILL-1 to speak to a VA representative about your eligibility for this valuable program.

Note: You may not receive GI Bill OJT benefits at the same time you receive other GI Bill education benefits.

NEW POST-9/11 GI BILL—CHAPTER 33

The Post-9/11 GI Bill is a new education benefit program that will provide service members with college tuition, stipends for housing, and books. This program went into effect on August 1, 2009. To qualify for this benefit you must serve a minimum of ninety days on active duty after September 10, 2001. This includes active duty service as a member of the Armed Forces or as a result of a call or order to active duty from a reserve component (National Guard and Reserve) under certain sections of title 10. The new Post-9/11 GI Bill will pay up to 100 percent for tuition, a monthly housing stipend based on the DoD Basic Allowance for Housing at the E-5 with Dependents payment rate, and up to $1,000 a year for books and supplies.

Your benefits under the Post-9/11 GI Bill will vary depending on your state of residence, number of education units taken, and amount of post September 11, 2001, active-duty service. Here is a quick reference showing the percentage of total combined benefit eligibility based on the following periods of post-9/11 service:

- 100%—36 or more cumulative months
- 100%—30 or more consecutive days with disability-related discharge
- 90%—30 or more cumulative months
- 80%—24 or more cumulative months
- 70%—18 or more cumulative months
- 60%—12 or more cumulative months
- 50%—six or more cumulative months
- 40%—90 or more days

However, some periods of active duty service are excluded. Periods of service under the following do not count toward qualification for the Post-9/11 GI Bill:

- NOAA, PHS, or Active Guard Reserve;
- ROTC under 10 U.S.C. 2107(b);
- service academy contract period;
- service terminated due to defective enlistment agreement;
- service used for loan repayment; *and*

- selected reserve service used to establish eligibility under the Montgomery GI Bill (MGIB chapter 30), MGIB for Selected Reserve (MGIB-SR Chapter 1606), or the Reserve Education Assistance Program (REAP chapter 1607).

Learn more about the Post-9/11 GI Bill by downloading the Department of Veterans Affairs Post-9/11 GI Bill Pamphlet (PDF): www.gibill. va.gov/pamphlets/CH33/CH33_Pamphlet.pdf.

FOR MORE INFORMATION

The VA can provide you with educational counseling after you leave the service. Contact the VA GI Bill Regional Processing Office by dialing toll-free 1-888-GIBill-1 (1-888-442-4551) or go to the MGIB website at www.gibill.va.gov. To contact the VA Regional Office closest to you, go to www1.va.gov/directory/guide/home.asp and click on "Facilities by State." Then, click on your state to locate the regional office nearest you.

In addition, information on MGIB and other veterans' educational benefit programs is available from your installation's Education Center or from the admissions office and/or veterans' coordinator at most colleges and universities.

Did You Know? You qualify for Federal Financial Student Aid such as Pell Grants and the Stafford Loan Program even if you are still on active duty. Visit www.fafsa.ed.gov/ to learn how to apply.

Additional Educational or Training Options

The transition from military to civilian life is an excellent time to take a serious look at your options for future success. Now is the best time to evaluate your educational options.

GUIDANCE COUNSELING

Before you leave the military, go to your local Education Center, Navy College Office, or Marine Corps Lifelong Learning Center. The counselors can provide assistance in determining the goals that are right for you. If you feel you need additional education or training, the Education Counselor will guide you to the appropriate curriculum and institution and help you with the paperwork necessary to enroll in an academic or vocational program.

Career Assessment

If you are not sure what you want to do upon leaving the military, then you should talk to a counselor at your local Education Center, Navy College Office, Marine Corps Lifelong Learning Center, or Transition Office. The counselor can recommend aptitude tests or vocational interest inventories to help clarify your career goals. These tests can help you pinpoint job skills in which you might excel and then relate them to specific occupations and careers in the civilian world.

Your installation's Education Center, Navy College Office, or Marine Corps Lifelong Learning Center may offer the Strong Interest Inventory, Self-Directed Search, or Career Assessment Inventory, as well as computerized counseling systems like Discover. These can help you select jobs and careers that more closely match your personality, background, and career goals.

Academic Planning

Once you have identified your career goal, you may find you need a formal education to achieve it. Your education counselor can explore the possibilities with you. Counselors can also advise you on nontraditional educational opportunities that can make it easier for you to get a diploma, vocational certificate, or college degree. These nontraditional opportunities include the following:

- **Take "challenge exams," such as a college-level equivalency exam:** You can convert knowledge learned outside the classroom into credits toward a college program. This can save you time and money.
- **Go to school part time while continuing to hold down a full-time job:** This approach might make adult education more practical.
- **See the veterans' coordinator at the college, university, or vocational school of your choice:** The coordinator can help you understand

your VA educational benefits and might lead you to special programs offered to former service members.

- **Determine if your military learning experiences can translate to course credit:** Check with your service Education Center, Navy College Office, or Marine Corps Lifelong Learning Center well in advance of your separation date to request copies of your transcripts.
- **Take advantage of distance-learning opportunities:** With today's technological advances, you can enroll in an educational program in which courses are offered by accredited educational institutions in a variety of formats, for example, CD-ROM, the Internet, satellite TV, cable TV, and video tapes.

Vocational Services

The Education Center, Navy College Office, or Marine Corps Lifelong Learning Center can tell you about vocational and technical school programs designed to give you the skills needed to work in occupations that do not require a four-year college degree. The counselors at these centers can also show you how to get course credits for nontraditional learning experience (such as military certifications and on-the-job training). The counselors can help you explore these options. The counselors may also help you find out about certification and licensing requirements—for example, how to get a journeyman card for a particular trade. The counselors can give you information on vocational and apprenticeship programs.

Note: Local trade unions may also offer vocational training in fields that interest you.

Licensing and Certification

Your military occupational specialty may require a license or certification in the civilian workforce. There are several resources available to assist you in finding civilian requirements for licensing and certification:

- **www.careeronestop.org/Toolkit/ACINet.aspx**: Department of Labor website. Go to "Explore Careers" section to look up licenses by state, requirements for the license, and point-of-contact information for the state licensing board.

- www.dantes.doded.mil: DANTES website has information on certification programs.
- www.cool.army.mil: Find civilian credentials related to your military occupational specialty, learn what it takes to obtain the credentials, and see if there are available programs that will help pay credentialing fees.
- www.cool.navy.mil: Find civilian credentials related to your Navy rating, learn what it takes to obtain the credentials, and see if there are available programs that will help pay credentialing fees.

Testing Available through Your Education Center

Testing can be an important first step in your career development. Some colleges and universities may require you to provide test results as part of your application. Prior to your departure from military service, you are encouraged to take advantage of the testing services offered by the Education Center, Navy College Office, and Marine Corps Lifelong Learning Center. These services include the following:

Vocational interest inventories: Most Education Centers, Navy College Offices, and Marine Corps Lifelong Learning Centers offer free vocation interest inventories that can help you identify the careers most likely to interest you.

Academic entry exams: Before applying for college or other academic programs, you may want to take a college admission test such as the Scholastic Aptitude Test (SAT), ACT, or the Graduate Record Examination (GRE). Some schools may require that you do so. Information on these tests is available from your Education Center, Navy College Office, or Marine Corps Lifelong Learning Center. You must start early. These exams are offered only a few times each year.

Credit by examination: Your Education Center, Navy College Office, and Marine Corps Lifelong Learning Center offers a variety of "challenge" exams that can lead to college credit. If you score high enough, you may be exempt from taking a certain class or other course requirements—resulting in a big savings of time and money as you earn your degree. The College Level Examination Program (CLEP) and the DANTES Subject Standardized Tests (DSST) are also free to service members on active duty.

Certification examinations: As a service member working in an important occupational field, you have received extensive training (service schools, correspondence course, OJT) that has proved valuable in developing your professional skills. Your local Education Center, Navy College Office, or Marine Corps Lifelong Learning Center can provide you information on certification examinations that "translate" military training into civilian terms. Examinations are available in many skill areas and upon successful completion the documentation you receive is readily understood and received in the professional occupational civilian community.

Save time and money: You can get up to thirty college credits by taking the five CLEP General Exams. If you are currently serving in the Armed Forces, you can take these exams for free.

Contact your installation Education Center, Navy College Office, or Marine Corps Lifelong Learning Office to ensure that they have the capability to offer examinations you need in paper and pencil or computer-base-testing (CBT) format.

DoD Voluntary Education Program Website

For separating service members, the Department of Defense Voluntary Education Partnership Memorandum of Understanding website, www. ccmeonline.org/sites/default/DoDMOU20110817Presentation.pdf, offers a wide variety of educational information of interest and use. The website was originally established to provide support for military education center staffs worldwide. As the website developed, it took on the mission of providing direct support to active and reserve components' service members and their families. This support includes information on all programs provided by the Defense Activity for Non-Traditional Educational Support (DANTES) including the Distance Learning Program, Examination Program, Certification Program, Counselor Support Program, Troops to Teachers, and a wide variety of educational catalogs and directories.

Links are provided to each of the services' education programs and to a wide variety of education-related resources. There is also a link for participating "Educational Institutions" on the website (www.dantes.doded. mil/index.html), which contains information on all of the services' education centers worldwide, including addresses, phone numbers, and e-mail.

The primary goal of the website is to provide on site, or through links, all the information service members may need to select, plan, and complete their program of study, either while on active duty or upon separation.

Service Unique Transcripts

Army: For everything you want to know about the free AARTS transcript (Army/American Council on Education Registry Transcript System), go to www.atrrs.army.mil. This free transcript includes your military training, your Military Occupational Specialty (MOS), and college level examination scores with the college credit recommended for those experiences. It is a valuable asset that you should provide to your college or your employer, and it is available for Active Army, National Guard, and Reserve Soldiers. You can view and print your own transcript at this website.

Save time and money: Unless you know for sure that you need to take a particular course, wait until the school gets *all* your transcripts before you sign up for classes; otherwise you may end up taking courses you don't need.

Navy and Marine Corps: Information on how to obtain the Sailor/Marine American Council on Education Registry Transcript (SMART) is available at https://jst.doded.mil/smart/welcome.do. SMART is now available to document the American Council on Education (ACE) recommended college credit for military training and occupational experience. SMART is an academically accepted record that is validated by ACE. The primary purpose of SMART is to assist service members in obtaining college credit for their military experience. Additional information on SMART can also be obtained from your nearest Navy College Office, or Marine Corps Education Center, or contact the Navy College Center.

Air Force: The Community College of the Air Force (CCAF) automatically captures your training, experience, and standardized test scores. Transcript information may be viewed at the CCAF website: www.au.af.mil/au/barnes/ccaf/index.asp.

Coast Guard: The Coast Guard Institute (CGI) requires each service member to submit documentation of all training (except correspondence course records), along with an enrollment form, to receive a transcript. Transcript information can be found at the Coast Guard Institute home page: www.uscg.mil/hq/cgi.

U.S. Department of Education Financial Aid Programs

Federal Student Aid, an office of the U.S. Department of Education, offers over $80 billion in financial aid that help millions of students manage the cost of education each year. There are three categories of federal student aid: grants, work-study, and loans. Even if you are still on active duty, you can apply for aid such as Pell Grants or Federal Stafford Loans. Find out more by visiting www.federalstudentaid.ed.gov.

Complete the Free Application for Federal Student Aid (FAFSA). You can apply online or on paper, but filing online is faster and easier. Get further instructions on the application process at www.fafsa.ed.gov. You should also apply for a Federal Student Aid PIN (if you haven't done so already). The PIN allows you to sign your application electronically, which speeds up the application process even more. Apply for a PIN at www.pin.ed.gov.

There is a series of eight questions on the application that ask about your dependency status. If you are a veteran, or are currently serving on active duty in the U.S. Armed Forces for purposes other than training, you are considered an independent student and would only include your information (and that of your spouse, if married). For more detailed information, go to www.fafsa.ed.gov.

Eligibility for federal student aid is based on financial need and on several other factors. The financial aid administrator at the college or career school you plan to attend will determine your eligibility. To receive aid from our programs, you must

- have demonstrated financial need (except for certain loans—your school can explain which loans are not need based).
- have a high school diploma or a General Education Development (GED) certificate, pass a test approved by the U.S. Department of Education, meet other standards your state establishes that the department approves, or complete a high school education in a home school setting that is treated as such under state law.
- be working toward a degree or certificate in an eligible program.
- be a U.S. citizen or eligible noncitizen.
- have a valid Social Security Number (unless you're from the Republic of the Marshall Islands, the Federated States of Micronesia, or the Republic of Palau).
- register with the Selective Service if required. You can use the paper or electronic FAFSA to register, you can register at www.sss.gov or call 1-847-688-6888. (TTY users can call 1-847-688-2567.)

- maintain satisfactory academic progress once in school.
- certify that you are not in default on a federal student loan and do not owe money on a federal student grant.
- certify that you will use federal student aid only for educational purposes.

When you complete your FAFSA, you will be asked what you will be receiving in veterans' educational benefits, which the Montgomery GI Bill falls under. Your school will take into consideration the amount you list on the application, along with any other financial assistance you are eligible to receive, in preparing your financial aid package.

The Veterans Upward Bound Program is a free U.S. Department of Education program designed to help eligible U.S. military veterans refresh their academic skills so that they can successfully complete the post-secondary school of their choosing.

The VUB program services include the following:

- Basic skills development, which is designed to help veterans successfully complete a high school equivalency program and gain admission to college education programs
- Short-term remedial or refresher classes for high school graduates that have put off pursuing a college education
- Assistance with applications to the college or university of choice
- Assistance with applying for financial aid
- Personalized counseling
- Academic advice and assistance
- Career counseling
- Assistance in getting veterans services from other available resources
- Exposure to cultural events, academic programs, and other educational activities not usually available to disadvantaged people

The VUB program can help you improve your skills in these areas:

- Mathematics
- Foreign Language
- Composition
- Laboratory Science

- Reading
- Literature
- Computer Basics
- Any other subjects you may need for success in education beyond high school
- Tutorial and Study Skills Assistance

To be eligible for VUB you must

- be a U.S. Military veteran with 181 or more days active-duty service and discharged on/after January 31, 1955, under conditions other than dishonorable;
- meet the criteria for low income according to guidelines published annually by the U.S. Department of Education, and/or be a first-generation potential college graduate;
- demonstrate academic need for Veterans Upward Bound and
- meet other local eligibility criteria as noted in the local VUB project's Approved Grant Proposal, such as county of residence, and so on.

For more information, as well as a link to individual program locations, visit http://navub.org.

What if I have children who will be getting ready for college soon? Will they qualify for aid? Federal Student Aid has a new tool called *FAFSA4caster*, designed to help students and their families plan for college. The *FAFSA4caster* provides students with an early estimate of their eligibility for federal student financial assistance. Military dependents who are enrolled in college and are eligible to receive Pell Grants should check out the two newest programs: Academic Competitiveness Grants and National Science and Mathematics Access to Retain Talent Grants (National SMART Grants). Visit the website at www.FederalStudentAid. ed.gov for more information.

WORK AND CAREER

If you are leaving the military, you can start the transition process twelve months prior to separation or twenty-four months prior to retirement. The sooner you start the better. There is a lot of information to absorb and you need time to plan and decide what is in the best interest of yourself and your family. A dedicated and highly trained transition staff is available to assist you.

The Transition Assistance Program demonstrates the Department of Defense, the Department of Labor, the Department of Veterans Affairs, and the Department of Homeland Security's continued commitment to our men and women in uniform.

Special transition benefits information, employment workshops, automated employment job-hunting tools and job banks, veteran benefits information, disabled veterans' benefits information, and many other types of transition and other related information is available to you. AND IT'S ALL FREE. Take full advantage of TAP and all it has to offer.

The Department of Defense Transition Assistance Program (TAP) for Active Component Service members (including AGR, AR, and FTS) consists of four components:

1. Pre-Separation Counseling—mandatory and conducted by the Military Services
2. Department of Labor (DOL) Transition Assistance Program Employment Workshops—facilitated and sponsored by DOL
3. Veterans Benefits Briefings—facilitated and sponsored by VA
4. Disabled Transition Assistance Program (DTAP)—facilitated and sponsored by VA

The transition process begins with the completion of DD Form 2648, "Pre-Separation Counseling Checklist." This is a mandatory legal requirement and a copy of your DD Form 2648 is required to be filed in your personnel file.

The Pre-Separation Guide was developed primarily to augment the four components of TAP with special emphasis on the pre-separation counseling component. The guide provides information on the various services and benefits available to separating and retiring service members and their families. Information contained in the guide may also be used by Department of Defense civilian employees affected by downsizing, reductions in force (RIFs), base closures, and base realignments.

All separating and retiring service members should make an appointment to see their local transition counselor for information on transition services and benefits. Transition counselors are located in the following offices at local military installations:

- **Army:** Army Career and Alumni Program (ACAP)
- **Air Force:** Airman and Family Readiness Center
- **Navy:** Fleet and Family Support Center
- **Marine Corps:** Career Resource Management Center (CRMC)/Transition and Employment Assistance Program Center
- **Coast Guard:** Worklife Division—Coast Guard Worklife staff can be found at the nearest Integrated Support Command.

Information Accuracy: The material contained in the guide is current as of May 2007. Subsequent changes in laws, policies, and regulations are not addressed herein. It is important to check with your local counselor to ensure you have the most up-to-date information.

Supplementation: Supplementing the Pre-Separation Guide or establishing Military, command, or local forms is prohibited without prior approval from the Office of the Under Secretary of Defense for Personnel and Readiness. Requests to supplement the guide or produce additional forms should be forwarded through the military service chain of command to the address below the section on "Comments and Suggestions."

Comments and Suggestions: Comments, suggestions, and recommendations from active-duty military personnel must be forwarded through the respective service's chain of command. Specific comments concerning websites listed in this document should be sent to the address listed below:

Office of the Under Secretary of Defense (Personnel and Readiness)
ATTN: DoD Transition Assistance Program Manager
4000 Defense Pentagon, Washington, DC 20301-4000

A transition counselor is a person responsible for conducting the transition program. Personnel may be military, civilian, or a contractor. Transition counselors may be assigned to family centers, Army Career and Alumni Program Centers, military personnel offices, on ships, and in transition centers. The term "Transition Counselor" is used throughout the guide. Individual Military Services may use a different title (see below) for a transition counselor.

- Army: ACAP Transition Counselor
- Air Force: Transition Assistance Staff or Career Consultant
- Navy: Command Career Counselor
- Marine Corps: Career Resource Management Center Specialist
- Coast Guard: Worklife Staff
- U.S. Coast Guard: The Coast Guard has its own version of the Pre-Separation Guide. Coast Guard personnel should contact the nearest Worklife Transition and Relocation Manager for a copy of the Coast Guard guide.

Processes

Pre-Separation Counseling: Your Best Beginning

Your first step in the separation process is to go to your installation's Transition Assistance Office. Each service has its own way of doing things; so too with the Transition Assistance Offices. In most cases, you will find the Transition Assistance Office located inside your installation's Family Center. Listed below is the name of each service's Transition Assistance Program:

- Army: Army Career and Alumni Program—The Army Career and Alumni Program (ACAP) is a military personnel function and the Centers are found under the Director of Human Resources (DHR) or the Military Personnel Office (MILPO). www.acap.army.mil/default.aspx
- Air Force: Airman and Family Readiness Center. You can find the nearest office using the military installation finder at www.militaryinstallations.dod.mil.
- Navy: Fleet and Family Support Center. Navy personnel should make an appointment with their Command Career Counselor for a pre-separation counseling interview and the Navy CONSEP (Career Options and Skills Evaluation Program) self-assessment at least 180 days prior to separation. www.nffsp.org.

- Marines: Career Resource Management Center (CRMC)/Transition and Employment Assistance
- Coast Guard: Worklife Division—Transition Assistance. Coast Guard Worklife staffs can be found at your nearest Integrated Support Command: www.uscg.mil/worklife.

The Transition Assistance Program (TAP) was developed by the Department of Defense (DoD) to help separating and retiring Service members and their families make a smooth transition from a military career to the civilian sector. For the Marine Corps, the program consists of five important components:

a. **Pre-Separation Interview**. This mandatory component is the beginning of USMC TAMP process. The pre-separation interview is conducted by the Unit Transition Counselor (UTC) and shall consist of an explanation of the transition requirements for separating and retiring service members including obtaining the Verification of Military Experience and Training (VMET) www.dmdc.osd.mil/appj/vmet/loginDisplay.do

b. **Pre-Separation Counseling Brief**: This briefing typically takes one full day and includes Subject Matter Experts outlining the benefits and entitlements available to transitioning service members. This brief is mandatory and must be completed before a service member can separate or retire.

c. **Transition Assistance Program (TAP) Employment Workshop**: Mandatory. Qualified comprehensive workshops conducted by Department of Labor (DOL) or TAMP personnel. In the workshop personnel will learn how to write a resume and cover letter, get information on skills assessment, job search techniques, and other important information about career and job services available through the DOL. Service members will learn how to access the DOL Career One-Stop Center in their local community to continue their job search if they have not found a job prior to separation or retirement.

d. **Veterans Affairs Benefits Briefing:** A briefing conducted by Department of Veterans Affairs personnel outlining VA benefits and entitlements available to transitioning service members. This component of TAP is sponsored by VA. All separating and retiring service members should attend a VA Benefits Briefing to learn about all the VA benefits they are, or may be, entitled to, the procedures for applying for benefits, information on the Montgomery GI Bill, and where to go to get VA assistance (healthcare, VA counseling at a Vet Center, etc.).

e. **Disabled Transition Assistance Program (DTAP):** Specifically for individuals who have or *think* they have a potential disability claim. DTAP is also sponsored by VA. All service members separating or retiring with a service-connected disability must attend this briefing. They will learn about eligibility for Chapter 31, Vocational Rehabilitation and Employment Service benefits by VA.

Finding a job might be your top priority. Many service members have never written a resume, filled out a job application, or attended a job interview. Fortunately, these skills can be learned. The following section will give you the resources and information you need to launch your new civilian career.

Today's job market demands increasingly sophisticated and technological skills—skills that are well suited for those leaving military service. American veterans are superbly qualified and capable of meeting the needs of the current and future civilian labor force. Today's defense occupations are diverse and numerous: senior management, executives, civil engineers, medical specialists, auditors, caseworkers, nuclear engineers, food service managers, mechanics, heavy equipment operators, qualified and skilled people in information technology and telecommunications, to name a few.

Most positions correspond closely to private sector occupations. It is true that a few military specialties have no direct application. However, the training and discipline required to master those specialties clearly demonstrate the potential to learn and master other skills required in the private sector. Look at it from an employer's point of view:

• Today's Soldiers, Sailors, Airmen, Marines, and Coast Guardsman are the highest quality military personnel in our nation's history.
• The men and women serving the Department of Defense (DoD) and Department of Homeland Security are competent, positive, selfless, and oriented toward mission accomplishment.
• They perform skillfully using today's sophisticated military equipment: computers, electronics, avionics, and so on.

• They demonstrate their ability to learn sophisticated skills on short notice.

Look at yourself. You have several things going for you. You are well trained, healthy, disciplined, and team oriented. What employer wouldn't want an employee like you?

The following programs and services are available to all transitioning service members.

Transition Assistance Offices

You might be reluctant to start your transition because you dread the thought of finding a job. Career changes are, however, a common part of American life. Most people change careers at least three times in their lives.

Transition Assistance Offices have programs and counselors to assist you and your family members in seeking employment in government and the private sector. Some of the employment assistance services available at your Transition Assistance Office are listed below:

• **Counseling**: The transition staff provides individual career development counseling, comprehensive assessment of employment skills, and identification of employment opportunities.
• **Services**: Transition Assistance Offices offer computerized listings of jobs, career workshops, and training opportunities, as well as automated resume writing. Many Transition Assistance Offices also provide access to a mini-reference library, word processing, and copying equipment to assist in job search preparation.
• **Job banks**: Job banks provide information and referrals on temporary, permanent, part-time, and full-time positions in the federal, state, and private sectors.

Separating service members are strongly encouraged to start their job search by using the following websites:

• www.dmdc.osd.mil/appj/dwp/index.jsp—look for job banks/boards under the employment hub
• DoD Transportal at www.dodtransportal.org

- Transition Bulletin Board at www.afcrossroads.com/employment/main.cfm
- www.usajobs.com
- www.go-defense.com

Whatever you do, start by putting your resume online in the Department of Labor's job bank under the DoD Job Search website.

Employers who are registered with the Department of Labor's job bank and looking to hire former military personnel go to this website to search for resumes. You can also visit these websites for more employment assistance: CareerOneStop, www.careeronestop.org, and Army Career and Alumni Program (ACAP), www.acap.army.mil/default.aspx

Workshops and seminars: A variety of workshops and seminars are available through your Transition Assistance Office to help you and your spouse become more competitive in the job market. Topics include enhancing job search skills, goal setting, and preparation of standard and optional forms for federal civil service employment, resumes, and interviewing techniques. One of the most popular job-hunting workshops is sponsored by the Department of Labor. Their two-and-a-half day Transition Assistance Employment Workshop is one component of the overall Transition Assistance Program (TAP). You can sign up for this important workshop through your Transition/ACAP Office or through your Command Career Counselor.

Training: Some locations offer occupational skills training for those seeking entry-level classes in typing, word processing, and data entry. In addition, you'll find helpful articles about writing resumes, dressing for success, interviewing techniques, and how to work a job fair at www.military.com/careers.

EMPLOYMENT ASSISTANCE AND
CREDENTIALING PROGRAMS

Army and Navy COOL: The Army and Navy both offer Credentialing Opportunities Online (COOL). These programs give you the opportunity to find civilian credentials related to your rating, or military occupational specialty. You can learn what it takes to get the credentials and learn about programs that will help pay credentialing fees. Check out the Army COOL website at www.cool.army.mil or Navy COOL website at www .cool.navy.mil to learn more.

Helmets to Hardhats: The Helmets to Hardhats (H2H) program lets your military service speak for itself. The program will help you find career opportunities that match your military background. Congressionally funded, H2H is the fastest, easiest way for transitioning military, Reservists, and Guardsmen to find a rewarding career in the construction industry. Visit http://helmetstohardhats.org to learn more.

USMAP: USMAP (United Services Military Apprenticeship Program) is available to members of the Navy, Marine Corps, and Coast Guard. Those who participate in this program are eligible to receive a Department of Labor (DOL) Certificate of Completion, which gives them a definite advantage in getting better civilian jobs since employers know the value of apprenticeships. Visit www.doleta.gov/OA/apprenticeship.cfm to learn more.

Library

Your local public and military libraries can be an excellent source of job search information. Most information of interest to job seekers is located in the reference section. Most public and military libraries offer access to the Internet. Helpful library resources include the following:

- **Occupational Information Network: Dictionary of Occupational Titles (O*NET):** This provides detailed descriptions of most occupations. Available online at http://online.onetcenter.org.
- **The Encyclopedia of Associations:** This lists the addresses of professional and industry associations: http://library.dialog.com/bluesheets/html/bl0114.html.
- **Dun and Bradstreet and Standard and Poor's Register of Corporations:** Both documents offer information on individual companies and organizations. No website available for this resource. Check the reference section of your local library.
- **The Occupational Outlook Handbook:** This book addresses the projected needs for various occupations. It may help you choose a career or open the door to a new one. You can also view the handbook online at www.bls.gov/oco.

Libraries also offer newspapers, trade journals, magazines, audio and video cassettes, and computer software packages that aid in career identification and planning. You also may find information on state training, employment, and apprenticeship programs, as well as statistics regarding employment availability, economic climate, and cost of living. Your librarian can show you where to find these resources and how to use them.

Fraternal Military Associations and Veterans' Services Organizations

Fraternal military associations and veterans' services organizations are good sources of employment information, assistance, and services. Many provide their own job referral and registration services; others sponsor events such as job fairs to expose you to prospective employers. All provide networking opportunities to learn about job requirements and opportunities.

Your transition counselor can help you locate local Veteran Service Organization offices. In addition, lists of Military and Veteran Service Organizations can be found at www.military.com/benefits/resources/military-and-veteran-associations.

Industry Associations

Industry associations are a source of industry-specific information. You can learn what an industry is all about from material provided by these associations. You can also learn the jargon and get insight into how people in the industry think. You also may find salary ranges, qualification requirements, locations of jobs, and the names and addresses of individual companies through these associations. More information can be found at www.bls.gov.

The "Hidden" Job Market

More than 70 percent of the jobs in the United States are never advertised or listed with employment agencies. They are simply announced (and filled) by word-of-mouth. This is the "hidden" job market.

Following are some steps you can take to tap this market.

Step 1. Make a list: List everyone you know who might have a job lead for you—friends of the family, people you went to school or church with, clubs you belong to, and so forth. Your friends who have recently left the military are likely to be a step ahead in the job-hunting process and may know who is hiring. Your colleagues may even have leads on job openings that would suit you perfectly.

Step 2. Send your resume: Send your resume to each person on your list and attach a cover letter explaining that you are looking for a job in your area of interest. Ask them to keep their eyes and ears open. They will help you; they are your friends.

Step 3. Make calls: Call each person to whom you send a resume and ask for his or her suggestions and guidance.

Step 4. Follow up: After you call, send each person a letter thanking him or her for the help. Call them periodically to see if they have heard of anything. Using this approach, you will have dozens of people helping you find the right job.

Step 5. Develop and maintain a network: The preceding steps have helped you develop a network. Networking is the most effective way to land the job you want.

Assessing Your Skills

To find a good civilian job, you need to clarify your skills. Skills assessment helps you answer the question "What do I do best?" Here is what a skills assessment can do:

- Help you determine the types of jobs in which you are likely to excel (manager, mechanic, nurse, salesperson, teacher, etc.)
- Help you prepare a focused resume (one that only includes the aspects of your background that specifically relate to the job or career you are looking for)
- Help you answer job interview questions such as "What do you like to do in your spare time?"

Translating military experience into civilian language is one of the most common stumbling blocks in the skills assessment process. One way to tackle this problem is to talk to friends who have already left the service. Ask them to tell you the dos and don'ts of what civilian employers want to hear.

You should also consider attending workshops and seminars. Here's a good approach to assessing skills:

Step 1. Assignments: List the projects you have worked on, problems you have solved, situations you have helped clarify, and challenges you have met.

Step 2. Actions: List the actions you have taken to carry out these tasks.

Step 3. Results: List the results that your actions helped to achieve.

The skills that appear on these three lists should be incorporated into your resume and job interviews. Skill assessment for many service members and their families requires assistance. The staffs at the Transition Assistance Office and Education Center can provide that assistance.

For more assistance in skills assessment, go to www.hireveterans.com and www.Military.com/careers.

RESUME WRITING FOR THE NEW MILLENNIUM

In the current job market, managers receive dozens of resumes. They do not have time to read lengthy listings of skills and complete life histories. For them, "less is more." Here are some tips on creating the most effective resumes:

- **Know the goal:** The goal of your resume should be to motivate employers to call you in for an interview. *Then* during your interview, you can discuss your background in as much detail as the employer desires.
- **Focus on skills:** Employers are more interested in what you *can* do than in what you want to do. Today's resume emphasizes skills, allowing the employer to compare your skills to those required for the job. (Remember, volunteering is considered real work experience, so don't forget to include appropriate volunteer work when preparing your resume.) Writing a skills-oriented resume is easier after you have completed your skills assessment.
- **Don't fuss over format:** Don't get hung up on which type of resume to use—functional, chronological, or whatever. Most employers appreciate a job history that tells them what you did and when. You should also state your accomplishments. Again, performing a skills assessment will help you do this.
- **Create a "scan-able" resume:** More and more, companies are scanning—rather than reading—resumes, especially if they get a

great number of them. There are many books available to help you design a "scan-able" resume. Research the company. Use their language where you can.

There is no "perfect" resume, but you have to feel comfortable with the format you choose and be familiar with what you have written. The employer will use your resume as the basis for asking detailed questions during your interview.

Create a one-minute verbal resume that quickly highlights your experience and skills. Then, practice delivering your one-minute resume aloud until you're comfortable. This will give you the confidence to answer the "Tell me something about yourself" interview question.

Resume Samples

Resume samples model the basic formats and principles of resume writing. Draw the best from each to help style your resume.

A template is a tool for crafting your resume. It isn't a fill-in-the-blank form, but it can help you get started. Ultimately, your resume should be unique to you and tailored to your particular strengths and experience.

The samples and templates below are organized by resume type. Choose the one that best matches your skills and qualifications.

Chronological Resume

- Emphasizes work history—where you worked and when
- Easy for employers to scan
- Often used by job seekers with steady work experience in their desired career field

Chronological Sample

Elizabeth DuShane

5555 Lakewood Road
Warren, OH 44481
(330) 555-5555

OBJECTIVE: Mechanical Engineer

ENGINEERING EXPERIENCE:
Industrial Engineer   1998–Current
Tool Incorporated, Warren, OH

- Designed a plant layout for the shipping department
- Developed a multi-step shipping process improvement plan

Design Engineer   1995–1998
Mechanical Systems, Columbus, OH

- Developed a complete safety package for a robot loader
- Designed hydraulic double stack lift
- Redesigned dairy open style conveyor
- Trained 10 engineers on AutoCAD Rev. 12
- Evaluated and purchased machine components

HVAC Engineer Assistant   1990–1995
Engineering Consultants, Columbus, OH

- Prepared building and equipment bid specifications
- Evaluated HVAC equipment options
- Incorporated EPA and OSHA regulations into safety procedures
- Created working drawings on AutoCAD Rev. 1

MANAGEMENT EXPERIENCE:
Supervisor   1987–1990
College Police Department, Cincinnati, OH

- Supervised more than 50 student security personnel
- Maintained security accounts and budgets
- Interviewed, hired, field trained, and conducted performance appraisals
- Prepared 25-page monthly report

Manager   1986–1988
Building Management Co., Cincinnati, OH

- Maintained and performed building improvements

EDUCATION:
Bachelor of Science Degree: Mechanical Engineering   1986–1990

Minor: Engineering Management
University of Cincinnati, Cincinnati, OH
Coursework: Thermodynamics, Heat Transfer, HVAC,
Machine Design, Fluid Power, IBM Compatible
AutoCAD 12, FORTRAN, Lotus, and Quattro Pro

Chronological Template

First and Last Name

Address Line 1
Address Line 2
City, State Zip Code
(555) 555-5555

OBJECTIVE: Include objective here.
WORK EXPERIENCE:
Job Title   Dates
Employer, City, State

  • List your responsibilities, accomplishments, and skills.

Job Title   Dates
Employer, City, State

  • List your responsibilities, accomplishments, and skills.

Job Title   Dates
Employer, City, State

  • List your responsibilities, accomplishments, and skills.

EDUCATION:
LICENSES AND CERTIFICATIONS:
AWARDS:
PROFESSIONAL MEMBERSHIPS:

Functional Resume

• Groups work experience and skills by skill areas or job function
• De-emphasizes lack of experience in a field

• Useful for first-time job seekers, those reentering the workforce, and career changers

Functional Sample

Charles Lopez

1234 Circle Drive
Minneapolis, Minnesota 55404
(612) 555-5555

OBJECTIVE
Dependable, enthusiastic worker with more than 10 years of experience seeking a Welding or Building Maintenance position. Self-starter, dedicated to achieving high-quality results.

SUMMARY OF QUALIFICATIONS
Welding—
Developed extensive experience in a wide variety of welding styles and positions including:

MIG	TIG	ARC	Heliarc
Oxyacetylene	Air ARC	Cutting and Gouging	Automatic Seam
Plasma Cutting	Underwater	Water Cooled Spot Welding	

Fabrication—
Skilled in layout and design of sheet metal and pipe. Developed extensive knowledge of sheet rollers and brakes. Followed Manufacturer's Operating Processes (MOP) to detail.

Equipment Operator—
Experienced forklift operator on various sized and styles of forklifts. Skilled in the use of a variety of power tools and metal fabrication equipment including drills, drill press, edge planer, end mill, benders, power saws, sanders, and grinders.

Equipment Maintenance—
Performed general maintenance on welding equipment and production machinery. Maintained high production levels through onsite machine repairs and preventive maintenance.

Building Maintenance—
Acquired experience in general construction including basic electrical repairs, carpentry, concrete, glass, spray and roller painting, plumbing, patching, and sheetrock.

SUMMARY OF EXPERIENCE
Lead Welder

- Maintained strict performance, quality, and production standards
- Trained new employees and monitored their performance during probationary period.

EDUCATION
Certificate:
Welding and Blueprint Reading
> Minneapolis Community and Technical College—Minneapolis, MN

Diploma:
Central High School—Saint Paul, MN

Functional Template

First and Last Name

Address Line 1
Address Line 2
City, State Zip Code
(555) 555-5555

OBJECTIVE
Include objective here.

SUMMARY OF QUALIFICATIONS
Qualification—
Short summary of skills, accomplishments, or responsibilities for this specific qualification.

Qualification—

Short summary of skills, accomplishments, or responsibilities for this specific qualification.

Qualification—

Short summary of skills, accomplishments, or responsibilities for this specific qualification.

SUMMARY OF EXPERIENCE

Job Title (can include employer and/or dates)

Main responsibilities or accomplishments

Job Title (can include employer and/or dates)

Main responsibilities or accomplishments

EDUCATION

LICENSES AND CERTIFICATIONS

AWARDS OR PROFESSIONAL MEMBERSHIPS

Combination Resume

- Combines the knowledge, skills, and abilities as highlighted in a functional resume with a shorter, chronological work summary.
- Easily incorporates other experiences, like volunteering or internships.
- Often used by job seekers with a varied employment history, and by career changers.

Combination Sample

SHIRLEY ADAMS

1234 56th Avenue
Apartment #203
Tucson, AZ 85725
(520) 555-5555

SUMMARY

Dependable **General Office Worker** with more than 10 years of transferable experience. Proven clerical, customer service, and communication skills in a variety of settings. Upbeat, positive attitude with a history of producing quality results and satisfied customers. Computer literate.

SELECTED SKILLS
General Office

- Organized and implemented group activities in an efficient manner
- Scheduled appointments and assured timely arrival
- Maintained accurate financial records and paid all invoices on time
- Answered phones and took accurate messages
- Prepared reports and created documents using MS Word and WordPerfect
- Located desired information using the Internet

Customer Service

- Welcomed customers and visitors in a friendly and courteous manner
- Provided customers/clients with desired information in a timely manner
- Listened, calmed, and assisted customers with concerns
- Established friendly and lasting relationships

Communication

- Utilized Internet e-mail as an effective communication tool
- Answered phones in a courteous and professional manner
- Established rapport with diverse individuals and groups
- Demonstrated ability to express ideas in a team environment and influence action

RELATED VOLUNTEER EXPERIENCE

General Office Volunteer	Salvation Army—Tucson, AZ	5 Years
Elected Secretary	Parent Teachers Association (ISD 01)—Tucson, AZ	5 Years
Event Coordinator	Neighborhood Involvement Program—Phoenix, AZ	3 Years
Group/Activities Leader	Girl Scouts of America—Phoenix, AZ	4 Years
Family Manager	Self-employed—Tucson, AZ	7 Years

EDUCATION
GED: Maricopa County Action Program, Phoenix, AZ

Combination Template

First and Last Name

Address Line 1
Address Line 2
City, State Zip Code
(555) 555-5555

SUMMARY or OBJECTIVE
Include employment objective and/or summary of qualifications here.

SUMMARY OF SKILLS AND/OR EXPERIENCE
Skill or Experience

- Description
- Description

Skill or Experience

- Description
- Description

Skill or Experience

- Description
- Description

EMPLOYMENT HISTORY
Job Title
Employer   City, State   Dates
Job Title
Employer   City, State   Dates
EDUCATION
Type of Award or Degree: Degree or Certification Name (GPA if relevant)
Minor if applicable
School Name—City, State
LICENSES
PROFESSIONAL MEMBERSHIPS OR ORGANIZATIONS

Text Format

- A plain-text version of a typical resume.
- Allows a computer to scan for certain terms and keywords more effectively.

Text Format Sample

IRMA PARKER
Phone: (763) 555-5555
Email: jobhunter@success.com

OBJECTIVE: Registered Medical Laboratory Technician requiring extensive experience with success in pediatrics and at a trauma emergency hospital.

SUMMARY OF SKILLS AND EXPERIENCE
LAB TECHNICIAN—Highly skilled lab technologist with experience serving ER, Urgent Care, and Stab-Room Trauma Unit. Processed cultures in microbiology, gram stains, urinalysis, and various manual tests.

PHLEMBOTOMY—Inpatient and outpatient, pre-op and post-op, blood draws. Recognized for exceptional skill in serving hard-to-draw patients and children.

INSTRUMENT MAINTENANCE—Skilled in troubleshooting and maintenance of technical equipment.

TEACHING—Responsible for training staff on equipment operation and procedures.

QUALITY CONTROL—Maintained high quality standards with an emphasis on accuracy. Maximized performance through organization, equipment testing, and procedures development.

EMPLOYMENT HISTORY
MEDICAL LABORATORY TECHNICIAN, ASCP
May 1995 to September 2006 Hennepin County Medical Center
*Increased lab efficiency through improved processing procedures, development of technical equipment, lab layout, and design.

*Maintained peak lab performance. Blood samples from Stab-Room Trauma Unit had to be accurately processed within two minutes!

*Assisted medical staff in the research and development of "Kiss of Life" mask used in respiratory emergency care.
PHLEBOTOMIST
August 1989 to March 1995 Minneapolis Children's Medical Center
EDUCATION
CERTIFIED: American Society of Clinical Pathologists
MEDICAL LABORATORY TECHNICIAN (GPA 3.5)
College of St. Catherine 1987
BIOLOGY/CHEMISTRY (117 credits)
Mankato State University 1985

WORKSHOPS

The Department of Labor-sponsored Transition Assistance Program Employment Workshops are sponsored in conjunction with the installation Transition Assistance staffs. The DOL TAP Employment Workshops normally run two-and-a-half days. However, some local installations may combine this workshop with other specialty workshops. During your first visit to the Transition Assistance Office, or with your Command Career Counselor, you should ask to be scheduled to attend the next available workshop (your spouse should attend if space is available). You should plan to attend employment workshops at least 180 days prior to separation. TAP addresses such useful subjects as the following:

- Employment and training opportunities
- Labor market information
- Civilian workplace requirements
- Resume, application, and standard forms preparation
- Job analysis, job search, and interviewing techniques
- Assistance programs offered by federal, state, local, military, and veterans' groups
- Procedures for obtaining verification of job skills and experience
- Obtaining loans and assistance for starting a small business
- Analysis of the area where you wish to relocate, including local employment opportunities, the local labor market, and the cost of living (housing, child care, education, medical and dental care, etc.)

At the TAP workshops, you will receive a participant manual. Among other valuable information, this manual contains points of contact around the nation for many of the services you will need after your separation.

Note: Not all installations and bases offer the Department of Labor TAP Employment Workshop. If the workshops are not available at your installation or base, the transition counselor will refer you to other sources where similar information is available.

MILITARY EXPERIENCE AND TRAINING HELP YOU WIN THAT JOB

Verification of your military experience and training is useful in preparing your resume and establishing your capabilities with prospective employers. Verification is also helpful if you are applying to a college or vocational institution. These institutions want information on your military training and experience, as well as how this might relate to the civilian world.

As a Service member, you have had numerous training and job experiences, perhaps too many to recall easily and include on a job or college application. Fortunately, the military has made your life a little easier in this regard. The DD Form 2586, "Verification of Military Experience and Training," is created from your automated records on file. It lists your military job experience and training history, recommended college credit information, and civilian equivalent job titles. This document is designed to help you, but it is not a resume!

To get your verification document, go to the VMET website at www. dmdc.osd.mil/tgps. All separating military personnel can electronically download and print their VMET document and personal cover letter from your military service from the VMET website. Simply click the "Request Document" and "Request Cover Letter" tabs and print each of these documents after they are downloaded.

You can get your verification document online as long as you have a current DoD Common Access Card (CAC) or have a current DFAS myPay PIN; however, you should retrieve it within 120 days prior to your separation. If you have problems getting your VMET and need assistance, check with your local transition counselor.

Once You Receive Your Verification Document

Identify the items that relate to the type of work or education you are pursuing and include them in your resume. If there are problems with information listed on the form, follow the guidance indicated below for your respective service:

- **Army:** Review and follow the guidance provided by the Frequently Asked Questions (FAQs) listed on the VMET online website.
- **Air Force:** Follow the instructions in the verification document cover letter or contact your transition counselor.
- **Navy:** Contact your Command Career Counselor or review and follow the guidance provided by the Frequently Asked Questions (FAQs) listed on the VMET online website.
- **Marine Corps:** Follow the instructions in the verification document cover letter. If you need further assistance, contact your administrative office.

Returning to Previous Employment

If you left a civilian job to fulfill Reserve or National Guard duty, you are entitled to return to the job after demobilization if you have

- given advance notice of military service to your employer (except when precluded by military necessity);
- not exceeded five years cumulative absence from the civilian job (with some exceptions);
- submitted a timely application for reemployment; and
- not received a dishonorable or other punitive discharge.

The Uniformed Services Employment and Reemployment Rights Act (USERRA) prohibits employers from denying any benefit of employment due to military service and protects employee rights when reclaiming civilian employment after an absence due to military service or training. These rights include the following:

- Upon completion of military service, employers must provide prompt re-employment. Your right to return to your job is protected by federal law.

- Individuals returning from military service are entitled to the seniority and seniority-based benefits held prior to military service and are also entitled to any additional seniority and seniority-based benefits that would have accrued had they not been called to active duty.
- You are entitled to any necessary retraining, employer-provided health-care plans, and employer-provided pension plans.
- If you can no longer perform the job, your employer must use reasonable efforts to help you upgrade or update your skills.
- You are entitled to special protection against discharge, except for cause.

Failure to report to work or make timely application to return to work does not automatically result in the loss of reemployment rights. However, it does subject you to the rules of conduct, policies, and general practices established by your employer, which may result in loss of USERRA protections.

If you believe that your rights under USERRA have been violated, there are options for resolving the issue:

- Speak directly with the employer. More often than not, discussions with employers can lead to acceptable solutions.
- Speak with your unit commander. Unit commanders may be able to discuss or articulate the issue with the employer in a different manner, or they may be able to suggest compromises and alternatives.
- If the first two options are not successful, contact Employer Support for the Guard and Reserve (ESGR). ESGR is a DoD organization that promotes cooperation between Guard and Reserve component members and their employers.

DoD Job Search

The Department of Defense (DoD) and the Department of Labor activated a new veterans and service member website called DoD Job Search. This website features job announcements, resume writing, and referral systems geared to transitioning military personnel and their spouses, DoD federal civilian employees and their spouses, and the spouses of relocating active-duty members. There are over 1 million jobs available on this website.

Check out the website at www.usajobs.gov for additional information and assistance.

DoD Transportal

DoD has created a web portal for military transitioners. This website is sponsored by the Department of Defense and is designed specifically to assist service members and their spouses leaving active duty. While DoD Transportal contains valuable information and resources, you should use this site as part of a comprehensive program of transition and employment assistance. The best place to start is your installation Transition Assistance Office. The DoD Transportal is another tool to assist you in your transition back into the civilian community. You can access this website at www.veteranprograms.com/id105.html.

This website has three features that can be accessed using the buttons on the left of the web page screen:

- **Transition Assistance:** This feature is a brief overview of the DoD Transition Assistance Program. Here you will find a general discussion of all benefits and services available to you.
- **At Your Service:** This feature provides the locations and phone numbers of all Transition Assistance Offices as well as links to transition assistance related websites.
- **Your Next Career:** This feature provides:
  - *Getting ready*: A mini-course on conducting a successful job search campaign including instructions on creating winning resumes.
  - *Tips on Using the Internet*: A mini-course on using the Internet to find a job including instructions on creating electronic resumes and avoiding Internet scams.
  - *Internet Career Links*: Links to the best job search websites on the net.
    - Websites with up to 1.5 million job listings.
    - Websites where you can post your resumes for employers to view.
    - Links to state job search websites.
  - *Corporate Recruiting Websites*: Links to recruiting websites operated by Fortune 500 companies.
    - Links to one hundred corporate recruiting sites selected among the Fortune 500 companies.

○ *Suggested Reading*: A list of books that you can use as job search resources.

Public and Community Service (PACS) Registry Program

The 1993 National Defense Authorization Act, PL 102-484 [10 USC, 1143 a(c)] requires the Secretary of Defense to maintain a registry of public and community service organizations. Service members selecting early retirement under the Temporary Early Retirement Act (TERA) are registered on the Public and Community Service Personnel Registry prior to release from active duty. Service members looking for employment in the public and community service arena to include those retiring under TERA, can access the PACS Organization Registry to see which organizations have registered for the purpose of hiring separating military personnel in public and community service jobs. In addition, service members with approved retirement under TERA can earn additional credit toward full retirement at age sixty-two by working in a public or community service job. Employers who wish to advertise job openings in the public and community service arena on the DoD Operation Transition Bulletin Board (TBB) at www.afcrossroads.com/employment/gov_dod.cfm will complete the DD Form 2581, "Operation Transition Employer Registration" and DD Form 2581-1, "Public and Community Service Organization Validation." Then, the organization will be included in the Operation Transition employer database and also be listed on the PACS organization registry. Completing the DD Forms is a requirement for posting employment opportunities (want ads) on the TBB.

PACS employers hiring service members who retired under the TERA program are required to complete both DD Forms 2581 and 2581-1. TERA retirees who are employed by approved PACS organizations during their enhanced retirement qualification period (ERQP) enables them to earn additional retirement credit and enhanced retirement pay beginning at age sixty-two. Retirees interested in gaining the additional credit toward full retirement can go to the TBB to look for PACS employment opportunities as well as see a list of approved PACS organizations. Please refer to the website at www.afcrossroads.com/employment/gov_dod.cfm.

The Public and Community Service organizational registry program is just another tool separating service members can use to get their names in front of nonprofit, public, and community service organizations such as schools, hospitals, law enforcement agencies, social service agencies, and many more for employment opportunities.

Transition Bulletin Board (TBB) Makes Job Hunting Easier

Searching through the employment section of the newspaper is not the only way to find work. Internet websites provide a quick and easy way to find the latest job openings and up-to-the-minute information useful to your job search. DoD's Transition Bulletin Board lists jobs, as well as registered Public and Community Service (PACS) organizations, and a list of business opportunities. Search ads are listed by job type and/or location; jobs are located both stateside and overseas. In addition, individuals retiring under the Temporary Early Retirement Authority (TERA) can fulfill the mandatory requirement to register for Public and Community Service (PACS) online at the TBB. Simply log onto the Operation Transition/TBB website, and click "TERA Individual Registration for PACS."

Your access to this resource is through any personal computer having Internet access. Access TBB from home, office, library, or your Transition Assistance Office. You can perform your own automated job search, tailored to your individual needs.

How to Use the TBB

Once you find a position that interests you, pursue the opportunity by following the employer's instructions listed in the TBB ad. Call or write the employer directly and send a copy of your full resume. To access the TBB, go to www.afcrossroads.com/employment/gov_dod.cfm. Click "Login as a Job Seeker." Enter your SSN, last name, date of birth, and click "Login." At the moment you click "Login," the information entered is encrypted so it is protected as it is transmitted over the Internet. Your information is matched against up-to-date personnel information at the Department of Defense.

Troops-to-Teachers Program

Background: Troops to Teachers (TTT) was established in 1994 as a Department of Defense program. The National Defense Authorization

Act for FY 2000 transferred the responsibility for program oversight and funding to the U.S. Department of Education but continued operation by the Department of Defense.

The No Child Left Behind Act provides for the continuation of TTT as a teacher recruitment program. TTT is managed by the Defense Activity for Non-Traditional Education Support (DANTES), Pensacola, Florida.

Goals and objectives: Reflecting the focus of the No Child Left Behind Act, the primary objective of TTT is to help recruit quality teachers for schools that serve students from low-income families throughout America. TTT helps relieve teacher shortages, especially in math, science, special education, and other critical subject areas, and assists military personnel in making successful transitions to second careers in teaching.

Function: TTT assists eligible military personnel to transition to a new career as public school teachers in targeted schools. A network of State TTT Offices has been established to provide participants with counseling and assistance regarding certification requirements, routes to state certification, and employment leads. Pending annual appropriation of funds, financial assistance is available to eligible individuals as stipends up to $5,000 to help pay for teacher certification costs or as bonuses of $10,000 to teach in schools serving a high percentage of students from low-income families. Participants who accept the stipend or bonus must agree to teach for three years in targeted schools in accordance with the authorizing legislation. The TTT link (www.proudtoserveagain.com) leads to the home page, which provides information and resource links, including links to state Departments of Education, state certification offices, model resumes, programs leading to teacher certification, and job listing sites in public education. An Internet Referral System has been established to enable participants to search for job vacancies online and post resumes for view by school districts searching for teachers. A "Mentor Connection" site provides access to TTT participants who have made the transition to teaching and are available to respond to questions from prospective teachers.

Eligibility: Military personnel within several years of retirement are encouraged to register with Troops to Teachers. Counseling and guidance is available to help individuals assess academic background, identify programs that will lead to state teacher certification, and identify potential employment opportunities.

Financial Assistance: Individuals eligible for immediate financial assistance are listed below:

- Retired military personnel, active and reserve
- Personnel within one year of retirement
- Active duty personnel separating with six years active duty and join a Selected Reserve component unit
- Current reserve component members with 10+ years of active and/or Selected Reserve service creditable toward retirement
- Veterans separated due to service-connected disability

Educational Requirements: Those interested in elementary or secondary-teaching positions must have a bachelor's degree from an accredited college. Individuals who do not have a baccalaureate degree, but have experience in a vocational/technical field, may also submit an application. There is also a growing need for teachers with backgrounds in areas such as electronics, construction trades, computer technology, health services, food services, and other vocational/technical fields.

Self-Determination Eligibility Guide: A guide to determining eligibility is available at www.proudtoserveagain.com.

Registration: Registration forms may be downloaded from the Troops to Teachers link at www.proudtoserveagain.com.

Current Information: The Troops to Teachers website is updated as new or revised information becomes available. The website also provides a standard PowerPoint briefing and other promotional materials.

Reemployment Rights Can Get You Your Old Job Back

Under certain circumstances, veterans have the right to return to their pre-service jobs after discharge or release from active duty. Your former employer must rehire you if you meet all of the following requirements:

- You must have left other-than-temporary employment to enter military service.
- You must have served in the Armed Forces (either voluntarily or involuntarily) no more than five years, unless at the request of and for the convenience of the government.

- You must have been discharged or released under honorable conditions.
- You must still be qualified to perform the duties of the job. If you became disabled while in military service, you must be able to perform some other job in your employer's organization (with comparable seniority, status, and pay).

Contact the U.S. Department of Labor, Veterans' Employment and Training Service (VETS), for assistance under the Uniformed Services Employment and Reemployment Rights Act of 1994. A complete list of VETS state directors is available on the Internet at www.dol.gov/vets.

Your reemployment rights also protect you against being discharged by your employer without cause for one year (six months in the case of a Reservist or National Guard member returning from training).

Private Employment Agencies

Overall, private employment agencies are responsible for approximately 3 to 5 percent of all hires nationally. If your skills and experience match those fields in which the agency specializes, you can expect some assistance. For example, a separatee with computing skills should seek an agency specializing in computer-related placements.

Most private employment agencies are reputable. They possess an extensive list of employers, and they charge those employers a fee for their services. Before registering with a private agency, confirm that all fees will be paid by the employer and not by you.

Finding Federal Employment Opportunities

Opportunities for employment with the U.S. government are available in all parts of the nation as well as overseas. Here are some ways to find out about different types of federal job listings.

Government jobs near you: Openings may be available at the installation from which you are separating. You can find out about these from your local civilian personnel office.

Opportunities overseas: To assist you in finding out about federal job opportunities elsewhere in the world, the Office of Personnel Management (OPM) maintains federal job information/testing offices in each state. You can view federal employment opportunities on the Internet at www.usajobs.com. You can also call OPM at 912-757-3000 or call the OPM Computer Bulletin Board at 912-757-3100.

Unique positions: OPM maintains an automated job referral system for hard-to-fill jobs. This system, to be expanded in the future, presently focuses on those positions requiring special skills. Applicants may register directly with the OPM computer center in Macon, Georgia. Write to Office of Personnel Management, Staffing Service Center, Macon, Georgia 31297.

Here are some other federal employment websites:

- Fed World: http://fedworld.ntis.gov
- Federal Employment Portal: www.opm.gov
- DoD Civilian Employment: www.godefense.com
- Army Civilian Personnel Online: www.cpol.army.mil/

Working for the DoD

The Department of Defense (DoD) welcomes veterans to join the DoD civilian workforce and continue serving the Defense mission! The DoD is the nation's number one employer of veterans, offering nearly seven hundred challenging occupations.

As a DoD civilian, you can serve with the Army, Navy, Air Force, Marines, or any one of the many other Defense agencies. Career opportunities exist in research laboratories, manufacturing facilities, office complexes, hospitals, military bases, and schools in almost every major population center in the United States—and in numerous countries throughout the world.

The department offers preference in employment to eligible veterans, along with world-class benefits; there are many opportunities for personal and professional growth, travel, and advancement. You have served our nation with honor and distinction. Now, the Department of Defense invites you to become part of the department's rich and proud tradition of civilian service.

goDefense.com

The Department of Defense (DoD) website, www.goDefense.com, offers veteran job seekers assistance with pursuing DoD civilian careers by providing online career opportunity information and resources. In addition, Recruitment Assistance Division (RAD) career counselors are available Monday through Friday, 7:00 a.m. to 5:00 p.m. EST to provide assistance with completing required forms and advisory guidance on how to respond to vacancy announcements. For more information, visit www.goDefense.com or call toll-free: 1-888-DOD4USA (1-888-363-4872); TTY for Deaf/Hard of Hearing: 703-696-5436, or send request by e-mail to daao@cpms.osd.mil.

Applying for Federal Jobs

You apply for most federal jobs by preparing and submitting the documents requested in the federal job announcement. If you have any questions, contact the civilian personnel office and/or the point of contact listed on the job announcement. If you believe your veterans' preference rights have been violated when applying for federal jobs, contact the U.S. Department of Labor, Veterans Employment and Training Service, for assistance under the Veterans' Employment Opportunities Act of 1998. A complete list of VETS state directors is available on the Internet at www.dol.gov/dol.vets.

How Federal Jobs Are Filled

Many Federal agencies fill their jobs like private industry by allowing applicants to contact the agency directly for additional job information and in understanding the application process. Most Federal agencies will accept the Optional Application for Federal Employment, Form OF-612 from individuals applying for federal employment. As an applicant you may submit the OF-612 or a resume.

While the process may be similar to that in private industry, there are still significant differences due to the many laws, executive orders, and regulations that govern federal employment.

Competitive, Excepted, and Senior Executive Service

Federal jobs in the Executive Branch fall into three categories: (1) those that are in the *competitive service*, (2) those that are in the *excepted service*, and (3) those that are in the *senior executive service*.

Competitive service jobs are under OPM's jurisdiction and subject to the civil service laws passed by Congress to ensure that applicants and employees receive fair and equal treatment in the hiring process. These laws give selecting officials broad authority to review more than one applicant source before determining the best-qualified candidate based on job-related criteria. A basic principle of federal employment is that all candidates must meet the qualification requirements for the position for which they receive an appointment.

Excepted service positions are excepted by law, by executive order, or by action of OPM placing a position or group of positions in excepted service Schedules A, B, or C. For example, certain entire agencies such as the Postal Service and the Central Intelligence Agency are excepted by law. In other cases, certain jobs or classes of jobs in an agency are excepted by OPM. This includes positions such as attorneys, chaplains, student trainees, and others.

NOTE: The excepted service is subject to the provisions of veterans' preference unless otherwise exempted. Some federal agencies such as the Central Intelligence Agency (CIA) have only *excepted service* positions. In other instances, certain organizations within an agency or even specific jobs may be excepted from civil service procedures.

The Senior Executive Service (SES) was established by Title IV of the Civil Service Reform Act (CSRA) of 1978. The SES was set up as a "third" service, completely separate from the competitive and excepted services. Top management positions are joined into a unified and distinct personnel system that provides for considerable agency authority and flexibility. SES positions are classified above GS-15 or equivalent. All SES vacancies are advertised on OPM's USAJOBS (www.usajobs.gov). From this site, you may download announcements for vacancies of interest to you. Veterans do not receive hiring preference for SES positions because 5 USC 2108(3), which defines the term "preference eligible," provides that this term does not include applicants for, or members of, the Senior Executive Service.

Vacancy Announcements

A posted vacancy announcement is an agency's decision to seek qualified candidates for a particular vacancy. The agency is under no obligation to make a selection. In some instances, an agency may cancel the posting and choose to reannounce the vacancy later.

Sources of Eligibles

In filling competitive service jobs, agencies can generally choose from among three groups of candidates:

1. A *competitive list of eligibles* administered by OPM or by an agency under OPM's direction. This list consists of applicants who have applied and met the qualification requirements for a specific vacancy announcement. It is the most common method of entry for new employees.
2. A list of eligibles who have *civil service status* consist of applicants who are eligible for noncompetitive movement within the competitive service because they either now are or were serving under career-type appointments in the competitive service. These individuals are selected under agency *merit promotion procedures and can receive an appointment* by promotion, reassignment, transfer, or reinstatement.
3. A list of eligibles that qualify for a special *noncompetitive appointing authority* is established by law or executive order. Examples of special noncompetitive appointing authorities include the Veterans' Recruitment Appointment (VRA) and Peace Corps.

Agencies in the competitive service are required by law and OPM regulation to post vacancies with OPM whenever they are seeking candidates from outside their own workforce for positions lasting more than 120 days. (*Agency*, in this context, means the parent agency—i.e., Treasury, not the Internal Revenue Service.) These vacancies are posted on OPM's USAJOBS.

If you are interested in excepted service positions and do not find any posted on USAJOBS, you should contact the respective federal agency directly. The U.S. Office of Personnel Management does not provide application forms or information on jobs in the excepted service.

Employment Preferences

Involuntarily and Certain Voluntarily Separated Members: Under chapter 58, Section 1143 (d) of title 10, U.S. Code, eligibility applies to members of the Armed Forces, and their dependents, who were on active duty on September 30, 1990, and who were involuntarily separated under honorable conditions on or after October 1, 1990. Preference eligible veterans shall be identified by possession of a DD Form 1173, "Uniformed Services Identification and Privilege Card," overstamped with "TA."

Preference applies to jobs graded at NF-3 and below, and to positions paid at hourly rates. Preference applies to any job that is open to competition in accordance with merit staffing practices. Spouse preference may be used once for each permanent relocation of the military sponsor. The spouse must have been married to the military sponsor before relocation to the duty station.

Military Spouses: Under DoD Instruction 1404.12, "Employment of Spouses of Active Duty Military Members Stationed Worldwide," eligibility applies to spouses of active-duty military members of the Armed Forces. Under this basic policy, preferences for military spouses are the same as the involuntarily and certain voluntarily separated members, except that military spouse preference has priority over that preference.

Visit the DoD's Spouse Career center at www.military.com/spouse to learn more about military spouse employment preferences.

Family Members in Foreign Areas: In accordance with DoD Instruction 1400.23 and DoD 1402.2-M, Chapter VII, family members of active duty military members and civilian employees stationed in foreign areas are eligible. Basic policy allows preference for all NAF jobs. Preferences apply when not at variance with the Status of Forces Agreements, country-to-country agreements, treaties, or as prescribed by DoD Instruction 1400.23.

Federal Jobs through the Non-Appropriated Fund and the Veterans Readjustment Act

Because of your military service, you may have an advantage over others when applying for federal employment. Congress provided this advantage by enacting veterans' hiring preference laws. These laws do *not* imply guaranteed placement of a veteran in every federal job. The veterans' hiring preference laws are not applicable to Non-Appropriated Fund (NAF) employment. Veterans applying for NAF jobs may be given preference at time of hire only.

If you are a Vietnam or post-Vietnam-era veteran: The Veterans Readjustment Appointment (VRA) program provides special employment opportunities and job training to veterans who were honorably discharged and who served for more than 180 days on active duty.

- If you are an eligible involuntary separatee: You and your family members are authorized a one-time employment preference for NAF positions that you are qualified to perform. For details, ask your installation's Transition Office to refer you to the local NAF personnel office.
- Eligible Vietnam-era veterans qualify for appointments under Veterans Readjustment Appointment (VRA) until ten years after their last discharge or separation from active duty or until December 31, 1995, whichever is later.
- Eligible post-Vietnam-era veterans qualify for ten years after the date of discharge or release from active duty or until December 31, 1999, whichever is later.
- Eligible veterans with a service-connected disability of 30 percent or more have no time limit.

For information about specific VRA job opportunities, contact the personnel office at the federal agency where you would like to work.

Veterans' Recruitment Appointment (VRA): The VRA is a special authority by which agencies may, if they wish, appoint an eligible veteran without competition. The candidate does not have to be on an eligibility list, but must meet the basic qualification requirements for the position. The VRA is a convenient method of appointment for both the agency and the veteran. However, use of the authority is entirely discretionary, and no one is entitled to a VRA appointment.

VRA appointees initially are hired for a two-year period. Successful completion of the two-year VRA appointment leads to a permanent civil service appointment. (Please note, however, that a veteran may be employed without competition on a temporary or term appointment based on VRA eligibility. Such an appointment is not a VRA appointment and does not lead to conversion to a permanent position.)

Eligibility Requirements

The following individuals are eligible for a VRA appointment:

- Disabled veterans
- Veterans who served on active duty in the Armed Forces during a war declared by Congress, or in a campaign or expedition for which a campaign badge has been authorized

- Veterans who, while serving on active duty in the Armed Forces, participated in a military operation for which the Armed Forces Service Medal was awarded
- Veterans separated from active duty within the past three years

There is no minimum service requirement, but the individual must have served on *active duty*, not active duty for training.

The Veterans' Preference Point System for Federal Employment

A "point system" is used to determine veterans' hiring preference:

- **Five-point preference:** Basically, five points are given to honorably separated veterans who have served more than 180 consecutive days of active duty before October 14, 1976 (including service during training under the six-month Reserve or National Guard programs), or during any war or expedition for which a campaign badge has been authorized (such as Desert Shield/Storm) and served continuously for twenty-four months or the full period called or ordered to active duty (including for training). Retired members of the Armed Forces above the rank of major or lieutenant commander are no longer eligible for the five-point preference. Their preference is contingent upon a disability.
- **Ten-point preference:** Ten points are given to disabled veterans and veterans who are awarded the Purple Heart and honorably separated. The point system program is administered by OPM. The VA issues letters to OPM indicating the degree of disability for veterans' preference purposes. The more points you have, the closer you get to the front of the line for possible job consideration with the federal government.

Hiring preference is not limited to veterans alone. It is also granted to the spouse of an unemployable disabled veteran, the unmarried widow or widower of a veteran, or the mother of a deceased or disabled veteran. Any federal agency personnel officer can give you more information on the point system. Visit the USAJOBS website at www.usajobs.gov/Veterans to learn more about Veteran Employment opportunities.

Veterans Get Priority at State Employment Offices

As a veteran, you receive special consideration and priority for referral, testing, and counseling from your state employment office. Your state employment office can provide many additional services, as noted below.

Veterans Employment and Training Service Office: There is at least one Veterans Employment and Training Service Office in every state (www.dol.gov/vets/aboutvets/contacts/main.htm). Veterans' employment representatives may also be found at local employment offices with large numbers of veteran job applicants. Their job is to monitor and oversee veterans' employment services, administer veterans' training programs, and protect the reemployment rights of veterans. They will assist you with any employment problem you may have.

Make sure you take your DD Form 214, "Certificate of Release or Discharge from Active Duty" (certified copy) with you for your first appointment with the state employment office.

DoD Job Search: This job bank, sponsored by the Department of Defense and the Department of Labor, lists millions of jobs across the nation that are not readily filled. Check out the website at https://dod.usajobs.gov for further detail and assistance.

Training opportunities: State employment offices can offer you seminars on subjects such as resume writing, interviewing skills, and career changes; information on vocational training opportunities; and proficiency tests in typing and shorthand for positions requiring such certification.

Information: At your state employment office, you will find data on state training, employment, and apprenticeship programs; and statistics regarding employment availability, economic climate, and cost of living. Some offices even have extensive information about the things you should know before moving to the state. To locate State Employment Offices visit www.statelocalgov.net/50states-jobs.cfm.To locate the local CareerOneStop Center visit www.careeronestop.org.

Service Family Members Get Job Assistance Too

Family members can take advantage of many of the outplacement services offered to transitioning service members. Most of these services are coordinated from the Transition Assistance Office at your installation. Family members can get help in developing their own Individual Transition Plans; they also have access to the following employment services:

Department of Labor TAP Employment Workshops: These two-and-a-half day Department of Labor (DoL) sponsored workshops are coordinated through the Transition Assistance and ACAP Offices and can help you with your employment objectives before you leave the military. Contact your Transition/ACAP Office or Command Career Counselor immediately to get scheduled for an appointment. Spouses are highly encouraged to attend the DoL Employment Workshop in order to prepare themselves for the transition from an active duty lifestyle to a civilian one.

TBB: The Transition Bulletin Board is an electronic listing of job vacancies and transition information. The Transition Bulletin Board is an electronic listing of job vacancies and transition information located at www.afcrossroads.com/employment/gov_dod.cfm.

Career counseling: The Transition Assistance Office will provide individual job/career development counseling, assist in assessing employment skills, and identify employment opportunities.

Job training: These services include workshops and seminars on enhancing job search skills; goal setting; preparing federal employment applications, resumes, interviewing techniques, and occupational skills training for family members.

Job banks: National job banks and local job banks provide information and referral on temporary, permanent, part-time, full-time, and volunteer positions in both the federal and private sectors. In addition, family members of separating personnel can receive a one-time priority for Non-Appropriated Funds jobs in the federal government. Ask your local civilian personnel office for details.

Where to Look for Great Jobs

Several places offer you the help you will need to find the job that's right for you. Check out these websites for more information:

- www.careeronestop.org
- www.bls.gov
- www.hireveterans.com
- www.doleta.gov/programs
- www.doleta.gov/

Military-Friendly Job Banks

* Veteran's Employment Resources (www.usajobs.gov/Veterans) provides multiple tools and valuable resources for all U.S. Veterans—job opportunities, forms, benefits, and program information as well as training assistance for private sector employment.
* Troops to Teachers (www.proudtoserveagain.com/index.html) helps military personnel begin new careers in education
* Helmets to Hardhats (www.helmetstohardhats.org) matches military skills to civilian jobs
* Calendar and location of military-friendly job fairs is available at www.militaryconnection.com/jobfairs
* USAJobs.com has federal jobs and employment information
* GoDefense.com (www.godefense.com) is a site for civilians and veterans working for National Defense
* MilitaryConnection.com's Virtual Job Fair (www.militaryconnection.com/virtualfairs) with links to government and private companies recruiting veterans

The Entrepreneurial Spirit

Since 1953, the U.S. Small Business Administration (SBA) has helped veterans start, manage, and grow small businesses. Today, the SBA provides specific programs for veterans, service-disabled veterans, and Reserve and National Guard Members, and they offer a full range of entrepreneurial support programs to every American, including veterans. Their job is to help you successfully transition from world's finest warrior to world's finest small business owner.

On August 17, 1999, Congress passed Public Law 106-50, The Veterans Entrepreneurship and Small Business Development Act of 1999. This law established the SBA Office of Veterans Business Development, under the guidance and direction of the Associate Administrator for Veterans Business Development, to conduct comprehensive outreach, to be the source of policy and program development, initiation, and implementation for the administration, and to act as an ombudsman for full consideration of veterans within the administration.

In addition, this law created the National Veterans Business Development Corporation, set goals for federal procurement for service-disabled veterans, established the Military Reservists Economic Injury Disaster

Loan, initiated new research into the success of Veterans in Small Business, and brought focus to veterans in the full range of SBA Capital, Entrepreneurial, and Government Contracting programs.

SBA has established Veterans Business Outreach Centers, special loans and Surety Bonding programs for veterans and reservists, government procurement programs for veterans, Veterans Business Development Officers stationed in every SBA District Office, special District Office outreach efforts, and counseling and training at more than 1,500 Small Business Centers and SCORE Chapters, including those online.

Special Localized Programs

Special local initiatives target veterans, service-disabled veterans, and Reserve and Guard members. Online and printed business planning guides are available, including "Balancing Business and Deployment" for self-employed Reserve and Guard to prepare for mobilization, and "Getting Veterans Back to Business" to assist in restarting or reestablishing your business upon return from active duty. These manuals include an interactive CD with a wealth of information on preparing your business and your employees for your absence, reestablishing a small business upon return from Title 10 activation, and information on various business assistance resources available to assist you. The CDs also contain information on loans, government procurement, and the full range of SBA's assistance to any veteran.

To learn more about the services and assistance SBA offers to veterans, service-disabled veterans, and reservists, please explore the links below, or follow up to our local district offices and programs located in or near the community you return home to.

SBA Veterans Advantage Loan Program

The SBA Veterans Advantage Loan Program was created by the SBA to offer financial, procurement, and technical assistance programs to the military community. It is a streamlined loan product with enhanced guarantee and interest rate characteristics.

The Veterans Advantage loan is available to veterans, service-disabled veterans, active-duty service members participating in the military's Transition Assistance Program, Reservists and National Guard members, current spouses of any of the above, spouses of any service member and the widowed spouse of a service member or veteran who died during service or from a service-connected disability.

The Veterans Advantage loan is offered by SBA's network of participating lenders nationwide. It features SBA's fastest turnaround time for loan approvals. Loans are available up to $500,000 and qualify for SBA's maximum guaranty of up to 85 percent for loans of $150,000 or less and up to 75 percent for loans over $150,000 up to $500,000.

The loan can be used for most business purposes, including start-up, expansion, equipment purchases, working capital, inventory, or business-occupied real-estate purchases.

The Veterans Advantage loans feature SBA's lowest interest rates for business loans, generally 2.25 percent to 4.75 percent over prime depending upon the size and maturity of the loan. Local SBA district offices will have a listing of lenders in their areas. More details on the initiative can be found at www.sba.gov/content/sba-veterans-advantage.

District Office Veterans Business Development Officers (VBDOs)

As a new veteran, we realize you may not know a lot about the assistance available to you from the SBA. To ensure that every veteran entrepreneur has access to the full range of SBA programs, and to receive the specific assistance and guidance you may be seeking, SBA has established a Veterans Business Development Officer (VBDO) in every one of the sixty-eight SBA District Offices around the nation. These VBD officers are responsible for providing prompt and direct assistance and guidance to any veteran or reservist seeking information about or access to any SBA program. To identify your local VBDO, please contact your local SBA district office (see the Blue Pages telephone directory) or contact the Office of Veterans Business Development (OVBD) at 202-205-6773. You can also visit www.sba.gov/offices/headquarters/ovbd/resources/47731.

Veterans Business Outreach Centers

OVBD provides funding to five Veterans Business Outreach Centers (VBOC) to offer and coordinate business development assistance to veterans, service-connected disabled veterans, and reservist entrepreneurs. Services include—face-to-face and online—outreach, concept development, business training, counseling, and mentoring. Please contact them directly:

The Research Foundation of the State University of New York
41 State Street
Albany, NY 12246
518-443-5398
Website: www.suny.edu
E-mail: brian.goldstein@nyssbdc.org

The University of West Florida in Pensacola
2500 Minnesota Avenue
Lynn Haven, FL 32444
1-800-542-7232 or 850-271-1108
Website: www.vboc.org
E-mail: vboc@knology.net

The University of Texas—Pan American
1201 West University Drive
Edinburg, TX 78539-2999
956-292-7535
Website: www.utpa.edu
E-mail: vboc@panam.edu

Vietnam Veterans of California
7270 E. Southgate Drive, Suite 1
Sacramento, CA 95823
916-393-1690
Website: www.vva.org
E-mail: cconley@vboc-ca.org

Robert Morris University
600 Fifth Avenue
Pittsburgh, PA 15219
(412) 397-6842

Website: http://rmu.edu
E-mail: vboc@rmu.edu

Small Business Development Centers

SBA provides funding to one thousand Small Business Development Centers (SBDC) in all fifty states and U.S. territories. This program provides a broad range of specialized management assistance to current and prospective small business owners. SBDCs offer one-stop assistance to individuals and small businesses by providing a wide variety of information, guidance, linkages, training, and counseling in easily accessible branch locations, usually affiliated with local educational institutions. The SBDC program is designed to deliver up-to-date counseling, training, and technical assistance in all aspects of small business management. SBDC services include, but are not limited to, assisting small businesses with financial, marketing, production, organization, engineering, and technical problems, and feasibility studies. To find your local SBDC, go to www.sba.gov/tools/local-assistance/sbdc or contact your district office VBDO.

SCORE: "Counselors to America's Small Business"

SCORE is the best source of free and confidential small business advice to help you build your business—from idea to start-up to success. SCORE is a nonprofit association dedicated to entrepreneurial education and the formation, growth, and success of small businesses nationwide. More than half of SCORE's network of 10,500 retired and working volunteers are veterans, and they are experienced entrepreneurs and corporate manager/executives. They have worn the uniform and they have succeeded in business. They provide free business counseling and advice as a public service to all types of businesses in all stages of development.

SCORE offers the following services:

- Ask SCORE e-mail advice online at (www.score.org/). Some SCORE e-counselors specifically target veterans, service-disabled veterans, and reserve component members.
- Face-to-face small business counseling at 389 chapter offices.

- Low-cost workshops and seminars at 389 chapter offices nationwide.
- A great online web based network.

SCORE provides small business counseling and training under a grant from the U.S. Small Business Administration (SBA). SCORE members are successful, retired and active business men and women who volunteer their time to assist aspiring entrepreneurs and small business owners. There are SCORE chapters in every state.

Find your local SCORE Chapter at www.score.org/chapters-map.

Women's Business Centers

The Office of Women's Business Ownership provides women-focused (men are eligible as well) training, counseling, and mentoring at every level of entrepreneurial development, from novice to seasoned entrepreneur, through representatives in the SBA district offices and nationwide networks of women's business centers (WBCs) and mentoring roundtables. Additionally, WBCs provide online training, counseling, and mentoring. Women's Business Centers represent a national network of more than a hundred centers designed to assist women in starting and growing small businesses. WBCs operate with the mission to level the playing field for women entrepreneurs, who face unique obstacles in the world of business. To find your local WBC, go to www.sba.gov/tools/local-assistance/wbc.

FINANCIAL ASSISTANCE

SBA administers three separate, but equally important loan programs. The agency sets the guidelines for the loans while our partners (lenders, community development organizations, and microlending institutions) make the loans to small businesses. SBA backs those loans with a guaranty that will eliminate some risk to our lending partners. As the agency's loan guaranty requirements and practices change as government alters its fiscal policy and priorities to meet current economic conditions, past policy cannot always be relied upon when seeking assistance in today's market. The loan guaranty that SBA provides transfers the potential risk of borrower non-payment, up to the amount of the guaranty, from the lender to the SBA. Therefore, when a business applies for an SBA loan, they are actually applying for a commercial loan, structured according to SBA requirements, but provided by our cooperating private or not-for-profit lending partner, which receives an SBA guaranty.

Basic 7(a) Loan Guaranty

The 7(a) Loan Guaranty Program serves as the SBA's primary business loan program to help qualified small businesses obtain financing when they might not be eligible for business loans through normal lending channels.

Loan proceeds can be used for most sound business purposes including working capital, machinery and equipment, furniture and fixtures, land and building (including purchase, renovation, and new construction), leasehold improvements, and debt refinancing (under special conditions). Loan maturity is up to ten years for working capital and generally up to twenty-five years for fixed assets. SBA does target veterans specifically in some of our loan programs. To find out more, visit www.sba.gov/loans-grants/see-what-sba-offers/sba-loan-programs/7a-loan-program, or contact your district office or any of the centers or chapters mentioned previously.

Certified Development Company 504 Loan Program

The Certified Development Company-504 (CDC/504) loan program is a long-term financing tool for economic development within a community. The 504 Program provides growing businesses with long-term, fixed-rate financing for major fixed assets, such as land and buildings. A Certified Development Company (CDC) is a nonprofit corporation set up to contribute to the economic development of its community. CDCs work with the SBA and private-sector lenders to provide financing to small businesses. There are about 270 CDCs nationwide. Each CDC covers a specific geographic area. Typically, a 504 project includes a loan secured with a senior lien from a private-sector lender covering up to 50 percent of the project cost, a loan secured with a junior lien from the CDC (backed by a 100 percent SBA-guaranteed debenture) covering up to 40 percent of the cost, and a contribution of at least 10 percent equity from the small business being helped.

Microloan Program

The SBA's Microloan Program provides very small loans and business counseling to start-up, newly established, or growing small business concerns. Under this program, SBA makes funds available to nonprofit community-based lenders (intermediaries) which, in turn, make loans to eligible borrowers in amounts up to a maximum of $35,000. The average loan size is about $13,000. Applications are submitted to the local intermediary and all credit decisions are made on the local level.

The maximum term allowed for a microloan is six years. However, loan terms vary according to the size of the loan, the planned use of funds, the requirements of the intermediary lender, and the needs of the small business borrower. Interest rates vary, depending upon the intermediary lender and costs to the intermediary from the U.S. Treasury.

International Trade

The Office of International Trade works in cooperation with other federal agencies and public- and private-sector groups to encourage small business exports and to assist small businesses seeking to export. Through sixteen U.S. Export Assistance Centers, SBA district offices, and a variety of service-provider partners, it directs and coordinates SBA's ongoing export initiatives to encourage small businesses going global.

SBA's Investment Programs

In 1958 Congress created the Small Business Investment Company (SBIC) program. SBICs, licensed by the Small Business Administration, are privately owned and managed (venture) investment firms. They are participants in a vital partnership between government and the private sector economy. All SBICs are profit-motivated businesses. A major incentive for SBICs to invest in small businesses is the chance to share in the success of the small business if it grows and prospers.

Equity (venture) capital or financing is money raised by a business in exchange for a share of ownership in the company. Ownership is represented by owning shares of stock outright or having the right to convert other financial instruments into stock of that private company. Two key sources of equity capital for new and emerging businesses are angel investors and venture capital firms.

Typically, angel capital and venture capital investors provide capital unsecured by assets to young, private companies with the potential for rapid growth. Such investing covers most industries and is appropriate for businesses through the range of developmental stages. Investing in new or very early companies inherently carries a high degree of risk. But venture capital is long term or "patient capital" that allows companies the time to mature into profitable organizations.

Surety Bond Guarantee Program

The Surety Bond Guarantee (SBG) Program was developed to provide increased bonding opportunities to small veteran and minority contractors to support contracting opportunities for which they would not otherwise bid. If your small construction, service, or supply company bids or performs projects requiring surety bonds, the U.S. Small Business Administration program could help make you more competitive.

A surety bond is a three-way agreement between the surety company, the contractor, and the project owner. The agreement with the SBA guarantees the contractor will comply with the terms and conditions of the contract. If the contractor is unable to successfully perform the contract, the surety assumes the contractor's responsibilities and ensures that the project is completed.

The SBA Surety Bond Guarantee Program covers four types of major contract surety bonds:

Bid Bond—guarantees the project owner that the bidder will enter into the contract and furnish the required payment and performance bonds.

Payment Bond—guarantees the contractor will pay all persons who furnish labor, materials, equipment, or supplies for use on the project.

Performance Bond—guarantees the contractor will perform the contract in accordance with its terms, specifications, and conditions.

Ancillary Bond—bonds that are incidental and essential to the performance of the contract.

The overall surety bond program has two programs:

The Prior Approval Program—The SBA guarantees 80 or 90 percent (for veterans) of a surety's loss. Participating sureties must obtain SBA's prior approval for each bond.

The Preferred Surety Bond Program—Selected sureties receive a 70 percent guarantee and are authorized to issue, monitor, and service bonds without the SBA's prior approval.

Program Eligibility Requirements

In addition to meeting the surety company's bonding qualifications, you must qualify as a small business concern, as defined by the SBA. For federal prime contracts, your company must meet the small business size standard for the North American Industry Classification System (NAICS) code that the federal contracting officer specified for that procurement. For more information about the Surety Bond Guarantee Program, visit www.sba.gov/category/navigation-structure/loans-grants/bonds/surety-bonds.

Business Planning and Disaster Assistance for Small Businesses Who Employ or Are Owned by Military Reservists

All of the technical assistance programs referenced above can provide pre- and post-mobilization business counseling and planning assistance to any reservist who owns their own business or to the small business they work for. It also offers assistance to the caretaker of the business who may manage the business while the reservist owner is activated.

The Office of Disaster Assistance also offers the Military Reservist Economic Injury Disaster Loan (MREIDL) program at very favorable rates and terms. The purpose of the MREIDL is to provide funds to eligible small businesses to meet its ordinary and necessary operating expenses that it could have met, but is unable to meet, because an essential employee was "called-up" to active duty in their role as a military reservist. These loans are intended only to provide the amount of working capital needed by a small business to pay its necessary obligations as they mature until operations return to normal after the essential employee is released from active military duty. The purpose of these loans is not to cover lost income or lost profits. MREIDL funds cannot be used to take the place of regular commercial debt, to refinance long-term debt, or to expand the business. Contact your district office or visit www.sba.gov/content/reservists-eligible-apply-sba-working-capital-loans-0.

Government Procurement

The Office of Government Contracting (GC) works to maximize participation by small disadvantaged woman-, veteran-, and service-disabled-veteran-owned small businesses in federal government contract awards and large prime subcontract awards. GC also advocates on behalf of small business in the federal procurement arena.

The federal government purchases billions of dollars in goods and services each year, and it is federal policy to ensure that all small businesses have the maximum practicable opportunity to participate in providing goods and services to the government. To ensure that small businesses get their fair share of federal procurements, government has established an annual 23 percent government-wide procurement goal to small business concerns, including small businesses owned and controlled by service-disabled veterans, qualified HUBZone small businesses, small businesses owned and controlled by socially and economically disadvantaged individuals, and small businesses owned and controlled by women.

The individual program goals are 5 percent of prime and subcontracts for small disadvantaged businesses; 3 percent of prime and subcontracts for Hubzone businesses; and 3 percent of prime and subcontracts for service-disabled veteran-owned small businesses. The SBA negotiates annual procurement goals with each federal agency and reviews each agency's results. The SBA is responsible for ensuring that the statutory government-wide goals are met in the aggregate. In addition, large business prime contractors are statutorily required to establish subcontracting goals for service-disabled and veteran-owned small businesses as part of each subcontracting plan submitted in response to a prime federal contract opportunity.

The GC administers several programs and services that assist small businesses in meeting the requirements necessary to receive government contracts, as prime contractors or subcontractors. These include the

Certificate of Competency, the Non-Manufacturer Rule Waiver, and the Size Determination programs.

The office also oversees special initiatives such as the Women's Procurement program, the Procurement Awards program, and the Annual Joint Industry/SBA Procurement Conference.

For resources and opportunities, contact your local SBA district office or visit www.sba.gov/contracting/resources-small-business. For the Federal Agency Procurement Forecast, go to www.sba.gov/content/federal-contracting-resources-small-businesses.

SBA Contacts and Representatives

A Subcontracting Opportunities Directory contains a listing of prime contractors doing business with the federal government: www.sba.gov/subcontracting-directory.

The Defense Logistics Agency, on behalf of the Secretary of Defense, administers the DoD Procurement Technical Assistance Program (PTAC). PTA centers are a local resource available to provide assistance to business firms in marketing products and services to the federal, state. and local governments: www.dla.mil.

SBA's Procurement Center Representatives (PCR), located in area offices, review and evaluate the small business programs of federal agencies and assist small businesses in obtaining federal contracts and subcontracts.

TPCR—Traditional Procurement Center Representative—TPCRs increase the small business share of federal procurement awards by initiating small business set-asides, reserving procurements for competition among small business firms; providing small business sources to federal buying activities; and counseling small firms.

BPCR—Breakout Procurement Center Representative—BPCRs advocate for the breakout of items for full and open competition to effect savings to the federal government.

CMRs—Commercial Marketing Representatives—CMRs identify, develop, and market small businesses to large prime contractors and assist small businesses in identifying and obtaining subcontracts. Contact your local SBA district office or visit site www.sba.gov/content/pcr-directory.

Office of Small and Disadvantaged Business Utilization (OSDBU)

OSDBUs offer small business information on procurement opportunities, guidance on procurement procedures, and identification of prime and subcontracting opportunities in various federal agencies. OSDBUs also have Veteran Small Business Representatives. If you own, operate or represent a small business, you should contact the Small Business Specialists for marketing assistance and information. The specialists will advise you as to what types of acquisitions are either currently available or will be available in the near future. Contact your local SBA office or visit www. osdbu.gov/members.html.

GC Programs

Section 8(a) Program/Small Disadvantaged Business Certification Program

The SBA administers two particular business assistance programs for small disadvantaged businesses (SDBs). These programs are the 8(a) Business Development Program and the Small Disadvantaged Business Certification Program. While the 8(a) Program offers a broad scope of assistance, including federal contracting assistance to socially and economically disadvantaged firms, SDB certification strictly pertains to benefits in federal procurement. Companies which are 8(a) firms automatically qualify for SDB certification. Contact your local SBA office or visit www.sba.gov/contracting/government-contracting-programs/8a-business-development-program.

Small Disadvantaged Business

The SBA certifies SDBs to make them eligible for special bidding benefits. Evaluation credits available to prime contractors boost subcontracting opportunities for SDBs. Qualifications for the program are similar to those for the 8(a) Business Development Program. A small business must be at least 51percent owned and controlled by a socially and economically disadvantaged individual or individuals. African Americans, Hispanic Americans, Asian Pacific Americans, Subcontinent Asian Americans, and

Native Americans are presumed to qualify. Other individuals, including veterans and service-disabled veterans, can qualify if they show by a "preponderance of the evidence" that they are disadvantaged. All individuals must have a net worth of less than $750,000, excluding the equity of the business and primary residence. Successful applicants must also meet applicable SBA size standards for small businesses in their industry.

HUBZone Empowerment Contracting Program

The HUBZone Empowerment Contracting Program stimulates economic development and creates jobs in urban and rural communities by providing federal contracting preferences to small businesses. These preferences go to small businesses that obtain HUBZone (Historically Underutilized Business Zone) certification in part by employing staff that live in a HUBZone. The company must also maintain a "principal office" in one of these specially designated geographic areas. A principal office can be different from a company headquarters, as explained in our section dedicated to Frequently Asked Questions.

Contact your local SBA Office or visit www.sba.gov/content/hubzone -maps. For Service-Disabled Veteran-Owned Small Business Concern Program go to www.sba.gov/sdvosb.

On May 5, 2004, the U.S. Small Business Administration (SBA) issued regulations in the Federal Register as an Interim Final Rule implementing Section 36 of the Veterans Benefits Act of 2003 (Public Law 108-183).

Section 308 of PL 108-183 amended the Small Business Act to establish a procurement program for Small Business Concerns (SBCs) owned and controlled by service-disabled veterans. This procurement program provides that contracting officers may award a sole source or set-aside contract to service-disabled veteran business owners, if certain conditions are met. Finally, the purpose of this procurement program is to assist agencies in achieving the 3 percent government-wide goal for procurement from service-disabled veteran-owned small business concerns.

Important Definitions

Veteran—a person who served in the active military, naval, or air service, and who was discharged or released under conditions other than dishonorable.

Service-Disabled Veteran—a person with a disability that is service-connected and was incurred or aggravated in the line of duty in the active military, naval, or air service.

Service-Disabled Veteran with a Permanent and Severe Disability—a veteran with a service-connected disability that has been determined by the U.S. Department of Veterans Affairs to have a permanent and total disability for purposes of receiving disability compensation or a disability pension.

Permanent Caregiver—a spouse, or an individual eighteen years of age or older, who is legally designated, in writing, to undertake responsibility for managing the well-being of a service-disabled veteran, to include housing, health, and safety.

Service-Disabled Veteran-Owned Small Business Contracts

Service-Disabled Veteran-Owned (SDVO) contracts are contracts awarded to an SDVO SBC through a sole source award or a set-aside award based on competition restricted to SDVO SBCs. The contracting officer for the contracting activity determines if a contract opportunity for SDVO competition exists.

SDVO SBC Set-Aside Contracts

The contracting officer may set-aside acquisitions for SDVO SBCs if

- the requirement is determined to be excluded from fulfillment through award to Federal Prison Industries, Javits Wagner-O'Day, Orders under Indefinite Delivery Contracts, Orders against Federal Supply Schedules, Requirements currently being performed by 8(a) participants, and Requirements for commissary or exchange resale items.
- the requirement is not currently being performed by an 8(a) participant, and unless SBA has consented to release of the requirement from the Section 8(a) Program.
- SBA has not accepted the requirement for performance under the 8(a) authority, unless SBA has consented to release of the requirement from the Section 8(a) Program.
- there is a reasonable expectation that at least two responsible SDVO SBCs will submit offers.
- the award can be made at a fair market price.

SDVO SBC Sole Source Contracts

A contracting officer may award a sole source contract to a SDVO SBC if the contracting officer determines that none of the SDVO SBC set-aside exemptions or provisions apply and the anticipated award price of the contract, including options, will not exceed $5.5 million for manufacturing requirements and $3.5 million for all other requirements. The SDVO SBC must be a responsible contractor able to perform the contract and the award must be made at a fair and reasonable price.

SDVO SBC Simplified Acquisition Contracts

If a requirement is at or below the simplified acquisition threshold, a contracting officer may set-aside the requirement for consideration among SDVO SBCs using simplified acquisition procedures or may award a sole source contract to a SDVO SBC. Contact your local SBA Office or visit www.sba.gov/sdvosb.

National Veterans Business Development Corporation

Many service members never consider small business ownership as a career when they transition out of the military, but you may discover that entrepreneurship is just the path for you. The following information and resources will help you develop a business plan, find financing, and determine if starting a franchise is your best option. This information is provided by the National Veterans Business Development Corporation, a federal contracted program for assisting veterans in starting a business or purchasing a franchise.

What Does It Take to Be an Entrepreneur?

The skills and strengths arising from military experience, such as leadership, organization, and the ability to work under pressure, lend themselves naturally to entrepreneurship, and as a result, many veterans find themselves attracted to business ownership when they leave the military. If you are considering entrepreneurship, it is important to assess your strengths and weaknesses to determine whether you are cut out to be a business owner. Although there are no guarantees in business, successful entrepreneurs tend to share many similar characteristics. The following is

a guide to help you determine if you share the entrepreneurial characteristics of other successful business owners.

Step 1: Think about why you want to be an entrepreneur

There are many reasons people take the plunge into entrepreneurship,
but not all reasons are the right reasons for opening your own business.
Below are the most common reasons people consider business ownership
as a career.

1. *You want to be your own boss.*

Although this is the number one reason given by new entrepreneurs
when making the change from employee to self-employed, there are a few
important things to consider. Without a boss watching over you, do you
have the self-discipline to get things done, to do them right, and to finish
them on time?

Without a boss to blame, are you willing to take responsibility for mistakes and fix problems yourself? If you eliminate the demands of your
boss, will you be able to handle demands from customers and clients,
suppliers and vendors, partners, and even yourself?

2. *You are tired of working 9 to 5.*

As an entrepreneur, you can usually set your own hours but that does
not necessarily mean shorter hours. Many entrepreneurs are forced to put
in twelve to eighteen hours a day, six or seven days a week. Are you ready
to work that hard, and is your drive for entrepreneurial success strong
enough to get you through the long hours? You may be able to sleep in
and work in the comfort of your home in your fuzzy slippers on occasion,
but probably not initially and probably not all the time.

3. *You are looking for an exciting challenge.*

Entrepreneurship is full of decisions that can affect your company's
success. Every day is a new adventure, and you can learn from your
mistakes as well as from your successes. Many successful entrepreneurs
claim they are adrenaline junkies, motivated by the excitement of business
ownership. That excitement requires risks, however, and you must know
your own tolerance for risk. Entrepreneurship, as exciting as it may be,
means putting everything on the line for your business. Sound too risky to
you? Or maybe it sounds like just the adventure you are craving.

4. *You want to make more money.*

Entrepreneurship can be an escape from structured pay charts and
minimal growth opportunities, and, as a small business owner, your hard

work directly benefits you. Despite the potential of big payoffs, however, entrepreneurs sometimes have to work months—even years—before they begin to see those profits. Oftentimes, entrepreneurs take a pay cut when they start out on their own. Are you willing to sacrifice your current level of pay until your business becomes a success?

5. *You really want to become an entrepreneur.*

This is perhaps the most important reason people should enter entrepreneurship. Entrepreneurship takes time, energy, and money, but it also takes heart. It must be something you want to do in order to succeed because it takes drive and motivation, even in the face of setbacks. If you are considering entrepreneurship just because you haven't found anything else that suits you, make sure you are honest with yourself about whether or not you are ready to be an entrepreneur.

Step 2: Assess your skills

Do your skills apply to entrepreneurial success? Many of the skills needed in entrepreneurship are those gained through military experience:

- Leadership
- Ability to get along with and work with all types of people
- Ability to work under pressure and meet deadlines
- Ability to give directions and delegate
- Good planning and organizational skills
- Problem solving
- Familiarity with personnel administration and record keeping
- Flexibility and adaptability
- Self-direction
- Initiative
- Strong work habits
- Standards of quality and a commitment to excellence

Think about other skills that might help you become a successful entrepreneur. Are you good with money? Do you have a strong credit history? Do you have a high energy level? Do you see problems as challenges and enjoy trying new methods for success? Listing your skills will not only help you assess yourself as an entrepreneur, but it might also tell you what kind of business you should start!

Step 3: Define your personality

Your personality often helps determine what type of work best suits you. People preferring structure might find the corporate environment most suitable while creative types might enjoy flexible jobs with relaxed policies. Like any job, there are certain types of personalities that thrive in entrepreneurship:

- Goal-oriented
- Independent
- Self-confident
- Innovative and creative
- Strong commitment
- Highly reliable
- Competitive
- Desire to work hard
- Problem solver
- Good manager
- Organized
- Honest
- Tolerance for failure, but a drive to achieve
- Idea-oriented
- Motivated by challenge
- Calculated risk-taker
- Courageous
- Persistent
- Adaptable
- Positive

Even if you do not have all of these characteristics, you can still be a great entrepreneur. Every entrepreneur is a blend of skills and strengths. Think about the skills or traits you don't have, and learn to improve them or work to overcome them on the road to entrepreneurship!

FRANCHISE OWNERSHIP

If you are considering business ownership but are hesitant to venture out on your own, you may want to consider becoming a franchisee, or franchise owner. Becoming a business owner can be an intimidating process, but when you purchase a franchise, you get a team of support, which includes marketing assistance, human resources tools, and training. Having others who are committed to your success as a business owner and who are willing and able to help when you run into problems is just one of the many advantages to franchise ownership.

Advantages of Franchises

1. *Higher rate of business success*

Perhaps the number one reason people become franchise owners is because franchises have a higher likelihood of succeeding than do traditional start-up businesses. In fact, according to the U.S. Department of Commerce, 95 percent of franchises are still in business after five years. Franchisors (the companies who sell or grant franchises to individuals) evaluate each prospective franchisee (individual franchise owners) and invest in those they think will thrive as franchise owners for their company. They look for specific skills, experience, motivation, financial capacity, and more to choose people who will be able to afford the franchise, follow the business operational model, and become successful.

2. *Established brand identity*

One of the key advantages of operating a franchise is the ability to give consumers a brand they know, quality they trust, and a consistency they have come to expect. Purchasing a franchise means purchasing the reputation of the brand, an established customer base, and a set of products or services that have been successfully tested in communities. While new business start-ups must work at building a reputation and generating awareness of the product or service they offer, franchises are often preceded by their reputation and can make an immediate impact.

3. *The dirty work is done*

Perhaps the most difficult thing new business owners face when opening a business of their own is the burden of starting from scratch. The tasks of starting a business can be lengthy and expensive. In a franchise system, however, the work has already been done to develop a product or service, identify and reach a target market, build a reputation, and create a replicable business model. While many new business owners spend the first year (or longer!) testing products, sales tactics, and marketing avenues, franchise owners already know exactly what works and how to effectively reach their target audience.

4. *Business support*

Business owners who start their own business take on a great deal of responsibility: they must market to new customers, provide products and services to existing customers, hire employees, and train those employees to do their jobs properly. In other words, new business owners must be sales representatives, accountants, human resource managers, marketing experts, and more. That is a lot of responsibility!

While some individuals may thrive in the multiple roles business owners must take on, others need support in some or all of the aspects of business ownership. Franchisees get the support they need in the form of training and even on-site assistance. In addition, most franchisors provide human resources tools, specialized software, marketing materials, and other valuable resources that independent business owners must find or develop for themselves.

5. *Easier to finance*

If you are looking to start a business with less than perfect credit and need to apply for a business loan, the established history of a franchise may help you get your loan. Because new business start-ups are extremely risky, banks are often hesitant to hand out loans without a history of business management and credit management in your past. Prospective franchisees applying for a business loan have the advantage of a tested product or service, a successful business model, and a core of support from the franchisor. Banks know that franchises have a higher likelihood of success than other new businesses; as a result, it is often easier to secure a business loan for a franchise than for a business start-up.

Disadvantages of Franchises

Does owning a franchise seem too good to be true? Although there are many advantages to owning a franchise, there are downsides as well. While these disadvantages may seem minor to some, they may turn others away from the notion of franchise ownership entirely. Read on to learn the negatives of franchise ownership and decide if it is the path for you.

1. *Factors beyond your control*

The value of a franchise lies in the value of the brand and the brand's reputation. When you purchase a franchise, you must take into account the reputation of the parent company and other branches of the franchise. If, over time, that reputation is damaged by factors beyond your control, the results on your business can be catastrophic. And because your franchise agreement is a long-term agreement, getting out of that franchise system may be more difficult than you thought.

2. *High costs*

Many people who pursue franchise ownership do so because they believe the costs associated with franchises will be less than those of a traditional start-up business. And for some franchises, that is true; for many others, however, the costs can soar when franchise fees, capital requirements, marketing fees, royalties, and other fees add up. In fact, one of the reasons that new franchises fail is insufficient funding and a lack of working capital. There are hundreds of reputable, low-cost franchises, but you must know what to look for and be smart from the very beginning.

3. *Restrictions on business*

If you are going into business to be independent, creative, and entrepreneurial, franchise ownership may not be right for you. Franchises are based on previously developed, successfully tested business ideas and plans. Most franchisors have strict regulations on how individual franchises may operate, and deviations are rarely allowed. Franchise owners, for example, must sell a specific product or service and advertise with specific marketing materials and slogans. While this may appeal to business owners who are eager for structure and support, others may find this too regimented for their individual business style.

4. *Reduced profits*

One of the greatest appeals of business ownership is that you benefit personally from your hard work, and many people seek entrepreneurship as a way to increase their earnings and have greater control over their financial destiny. Franchise ownership is actually a middle step between the financial freedom of business ownership and the rigid pay structure of other jobs. As a franchise owner, your hard work will directly result in higher profits for your business, but most franchisors will require continuous monthly royalty payments equaling 5 percent to 10 percent of your profits.

Writing a Business Plan

Business plans are the face of your company and can make the difference in whether or not you receive a loan or whether someone chooses to invest in your company. The importance of a good business plan cannot be overstated, as it defines your business, sets your objectives, and enhances your ability to make sound business decisions in line with your overall business goals. Although all business plans vary slightly, there are six primary sections that should be included in all plans.

Executive Summary

The executive summary is perhaps the most critical part of your business plan, as it is sometimes the only section that will be read before deciding whether or not to consider your business for a loan. If a lender or investor likes what is written in the executive summary, he or she will continue reading; otherwise, you may not get another chance to impress them with your business idea.

The executive summary should describe your business and highlight the key points from each section of your business plan. For example, the executive summary would not include an exhaustive list of your competitors and their products—that is for the marketing and sales section—but it would mention how your product differs from others on the market and what you have to offer that is special. The executive summary should be no more than one or two pages, and although it comes at the beginning of your business plan, it is recommended that you write this section last to ensure you highlight the most important points of each section.

Business Opportunity

First, the business opportunity should answer the question, is my business idea viable? This section should define the simple vision for your company. Provide an overview of your business, including its history, progress to date, and vision for the future. Questions to be answered in the overview of your business include these: Have you started conducting business? If not, when? If so, what progress have you made? Did you acquire this business from a previous owner or start from scratch? If you acquired it, what is the history of the business previously?

Second, the business opportunity must address your product, including why it is different, why customers will buy your product, whether or not your product is already developed, and whether you hold or plan to hold any patents, copyrights, or trademarks. Questions to be answered in the overview of your product include the following: Have you already developed this product? If yes, have you begun selling the product, and how has it been received? If no, what are your plans and timeline for development? How is this product unique, and what are the benefits to using this product instead of a competitor's product?

Marketing and Sales Plan

First, define your business and the product and/or service you are going to sell and create an overview of your market area. Identify your competition and the products or services they offer, then describe what you can offer.

A marketing plan is critical to entrepreneurial success because it tells you who you need to reach and how you are going to reach them. Without customers, you have no business. What have you got that the competition does not, and how will you attract customers away from the competition? Include the price of your product, how it compares to the competition's price, and why you can offer it for less money or how you plan to attract customers despite a higher price. Finally, give an overview of how you will sell your product or service (online, face-to-face, etc.) and how that relates to the competition's sales methods.

Next, describe your customers, including their demographics, needs, patterns, and preferences. Describe the size of your target market and what they will find attractive about your product opposed to products currently on the market. How does your product better respond to their needs and preferences?

Third, outline your marketing strategy by identifying the methods you will use to market your product to your customers. Will you advertise only on television? Will you place ads in the newspaper or local periodicals? Would billboards be appropriate, or should you send out bulk mailings? Include in your strategy whatever ways you see appropriate to reach your customer base, and identify what percentage of your total marketing dollars you will dedicate to each marketing method.

Last, create your marketing budget. Effective marketing is critical from the first day; otherwise, no one will know about your business! Research marketing costs in your area. If you plan to rent a billboard on the main interstate for three months, find out exactly how much it costs. Do not guess on marketing costs—research and determine the exact numbers it will take to market your product to your target audience. If costs seem too high, eliminate high-cost options or look for marketing strategies that reach fewer people overall but reach a higher number of people in your targeted customer base.

Management Team and Personnel

It is important to demonstrate that your management team and/or staff have the skills and qualifications to handle every facet of your business. Is there evidence of expertise in marketing, finance, operations, and development? This section of your business plan should outline the structure and key skills of your staff.

Define the positions of your staff, their role in the company, and a summary of each person's background, experience, and qualifications. Include the time commitment of each individual (e.g., full-time, part-time, one day a week); also include descriptions and qualifications for consultants and partners. If you have not begun hiring employees, include the structure and key skills of staff you plan to hire, a timeline for hiring, and the salaries you estimate to assign to each position. Identify recruitment and training procedures, timelines for doing so, and the costs of employee training.

Operating Plan

Your business plan must include a section covering your operating capabilities and plans. The areas you should cover in this section include office space and location, production facilities, and information technology (IT) infrastructure.

Office space and location will include where you will house your office (e.g., in your home, an office building, etc.), the costs associated with this location, the benefits and disadvantages to being housed in that location, whether you rent or own the space, and (if you rent) the duration of your lease. If you have plans for upgrading your space or relocating, that should be included as well.

If your business requires you to create a product, you will have to include a paragraph on your production facilities. This should include whether you already have facilities and whether you plan to do your own production or outsource it to another company. It should describe the benefits and disadvantages to handling your own production versus outsourcing it, as well as the facilities you have or need, the capacity of the facilities versus anticipated demand, and whether you plan on making an investment into enhancing your production capabilities.

Finally, this section should include a description of your IT infrastructure, including the strengths and weaknesses of your system, your plans to upgrade the system, and how your system will be used as a business tool.

Finances

The final component of your business plan should be your financial forecasts. The purpose of this section is to inform lenders and investors of how much capital you need, how secure their loans or investments are, how you plan to repay the loans, and what your projected sources of revenue and income will be. To do so, you should include detailed financial projections by month for the first year and by quarter for years two and three, as well as the assumptions upon which your projections were made, including the breakdown of anticipated costs and revenues for all three years. You should also include cash flow statements, loan applications, capital equipment and supply lists, and profit and loss statements.

Financing Your Small Business

One of the most common mistakes entrepreneurs make is underestimating the costs of their business and creating a financial plan based on low cost projections. Every entrepreneur has different costs associated with his or her business. For example, establishing a home-based business will have little to no cost for acquiring office space; renting office space will entail low to moderate costs; and building an office will require a high cost. Regardless of your specific needs, every entrepreneur must take two costs into account: start-up costs and recurring costs. Start-up costs are all of the one-time costs required to start your business, such as a security deposit on office space, furniture and equipment purchase, signage, and so forth. Recurring costs are all of the costs you encounter monthly, such as salary and benefit expenses, insurance fees, monthly rent, and so on.

Once you have determined your costs, decide whether you will need to borrow money to start your business. If so, there are several different funding options to consider. Each funding source brings with it a series of pros and cons that should be weighed in order to find a lender to meet your start-up needs.

Option 1: Banks

Banks are usually the first place people look when they want to borrow money. Banks offer a variety of loans and can often advise you as to which type of loan would be best for your needs. Some loans, for example, require you to make set payments of both the principal and interest, whereas others require you to pay back only the interest with a lump payment of the entire principal at the end. The obvious advantage of approaching banks for loans is that banks are designed for just that purpose. The downside is that if you have a bad credit history or have accumulated debt, it can be difficult to get approval for a loan at most banks. The best way to determine whether bank loans are appropriate for your needs is to do your research: locate the banks in your region, find out what types of loans they offer, and learn what requirements they have for approving loans.

Option 2: Venture Capital Firms

Venture capital firms invest in small companies in return for equity. They look for companies with the potential for high growth and high profitability. Although some venture capitalists will invest in companies that are just beginning, they generally seek to fund companies that have been in business for some amount of time in order to assess progress, growth, and earned revenues. For that reason, acquiring start-up funding from venture capitalists can be very difficult; also, the earlier the stage of investment, the more equity venture capital firms require. If you are serious about acquiring venture capital funds for your business start-up, look for firms that specifically cater to business in the start-up phase. If you have a thorough, viable business plan, and your management team has extensive experience fostering rapid growth in small businesses and creating substantial profits, you will have a much higher chance of receiving venture capital funding.

Option 3: Angel Investors

Angel investors are individuals who invest their own money in entre-preneurial ventures in return for equity. Angel investors can be persons you know or persons you don't know and can also work as an individual or be part of an angel group. Angel investors generally invest smaller amounts of money in companies than do venture capitalists, making them an ideal source for funding when you have exhausted funding from your friends, family, and self, but are not yet ready to approach a venture capital firm.

Option 4: Partners

In some cases, funding can be secured by current or potential partners seeking a share of the business. The advantages to partner financing are that partners considering investment are already knowledgeable about the business idea and have confidence in its future, and the approval process may be easier than with a bank or lending firm. The decision you as an entrepreneur must make is whether or not you are willing to give up a portion of your company in order to obtain this funding, or whether you would rather go to banks or other lenders and maintain your control.

Option 5: Friends and Family

Many people warn against the risks of borrowing money from friends and family, but there are also benefits to acquiring loans this way, and it is an extremely popular source of funding for small businesses. Friends and family already know you, your character, and your history of credit, debt, and financial management. Nevertheless, even friends and family considering making a loan should ask to see a business plan to make sure it is well thought out. The terms on which you must pay back loans from friends and family will likely be more relaxed, and they may not demand interest on the repayment of the loan. The obvious downside to borrowing from friends and family is the potential inability to repay the loan, damag-ing not only your finances but their finances as well—and the relation-ships you share with those individuals.

Option 6: Self-Financing

Self-financing is the most popular form of financing for small business owners, and it can serve to be extremely advantageous when you approach other lenders. By investing your own money and assets into your business, it demonstrates your faith that your business will succeed. Different forms of self-financing include borrowing against your retirement fund, taking out personal lines of credit, and utilizing a home equity loan. The disadvantage to financing your business this way is that if your business flounders and you are unable to repay the money, you can lose a lot more than your business. Before putting your home on the line for your business or risking your personal credit history, carefully consider whether self-financing is the right option for you.

Entrepreneurship Resources

The Veterans Corporation (TVC)

The National Veterans Business Development Corporation, doing business as the Veterans Corporation, is a federally chartered 501(c)(3) organization that was created by Public Law 106-50, the Veterans Entrepreneurship and Small Business Development Act of 1999. This act recognized that America "has done too little to assist Veterans . . . in playing a greater role in the economy of the United States." The corporation is charged with creating and enhancing entrepreneurial business opportunities for veterans, including service-disabled veterans. Toward this mission, TVC provides veterans with the tools and resources they need to be successful in business:

- Access to capital
- Access to business services
- Entrepreneurial education
- Surety bonding
- Insurance and prescription coverage
- Veterans' business directory

Contact TVC toll-free at 866-283-8267 or on the web at www.veterans corp.org.

Small Business Administration (SBA)

The primary federal agency providing financial and business development assistance to small firms and aspiring entrepreneurs is the U.S. Small Business Administration, an independent agency chartered in 1953. The SBA encourages participation by qualified veterans in all of its various financial and business development programs. A variety of special outreach programs for veterans are coordinated by SBA's Office of Veterans Business Development (OVBD), established for this and other purposes pursuant to Public Law 106-50. OVDB supports Veteran Business Outreach Centers, and it further leverages its resources and extends its outreach efforts throughout the nation by the use of designated Veteran Business Development Officers in each of the SBA's seventy district offices. SBA provides financial assistance, business development counseling, procurement assistance, and other support to veteran entrepreneurs. Contact SBA toll-free at 800-827-5722 or on the web at www.sba.gov.

Center for Veterans Enterprise

The Department of Veterans Affairs established the Center for Veterans Enterprise (CVE) in 2001. CVE is dedicated to helping veterans succeed in business and specializes in assisting with procurement opportunities. To help coordinate prime and subcontracting business opportunities with veterans for government and private-sector buyers, CVE maintains an electronic business registry. All veteran entrepreneurs, including reservists and members of the National Guard who have been called to active duty of any duration, are encouraged to register their firms and capabilities in this database which is called the VETBiz Vendor Information Pages (VIP). In addition to procurement assistance, CVE provides business coaching, networking, outreach, and other business assistance to veterans. Contact CVE toll-free at 866-584-2344 or on the web at www.vetbiz.gov.

SCORE

SCORE is a 501(c)(3) nonprofit organization headquartered in Washington, D.C., that provides a public service to America by offering small business advice and training. SCORE was formed in 1964 to help small businesses flourish and now has more than ten thousand volunteers who can assist business owners with more than six hundred business skills. Volunteers are working or retired business owners, executives, and corporate leaders who share their wisdom and lessons learned in business. As a result, SCORE "Counselors to America's Small Business" is America's premier source of free and confidential small business advice for entrepreneurs. To date, SCORE has helped more than 7.5 million small businesses through face-to-face small business counseling, low-cost workshops nationwide, and online support and business guidance. Contact SCORE toll-free at 800-634-0245 or on the web at www.score.org.

Association of Small Business Development Centers

The mission of the Association of Small Business Development Centers (ASBDC) is to represent the collective interest of our members by promoting, informing, supporting, and continuously improving the SBDC network, which delivers nationwide educational assistance to strengthen small/medium business management, thereby contributing to the growth of local, state, and national economies.

The ASBDC is a partnership program uniting private enterprise, government, higher education, and local nonprofit economic development organizations. ASBDC is dedicated to the sound development of small business throughout America. Founded in 1979, the ASBDC provides a vehicle for continuous improvement of the Small Business Development Center program, exchange of information among members regarding objectives, methods and results in business management and technical assistance, and advocacy of America's small business community. Over 500,000 businesses are assisted by ASBDC member programs on an annual basis. A sizable number of them are in the dynamic start-up mode, while most are existing businesses searching for stability or planning for growth. Contact ASBDC by phone at 703-764-9850 or on the web at www.asbdc-us.org.

International Franchise Association

The International Franchise Association (IFA), founded in 1960, is a membership organization of franchisors, franchisees, and suppliers. IFA's website is dedicated to providing members and guests with a one-stop shopping experience for franchise information. For more than forty years, the International Franchise Association has protected, enhanced, and promoted franchising worldwide. IFA is the official "Spokesperson for Responsible Franchising."

Franchisors join for the legislative, educational, and networking benefits available as an IFA member. IFA's government and public relations programs are designed to educate and influence public policy makers, and to reduce or eliminate regulations that threaten responsible franchise development. IFA provides information necessary to stay abreast of the changes facing the global franchise community through their educational programs, annual convention, legal symposium, and regional and local meetings. For veterans, IFA's Veterans Transition Franchise Initiative program is comprised of more than one hundred franchise companies that offer veterans financial incentives to buy and operate their franchises. Contact IFA by phone at 202-628-8000 or on the web at www.franchise.org.

Boots2Business

Boots2Business (www.boots2business.org) is a comprehensive online resource, providing education and workplace training that is uniquely tailored to meet the needs of America's military personnel including those in theater in Iraq and Afghanistan, as well as veterans, members of the National Guard and Reserve, service-disabled veterans, and their families. Boots2Business combines elements from successful programs used independently in thousands of vocational schools, job-training centers, community colleges, detention and correctional facilities, Job Corps centers, and adult education programs nationally. TVC has integrated these elements into a cohesive and interactive online program that provides support to the basic, transitional, workforce, family, and entrepreneurial needs of Guard and Reserve Veterans, service-disabled veterans, and their families.

This program has five key areas:

- Basic Skills, Catching Up/Stepping Up
- Transition Skills, Job and Career Preparation
- Workforce Success Skills, Getting a Job and Keeping It
- Entrepreneurial Skills, Start and Grow a Small Business
- Family Resource Center, Life and Family Support

Within these five sections are thirty-one clusters with one thousand course lessons and many tutorials to guide the student through their specific needs. Access to this site is in the form of a scholarship to the veteran and their family. Each scholarship is for one year and is provided by granting organizations or by TVC directly. The cost for each scholarship is $100. Were a veteran to purchase access to all the elements of Boots-2Business without TVC, the cost would exceed $132,000 per year. TVC currently has three hundred scholarships for veterans and service-disabled veterans in New Jersey that are provided by the Henry H. Kessler Foundation. TVC is directly sponsoring a block of six hundred scholarships divided equally between its three hubs. Each hub will coordinate a statewide outreach giving Boots2Business a four-state network. An additional two hundred scholarships have been made possible through a grant from the NEC Foundation of America for national outreach. TVC is currently working with a number of corporations and foundations to extend this valuable scholarship program to all veterans and their families.

Access to Surety Bonding

TVC provides veteran contractors with access to surety bonding through an exclusive partnership with the Surety and Fidelity Association of America. Unlike other bonding programs available, this program is designed solely for veterans, including members of the National Guard and Reserve. It is a fully mentored program with no cap on the amount of the bond you can receive. Last year, the value of construction put into place, excluding single family residential construction, was about $550 billion. For veteran contractors to secure some of that work, especially in the public sector, they must be surety bonded.

Surety bonds provide financial security and construction assurance to project owners by verifying that contractors are capable of performing the work and will be subcontractors, laborers, and material suppliers. There are three basic types of contract surety bonds: bid bond, performance bond, and payment bond.

Surety bonds are extremely important for contractors and subcontractors. By the Miller Act of 1935, federal law mandates performance bonds for public works contracts over $100,000 and payment bonds for contracts over $25,000. In addition, most states require performance and payment bonds on all state and local public works projects.

TVC's partnership with SFAA (Surety & Fidelity Association of America) provides both current and emerging veteran contractors and subcontractors with the education and training they need to do business with the government. TVC members can become experts in government contracting and surety bonding with four unique two-hour training modules conducted by SFAA:

- Module A—Introduction to Surety Bonding: presents the basics of surety bonding including how to obtain a bond, the costs of bonding, and how to develop a surety bond relationship
- Module B—Construction Accounting and Financial Management: provides accounting fundamentals from job costing to financial reporting as well as construction-specific practices for contractors
- Module C—Project Management: covers such topics as project planning methods, estimating bids, job costing, and scheduling
- Module D—Why Contractors Fail: identifies the most common reasons why contractors fail, the ways to avoid common pitfalls, and the role surety bonding plays in ensuring contractor success. If you are interested in doing business with the government, you won't want to miss out on TVC's comprehensive, fully mentoring bonding program. They can help you thoroughly prepare for your bond, identify a knowledgeable surety bond producer, and have your bond application submitted to a surety company for underwriting.

ConnectVets Business Forum

ConnectVets Business Forum is a mentored online meeting place for veteran entrepreneurs to interact with each other through a peer network. The forum is a place where veterans can post business questions, offer advice, and share business experiences. Monitored by volunteer veteran business owners and TVC staff, the forum is designed specifically for the growing community of veteran entrepreneurs with topics covering everything from education to business plans to government contracting and more. To join the forum and get in touch with other veterans in business, visit www .connectvets.org/jobs.html.

Virtual Business Resource Center

TVC, in partnership with SCORE, created a veteran front-end portal to assist veteran entrepreneurs in getting the one-on-one support they need to become successful in their business ventures. Through this direct link on TVC's website, veterans are able to access SCORE's network of experienced and qualified mentors who can answer business questions, provide advice, and offer guidance. This program provides a key advantage for service men and women who are members of the National Guard and Reserve as they pursue their dreams for business ownership through entrepreneurship. Get connected to a SCORE mentor by visiting www.score.org/vetsfastlaunch.

EMPLOYMENT RESTRICTIONS AFTER LEAVING THE MILITARY

Post Government (Military) Service Employment Restriction Counseling should be completed during the transition process. You will be informed about this requirement when completing your DD Form 2648, "Pre-Separation Counseling Checklist."

Post-government (military) employment restriction information will be provided by the military services as appropriate. Transition/Command Career Counselors shall refer separating and retiring service members to an installation legal office (Staff Judge Advocate or Counselor's Office) to ensure they receive a post-government (military) employment restrictions briefing, counseling, or appropriate information from an ethics official. Additional information about employment restrictions after leaving the military is provided below.

Personal Lifetime Ban

Simplified Rule: After you leave government service, you may not represent someone else to the government regarding *particular matters* that you worked on while in government service.

Rule: Former service members may not knowingly make a communication or appearance on behalf of any other person, with the intent to influence, before any officer or employee of any federal agency or court in connection with a *particular matter* in which the officer or employee *personally and substantially* participated, which involved a *specific party* at the time of the participation and representation, and in which the United States is a party or has a direct and substantial interest (18 U.S.C. 207(a) (1)). (This rule does not apply to former military enlisted personnel.)

Official Responsibility Two-Year Ban

Simplified Rule: For *two years* after leaving government service, you may not represent someone else to the government regarding *particular matters* that you did not work on yourself, but were *pending under your responsibility* during your last year of government service.

Rule: For a period of two years after termination of government service, former government officers and employees may not knowingly make a communication or appearance on behalf of any other person, with the intent to influence, before any officer or employee of any federal agency or court, in connection with a particular matter which the employee reasonably should have known was actually pending under his or her *official responsibility* within one year before the employee left government service, which involved a specific party at that time, and in which the United States is a party or has a direct and substantial interest (18 U.S.C. 207(a) (2)). (This rule does not apply to former military enlisted personnel.)

Trade or Treaty 1 Year Ban

Simplified Rule: For *one year* after leaving government service, you may not aid, advise, or represent someone else regarding trade or treaty negotiations that you worked on during your last year of government service.

Rule: For a period of one year after leaving government service, former employees or officers may not knowingly represent, aid, or advise someone else on the basis of *covered information*, concerning any ongoing *trade or treaty negotiation* in which the employee participated personally and substantially in his last year of government service (18 U.S.C. 207(b)). (This rule does not apply to former military enlisted personnel.)

Compensation for Representation to the Government by Others

Rule: After you leave government service, you may not accept compensation for representational services, which were provided by anyone while you were a government employee, before a federal agency or court regarding particular matters in which the government was a party or had a substantial interest. This prohibition may affect personnel who leave the government and share in the proceeds of the partnership or business for representational services that occurred before the employee terminated federal service. (Examples: lobbying, consulting, and law firms) (18 U.S.C. 203). (This rule does not apply to former enlisted military personnel.)

Additional Restrictions for Retired Military Personnel and Reservists

Simplified Rule: Foreign Employment—Unless you receive prior authorization from your service secretary and the secretary of state, you may forfeit your military pay during the time you perform services for a foreign government.

Rule: The U.S. Constitution prohibits retired military personnel and reservists from receiving pay from *foreign governments* without Congressional authorization. This can extend to receipt of pay from a U.S. contractor or subcontractor for providing services to a foreign government. In 37 U.S.C. 908, Congress authorizes the secretary of state and secretary of the appropriate military department to approve such receipt of pay. Each military service has implementing directives. Retired personnel and reservists who violate this Constitutional proscription may forfeit pay equal in amount to their foreign pay.

Employment by DoD: To avoid the appearance of favoritism, 5 U.S.C. 3326 prohibits the appointment of retired military personnel to civil service positions (including a non-appropriated fund activity) in any DoD component for six months after retirement. (This restriction has been temporarily waived due to the current national emergency following the attacks of 9/11.)

The secretary concerned may waive this prohibition. However, DoD Directive 1402.1 requires the secretary concerned to conduct intensive external recruitment before granting the waiver.

Employment during Terminal Leave

Holding a civil office in state or local government: While on active duty (including terminal leave) military *officers* are prohibited by 10 U.S.C. 973(b) from holding a "civil office" with a state or local government.

Civilian position in the U.S. government: Military personnel on terminal leave are authorized to accept a civilian position in the U.S. government and receive the pay and allowances of that position as well as their military pay and allowances (5 U.S.C. 5534a).

Note: Please remember that while on terminal leave, you are still an active-duty service member, and the restrictions that apply to you while on active duty still apply. For example: restrictions on political activities.

Outside employment: If you are currently required to obtain permission prior to engaging in outside employment, that requirement will most likely carry over to you during terminal leave. Check with your supervisor.

Restriction on representing others to the federal government: You may not represent anybody outside the government to the government on any particular matter involving the government. Military officers working on terminal leave (like all federal employees) are prohibited by 18 USC 205 and 18 USC 203 from representing their new employer to the government. In almost every case, this precludes a member from interacting or appearing in the federal workplace as a contractor. Being present in government offices on behalf of a contractor inherently is a representation. Of course, military officers on terminal leave may begin work with the contractor, but only "behind the scenes" at a contractor office or otherwise away from the government workplace. *Enlisted members are not subject to 18 USC 203 or 205.*

Prohibition on working for a foreign principal: Over and above the restriction of receiving compensation from a foreign government, there is also a specific prohibition of a public official from being or acting as an agent of a foreign principal required to register under the Foreign Agents Registration Act of 1938 (expanding the restriction beyond foreign governments to include persons, partnerships, and corporations (18 U.S.C. 219).

Military Spouses

Frequent relocation, extended deployments, and other unique aspects associated with the military lifestyle can create significant career and employment challenges for military spouses. Wives of military personnel are less likely to be employed than wives of civilians and those that are employed earn significantly less than wives of civilians. Spouses of reservists have also reported difficulty in maintaining full-time employment during a spouse's deployment due to child care issues.

The average age of active-duty military spouses is 31.9. Of the 711,375 active-duty spouses, 66 percent are already in the workforce. A DoD survey in September 2008 identified that 84 percent of all military spouses have at least some college education; 25 percent hold a bachelor's degree; and 10 percent hold advanced degrees. The majority of military spouses work outside of the home to supplement their family income and wish to stay in their current career of choice regardless of relocation. Seventy-seven percent of military spouses surveyed report they want or need to work. Ninety three percent of the military spouse population is female and recent studies reveal the extent of the disparity in pay. The overall wage gap between civilian and military wives is 42 percent. This gap represents both lower labor force participation by military wives and lower earnings for employment. Among households that moved the year prior to the survey, a common situation in the military, the wage gap rises to over 47 percent.

The challenge is to reduce the barriers that currently prevent military spouses from maintaining a career or employment on a normal progression path regardless of relocation. The lack of broad-based reciprocity among the states to recognize professional licenses or certificates held by military spouses creates a significant barrier to employment. Additionally, frequent moves result in military spouses incurring high costs for recertification and increased delays before they are able to work due to state licensing requirements in fields such as teaching and medical services. Finally, employers may need more exposure to the benefits of hiring military spouses.

The DoD will assist spouse education counseling for all ranks and provide stipends for those pursuing portable career opportunities for entry-level ranks usually six years or less of service. Specifically, the Military Spouse Career Advancement Accounts program will be focused on E1–E5, W1–W2, and O1–O2 ranks for financial assistance to encourage spouses working on two-year degrees, licenses, and certifications. The Departments of Education and Veterans Affairs will work with Defense to assist Military Spouse Career Advancement Account education counselors to help military spouses maximize federal financial aid options, to include assistance with GI Bill and Pell Grants.

Finding a Job as a Military Spouse

Finding a job is difficult at the best of times with the current state of the economy, and it poses even more problems if you keep relocating because of permanent changes of station (PCSs). If you work for a national or multinational company with lots of offices, you may be able continue working with them at your new location. While some jobs are almost recession-proof—teaching, nursing and so on—getting hired for other jobs can be a challenge. One of the challenges is deployment. Many employers might be reluctant to hire you if they think your partner is likely to be deployed, leaving you to look after the home and family and unable to continue with your job. The fact that your partner may suddenly be posted to another base is also a handicap because some employers feel it is a waste of time training you for a job if you are not likely to be with them very long.

However, if you want to find work, there are a lot of resources at your disposal. There are opportunities for working on base, which is more convenient. There are also jobs off base, but many bases are in remote areas and transportation could be a problem and the more remote the area, the fewer the jobs available in any case.

For jobs on base, contact the Family Support Center for how to get in touch with the employment assistance program office. It will have information on job opportunities on and off base, as well as how to apply for federal positions. Let everyone know you are looking for a job. Your friends may hear about an opportunity and can then pass it on to you. For off-base jobs, contact the local labor office, scan the local newspapers— their websites often post jobs before they appear in print—and send your resume around to prospective employers. One way to test the water is to register with a temp agency. Lots of temp jobs lead to permanent employment, and it gives you an opportunity to decide whether you like working for the company and it gives them the chance to test your competencies.

Depending on your skill sets, there are lots of working from home jobs provided you have a computer and Internet connection. Opportunities in this area include translation and transcription services, bookkeeping, data entry, call center services, and so on. Be careful though, as there are a lot of scams involving working from home. Check your prospective employer out carefully.

Consider going back to school or taking training courses to qualify you for more jobs. The DoD offers tuition assistance for military spouses and there are many online and offline training and further education opportunities.

Finding a Job Overseas

Finding a job overseas can be even more challenging because of language, U.S. qualifications not being recognized, and just different ways of doing things. Do your homework carefully to discover what is available, what you think you are qualified to do, and be flexible. If the job that you would like is not available, consider other options—either a career change or going back to school. Talk to other spouses about what is available; join discussion groups and the spouses' club if there is one.

Most overseas bases have commissaries or exchanges as well as civilian and defense contractors who may have positions open. There may be other U.S. bases nearby run by other branches of the military, but don't let that stop you applying if there is a job.

Check out the Office of Personnel Management website at www.opm. gov. You'll be amazed how many federal jobs are posted and how many of them are overseas.

If you do get a job, make sure you comply with that country's tax laws. If you are employed by a U.S. company, you might be paid in dollars, which are exempt from federal taxes. If you are employed by a local company and are paid in that country's currency, you will probably be subject to their tax laws.

Military Spouse Preference Program

The Military Spouse Preference (MSP) Program is derived from Title 10, United States Code, Section 1784, "Employment Opportunities for Military Spouses," and applies to spouses of active-duty military members of the U.S. Armed Forces (including Coast Guard) who relocate to accompany their sponsor on a permanent change of station (PCS) move. The program is intended to lessen the career interruption of spouses who relocate with their military sponsors. MSP is a Department of Defense (DoD) program. Consequently, it applies only to DoD vacancies. Military spouses are eligible to request MSP regardless of current employment status.

If you are a spouse of an active-duty military member, you may be eligible for Military Spouse Preference (MSP). The MSP Program applies only if

- the spouse was married to the military sponsor prior to the reporting date to the new assignment;
- the relocation was based on PCS move and not for separation or retirement;
- the vacancy is within the commuting area of the sponsor's permanent new duty station; and
- the spouse is among the "best qualified" group and is within reach for selection.

MSP applies if you are ranked among the "best qualified" for this vacancy, and the list established from this announcement is used to fill the vacancy. To be rated "best qualified," MSP applicants must attain an eligibility rating on this examination of 80 or higher, not including points for veteran's preference. MSP does not apply, however, when preference would violate statutes or regulations on veterans' preference or imply nepotism.

Note: Applicants claiming military spouse preference will be required to produce a copy of military sponsor's PCS orders to substantiate eligibility prior to appointment in the federal service. Failure to provide these orders may result in the cancellation of any pending appointment to a federal service position.

If you can't find employment, consider working from home, either working for yourself or an employer. You could give English-language lessons, or if you have special skills, you could offer music lessons or coaching in math, science, and so on. As mentioned above, there are also opportunities for working from home but employed by a company that requires you to do translating, transcription, data entry, and so forth. Before embarking on this, however, make sure that you have the necessary permissions and licenses.

Resources

GENERAL

American Red Cross

While providing services to 1.4 million active-duty personnel and their families, the Red Cross also reaches out to more than 1.2 million members of the National Guard and the Reserves and their families who reside in nearly every community in America. Red Cross workers in hundreds of chapters and on military installations brief departing service members and their families regarding available support services and explain how the Red Cross may assist them during the deployment.

Both active-duty and community-based military can count on the Red Cross to provide emergency communications that link them with their families back home, access to financial assistance, counseling, and assistance to veterans. Red Cross Service to the Armed Forces personnel work 'n 756 chapters in the United States, on 58 military installations around the world, and with our troops in Kuwait, Afghanistan, and Iraq.

www.redcross.org

Angels 'n Camouflage

A cooperative initiative with various organizations across the country, Angels 'n Camouflage, Inc. reinforces the importance and advantages of supporting our veterans and deployed service members. Since its inception in 2002, Angels 'n Camouflage, Inc. has helped thousands of veterans and troops through "Mail Call" and emergency assistance for those veterans homeless or injured from combat.

www.angelsncamo.org

Twitter: @Angelsncamo

Army National Guard Websites

Army National Guard

National Guard Website

www.nationalguard.com

National Guard Family Program

One stop to find information on programs, benefits, and resources on National Guard family programs.

www.jointservicessupport.org/fp/

ESGR (Employment Support for the Guard and Reserve)

www.esgr.mil

Army Reserve Websites

U.S. Army Reserves

Army Reserve Family Programs Online

Army Reserve Family and Readiness Program

www.arfp.org

Deployment Health Clinical Center

Health Clinical Center of the Department of Defense: Health information for clinicians, veterans, family members, and friends.

www.pdhealth.mil

Military OneSource

Military OneSource is a "one-stop shop" for information on all aspects of military life.

From information about financial concerns, parenting, relocation, emotional well-being, work, and health, to many other topics, Military OneSource can provide a wealth of information. There are many informative topics on the website specific to wounded service members and families. For example, by clicking on Health and Wellness/Wounded Warrior and selecting Caring for an Injured Service Member, you can access topics such as "Compassion Fatigue and Caregivers," "Financial Resources and Assistance for Military Family Caregivers," and "How to Talk to a Child about a Parent's Severe Injury."

In addition to the comprehensive information available online, representatives are available twenty-four hours a day, seven days a week (24/7). Find a representative at the 800 number provided below.

Calling will provide you with personalized service specific to answering your needs. You can call the same representative back for continuity of service, as each person has their own extension. Military OneSource is closely aligned with the Military Severely Injured Center. You can call Military OneSource as a parent, spouse, or service member. The information you need is a phone call away: 1-800-342-9647. www.militaryonesource.mil

The Military Order of the Purple Heart—703-642-5360

The Military Order of the Purple Heart provides support and services to all veterans and their families. This website includes information on VA benefits assistance, issues affecting veterans today, and links to other key websites for veterans.

www.purpleheart.org

Noncommissioned Officers Association (NCOA)

NCOA was established in 1960 to enhance and maintain the quality of life for noncommissioned and petty officers in all branches of the Armed Forces, National Guard, and Reserves. The Association offers its members a wide range of benefits and services designed especially for current and former enlisted service members and their families. Those benefits fall into these categories: social improvement programs to help ensure your well-being during your active military career, your transition to civilian life, and throughout your retirement; legislative representation to serve as your legislative advocate on issues that affect you and your family, through their National Capital Office in Alexandria, Virginia; Today's Services to help save you money through merchant program discounts. Contact NCOA at 1-800-662-2620.

www.ncoausa.org

Returning Veterans Resource Project NW

Provides free counseling for veterans and families in Oregon.

www.returningveterans.com

Veterans Health Information

A list of links to civilian and military health care information.

www.va.gov

Veterans of Foreign Wars (VFW)

The Veterans of Foreign Wars has a rich tradition of enhancing the lives of millions through its legislative advocacy program that speaks out on

Capitol Hill in support of service members, veterans, and their families, and through community service programs and special projects. From assisting service members in procuring entitlements, to providing free phone cards to the nation's active-duty military personnel, to supporting numerous community-based projects, the VFW is committed to honoring our fallen comrades by helping the living. Contact the VFW at (202) 453-5230, or fax at (202) 547-3196.

www.vfw.org

Veterans Outreach Center

The Veterans Outreach Center (VOC) proactively seeks out veterans in need who continue to suffer in silence, battling personal wars that can be won—with help. VOC's collaborative approach to treatment cares for the whole person; veterans receive the breadth of services needed to regain their mental, physical, and economic health; reconnect with themselves and the community; and resume productive lives.

www.veteransoutreachcenter.org

Vets 4 Vets

Outreach-Support groups run by vets for Iraq-era vets

www.vets4vets.com

Women Veterans Health Program

Provides full range of medical and mental health services for women veterans.

www.va.gov

DOCUMENTS

Air Force: The Community College of the Air Force (CCAF) automatically captures your training, experience, and standardized test scores. Transcript information may be viewed at the CCAF website: www.au.af. mil/au/barnes/ccaf/index.asp.

Army: For everything you want to know about the free AARTS transcript (Army/American Council on Education Registry Transcript System), go to http://www.atrrs.army.mil. This free transcript includes your military training, your Military Occupational Specialty (MOS), and college-level examination scores with the college credit recommended for those experiences. It is a valuable asset that you should provide to your college or your employer, and it is available for Active Army, National Guard, and Reserve soldiers. You can view and print your own transcript at this website.

Save time and money: Unless you know for sure that you need to take a particular course, wait until the school gets all your transcripts before you sign up for classes. Otherwise you may end up taking courses you don't need.

Coast Guard: The Coast Guard Institute (CGI) requires each service member to submit documentation of all training (except correspondence course records), along with an enrollment form, to receive a transcript. Transcript information can be found here at the Coast Guard Institute website: www .uscg.mil/hq/cgi/active_duty/go_to_college/official_transcript.asp.

Navy and Marine Corps: Information on how to obtain the Sailor/ Marine American Council on Education Registry Transcript (SMART) is available at www.navycollege.navy.mil. SMART is now available to document the American Council on Education (ACE) recommended college credit for military training and occupational experience. SMART is an academically accepted record that is validated by ACE. The primary purpose of SMART is to assist service members in obtaining college credit for their military experience. Additional information on SMART can also be obtained from your nearest Navy College Office or Marine Corps Education Center, or contact the Navy College Center.

ADVOCACY

General

American Bar Association

The mission of the ABA Standing Committee on Legal Assistance for Military Personnel (LAMP Committee) is to help the military and the Department of Defense improve the effectiveness of legal assistance provided on civil matters to an estimated 9 million military personnel and their dependents.

www.americanbar.org/groups/legal_assistance_military_personnel/
about_us.html

The American Legion

Since its founding in 1919, The American Legion has been an advocate
for America's veterans, a friend of the U.S. military, a sponsor of community-based youth programs, and a spokesman for patriotic values.
It is the nation's largest veterans organization with nearly 2.7 million
members and about 15,000 local "posts" in most communities and six
foreign countries. The Legion provides free, professional assistance—
for any veteran and any veteran's survivor—in filing and pursuing
claims before the VA; it helps deployed service members' families with
things ranging from errands to household chores to providing someone
to talk to; and offers temporary financial assistance to help families
of troops meet their children's needs. Contact the American Legion at
(202) 861-2700, Ext. 1403, or fax at (202) 833-4452.

www.legion.org

American Legion Auxiliary

The women of the American Legion Auxiliary educate children, organize
community events, and help our nation's veterans through legislative action and volunteerism. It is the world's largest women's patriotic service
organization with nearly 1 million members in 10,100 communities.

www.alaforveterans.org

AMVETS

As one of America's foremost veteran's service organizations, AM-
VETS (American Veterans) assists veterans and their families. A
nationwide cadre of AMVETS national service officers (NSOs) offers
information, counseling, and claims service to all honorably discharged
veterans and their dependents concerning disability compensation, VA
benefits, hospitalization, rehabilitation, pension, education, employment, and other benefits.

301-459-9600, Toll-Free: 1-877-726-8387

www.amvets.org

Hope for The Warriors®

The mission of Hope for The Warriors® is to enhance quality of life
for U.S. service members and their families nationwide who have been
adversely affected by injuries or death in the line of duty. Hope for The
Warriors® actively seeks to ensure that the sacrifices of wounded and

fallen warriors and their families are never forgotten nor their needs unmet, particularly with regard to the short- and long-term care of the severely injured.

On their own, our service members and their families are awe inspiring in the face of their disabilities and hardships—courageous and resolute. But, it is with the support of a grateful nation that they remain unfaltering in their determination and find hope and purpose beyond recovery. As a united support network, all individuals, whether of great or small means, can find an opportunity to honor those who have willingly sacrificed to defend and protect our freedom. They have designed special projects and programs that allow and encourage community involvement.

www.hopeforthewarriors.org

Military Order of the Purple Heart of the USA (MOPH)

The Military Order of the Purple Heart represents combat wounded veterans in the nation's capitol. This means that the voice of the combat wounded veteran is heard in Congress, at the Department of Defense and at the Veterans Administration. The MOPH is constantly alert to any legislation that affects its members. The MOPH also works on combat wounded veterans' behalf. Contact MOPH at (703) 642-5360.

www.purpleheart.org

National Veterans Foundation

The National Veterans Foundation serves the crisis management, information, and referral needs of all U.S. veterans and their families through management and operation of the nation's only toll-free helpline for all veterans and their families; public awareness programs that shine a consistent spotlight on the needs of America's veterans; and outreach services that provide veterans and families in need with food, clothing, transportation, employment, and other essential resources.

1-888-777-4443

www.nvf.org

VETERAN SERVICE OFFICERS ORGANIZATIONS

American Legion
www.legion.org

American Veterans
www.amvets.org
Disabled American Veterans
www.dav.org
Military Order of the Purple Heart
www.purpleheart.org
Military Coalition Members
www.themilitarycoalition.org/tmc-members.html
National Association of State Directors of Veterans Affairs
www.nasdva.net
Paralyzed Veterans of America
www.pva.org
Veterans of Foreign Wars
www.vfw.org

TRICARE PROGRAMS

Active Duty Dental Program
https://secure.addp-ucci.com/dwaddw/home.xhtml
Tricare
www.tricare.mil
Tricare Dental
www.tricare.mil/Plans/DentalPlans.aspx
Tricare North Region
www.healthnetfederalservices.com
Tricare Pharmacy
www.express-scripts.com
Tricare Retiree Dental
www.trdp.org
Tricare South Region
www.humana-military.com
Tricare West Region
www.triwest.com
Military Medical Support Office (MMSO)
www.tricare.mil/tma/MMSO/index.aspx

WOUNDED WARRIOR SERVICE PROGRAMS

Air Force Wounded Warrior Program
www.woundedwarrior.af.mil
Army Wounded Warrior Program
www.wtc.army.mil/index.html
Marine for Life
www.marineforlife.org
Navy Safe Harbor—for Severely Injured Support
http://safeharbor.navylive.dodlive.mil

ORGANIZATIONS SPECIFIC TO DISABILITY

Blind Veterans Association
www.bva.org
Colorado Traumatic Brain Injury Trust Fund Program
www.tbicolorado.org
Defense and Veterans Brian Injury Center
www.dvbic.org
Helping Hands
www.monkeyhelpers.org
National Amputation Foundation
www.nationalamputation.org
Operation TBI Freedom—Denver Options
www.rmhumanservices.org/program/operation-tbi-freedom/

VACATIONS FOR WOUNDED SERVICE MEMBERS

Vacations for Veterans
Vacations for Veterans enables veterans of the United States Armed
Forces recently wounded in combat operations and who have received
the Purple Heart Medal in the Afghanistan or Iraq Campaigns to receive
free lodgings donated by vacation homeowners.
www.vacationsforveterans.org

TRANSPORTATION

Air Ambulance Service
  www.aircompassionamerica.org
Air Charity Network
  www.aircharitynetwork.org
Angel Flight West
  www.angelflightwest.org
Operation Hero Miles
  www.fisherhouse.org/programs/hero-miles
Mercy Medical
  www.mercymedical.org
Veterans Airlift Command
  www.veteransairlift.org

COUNSELING

Art of Redirection Counseling
  www.artofredirection.com
One Freedom
  www.onefreedom.org
Give an Hour
  www.giveanhour.org
People House
  www.peoplehouse.org
Pike Peak Behavioral Health Group
  www.ppbhg.org
Soldiers Project
  www.thesoldiersproject.org
Veterans and Families
  www.veteransandfamilies.org

SPECIAL PROGRAMS FOR OEF/OIF WOUNDED

Angels of Mercy
  www.supportourwounded.org

Bob Woodruff Foundation
   http://remind.org
Cadence Riding
   www.cadenceriding.org
Challenge Aspen
   www.challengeaspen.com
Challenged Athlete Foundation
   www.challengedathletes.org
Coalition to Salute America's Heroes
   www.saluteheroes.org
Disabled Sports USA
   www.disabledsportsusa.org
Family and Friends for Freedom Fund, Inc.
   www.injuredmarinesfund.org
Fisher House
   www.fisherhouse.org
Hearts and Horses
   www.heartsandhorses.org
Hope for the Warriors
   www.hopeforthewarriors.org
Independence Fund
   www.independencefund.org
Lakeshore Foundation
   www.lakeshore.org
Northup Gumman—assisting with employment
   http://operationimpact.ms.northropgrumman.com
Operation Family Fund
   www.operationfamilyfund.org
Operation First Response
   www.operationfirstresponse.org
Outdoor Buddies
   www.outdoorbuddies.org
Pentagon Foundation
   www.pentagonfoundation.org
Pike Peak Therapeutic Riding Center
   www.pptrc.org
Rebuild Hope
   www.rebuildhope.org

Sentinels of Freedom
www.sentinelsoffreedom.org
Sentinels of Freedom–Scholarships
www.sentinelsoffreedom.org
Semper Fi Fund (must be a marine or have been attached to a marine unit on deployment when injuries took place)
www.semperfifund.org
Strikeouts for Troops
www.strikeoutsfortroops.org
Sun Valley Adaptive Sports
www.highergroundsv.org
Therapeutic Riding and Education Center
www.trectrax.org
Tirr Foundation
www.tirrfoundation.org
Wounded Heroes Foundation
www.woundedheroesfund.net
Wounded Warrior Project
www.woundedwarriorproject.org
Wounded Warrior Resource Center
www.woundedwarriorresourcecenter.com
Wounded, Ill, and Injured Compensation and Benefits Handbook
http://warriorcare.dodlive.mil/benefits/compensation-and-benefits/

FAMILIES

Army Family and Morale, Welfare and Recreation
Army recreation programs
www.armymwr.com
Azalea Charities
Provides comfort and relief items for soldiers, sailors, airmen, and marines who are sick, injured, or wounded from service in Iraq and Afghanistan. It purchases specific items requested by Military Medical Centers, VA Medical Centers, and Fisher House rehabilitation facilities each week. It also provides financial support to *CrisisLink*, a hotline for

wounded soldiers and their families, and Hope for The Warriors®—
special projects for wounded soldiers.

www.azaleacharities.com/about/mission.shtml

Blue Star Mothers of America

A nonprofit organization of mothers who now have, or have had, children honorably serving in the military. Their mission is "supporting each other and our children while promoting patriotism."

www.bluestarmothers.org

Military Connection

Comprehensive military directory providing information on job postings, job fairs, and listings.

www.militaryconnection.com

Military Family Network

One nation, one community, making the world a home for military families.

www.emilitary.org

Military Homefront

Website for reliable quality of life information designed to help troops, families, and service providers.

www.militaryonesource.mil

My Army Life Too

Website of choice for Army families providing accurate, updated articles and information on various topics.

www.myarmyonesource.com

National Military Family Association

Serving the Families of Those Who Serve, The National Military Family Association (NMFA)—"The Voice for Military Families"—is dedicated to serving the families and survivors of the seven uniformed services through education, information, and advocacy. NMFA is the only national organization dedicated to identifying and resolving issues of concern to military families. Contact NMFA at 1-800-260-0218, (703) 931-6632, or fax at (703) 931-4600.

www.militaryfamily.org

National Remember Our Troops Campaign

The National Remember Our Troops Campaign works to recognize military service members and their families by providing an official U.S.

Blue or Gold Star Service Banner. The Star Service Banner displayed in the window of a home is a tradition dating back to World War I.
www.nrotc.org

FAMILY ASSISTANCE

American Red Cross
www.redcross.org
Armed Forces Foundation
www.armedforcesfoundation.org
Army One Source
www.myarmyonesource.com
Cell phones/calling cards for soldiers
www.cellphonesforsoldiers.com
ChildCare Aware of America
http://usa.childcareaware.org
Freedom Calls Foundation
www.freedomcalls.org
Freedom Hunters
www.freedomhunters.org
Grand Camps for kids and grandparents
www.grandcamps.org
Homes for our Troops
www.hfotusa.org
Military Family Network
www.emilitary.org
Military Impacted Schools Association
http://militaryimpactedschoolsassociation.org
Military news with benefit information
www.military.com
Military One Source
www.militaryonesource.com
Military Spouse Career Center
www.military.com/spouse
Military Spouse Resource Center—assist with employment, education,
www.careeronestop.org/militaryspouse/

National Military Family Association
www.militaryfamily.org
National Resource Directory
www.nationalresourcedirectory.org
Our Military Kids
www.ourmilitarykids.org
Project Focus
www.focusproject.org
Project Sanctuary
www.projectsanctuary.us
Rebuilding Together
www.togetherwetransform.org
Snowball Express
www.snowballexpress.org
Social Security
www.ssa.gov
Soldiers Angels
www.soldiersangels.com
Swords to Plowshares (employment, training, health, and legal)
www.swords-to-plowshares.org
Tragedy Assistance Program for Survivors
www.taps.org
United Services Organization
www.uso.org
Veterans Holidays (discounted rates)
www.veteransholidays.com
Waves of Honor
www.wavesofhonor.com
Women, Infants, and Children (WIC)
www.fns.usda.gov/wic

FINANCIAL ASSISTANCE

American Legion Temporary Financial Assistance (TFA)
www.legion.org/tfa
American Military Family
www.AMF100.org

American Soldier Foundation
www.ussoldiersfoundation.org

AnnualCreditReport.com
www.annualcreditreport.com

Coalition to Salute America's Heroes
www.saluteheroes.org

Elks Lodge—have financial assistance available
www.elks.org

EQUIFAX Credit Information Service
www.equifax.com

Experian National Consumer Assistance
www.experian.com

Home Front Cares
www.thehomefrontcares.org

Impact a Hero
www.impactahero.org

Military One Source
http://militaryonesource.mil

National Association of American Veterans
www.naavets.org

National Veterans Foundation
www.nvf.org

Operation Home Front
www.operationhomefront.net

Reserve Aid
www.reserveaid.org

TRANSUNION
www.transunion.com

Unmet Needs
www.vfw.org/UnmetNeeds/

USA Cares
www.usacares.org

VA Form 26-1880
Request for Certificate of Eligibility: www.vba.va.gov/pubs/forms/
vba-26-1880-are.pdf
Get your W-2 from myPay: https://mypay.dfas.mil/mypay.aspx

VA Home Loan Resources
http://benefits.va.gov/homeloans/

EDUCATION

Air Force (CCAF) Transcript
www.au.af.mil/au/barnes/ccaf/index.asp
Application for Education Benefits, VA 22-1990
www.vba.va.gov/pubs/forms/VBA-22-1990-ARE.pdf
Application for Pell Grants or Federal Stafford Loans (FAFSA)
www.fafsa.ed.gov
Coast Guard Institute Transcript
www.uscg.mil/hq/cgi/active_duty/go_to_college/official_transcript.asp
Defense Activity for Non-Traditional Education Support (DANTES)
www.dantes.doded.mil
DoD Voluntary Education Partnership Memorandum of Understanding (MOU)
www.dodmou.com
Federal Financial Student Aid
https://studentaid.ed.gov/sa/redirects/federal-student-aid-ed-gov
VA Education Services (GI Bill)
www.benefits.va.gov/gibill/
VA Regional Office Finder
www1.va.gov/directory/guide/home.asp
Veterans Upward Bound
www.navub.org/

EDUCATION RESOURCES

AHEAD—Association on Higher Education and Disability
www.ahead.org
American Council on Education
www.acenet.edu
National Center for Learning Disabilities
www.ncld.org
Online Disability Information System (ODIS)
www.ccids.umaine.edu
OSERS: National Institute on Disability & Rehabilitation Research (NIDRR)
www2.ed.gov/about/offices/list/osers/nidrr/index.html?src=mr

UNIVERSITY RESOURCES

Centennial College, Centre for Students with Disabilities (CSD)
www.centennialcollege.ca/student-life/student-services/centre-for-stu
dents-with-disabilities/
Coalition of Rehabilitation Engineering Research Organizations
www.crero.org
Curry School of Education
http://curry.virginia.edu
George Washington University, Rehabilitation Counselor Education Programs
www.gwu.edu/graduate-programs/rehabilitation-counseling
Iowa State University, Student Disability Resources
www.sdr.dso.iastate.edu/
Johns Hopkins University, Physical Medicine and Rehabilitation
www.hopkinsmedicine.org/physical_medicine_rehabilitation/
Nebraska Assistive Technology Project
www.atp.ne.gov/
Northwestern University Prosthetics-Orthotics Center
www.nupoc.northwestern.edu/
Ohio State University, Disability Services
www.ods.ohio-state.edu/
Oklahoma Department of Rehabilitation Services, National Clearinghouse of Rehabilitation Training Materials (NCRTM)
www.okdrs.org/drupal/guide/national-clearinghouse-rehabilitation
-training-materials-ncrtm
Tarleton State University
www.tarleton.edu
Thomas Edison State College, Online Degrees
www.tesc.edu/academics/online-degrees.cfm
University of California, Berkeley, School of Psychology
http://psychology.berkeley.edu/
University of California, Los Angeles, Disabilities and Computing Program (DCP)
www.dcp.ucla.edu
University of Georgia, Disability Resource Center
https://drc.uga.edu/

University of Illinois at Urbana–Champaign
www.illinois.edu
University of Kansas Medical Center, School of Health Professions
www.kumc.edu/school-of-health-professions.html
University of Minnesota, Disability Resource Center
https://diversity.umn.edu/disability/home
University of New Hampshire, Institute on Disability
http://iod.unh.edu/
University of Virginia, Special Education Website
http://special.edschool.virginia.edu
University of Washington, Department of Rehabilitation Medicine
http://rehab.washington.edu
Victorian University, TAFE Services
www.vu.edu.au/courses/fees-assistance/vocational-education-vetafe
-course-fees
West Virginia University International Center for Disability Information
www.icdi.wvu.edu/

EDUCATION/SCHOLARSHIPS

Air Force Aid Society
The Air Force Aid Society provides need-based grants of up to $1,500 to selected sons and daughters of current, former, and deceased Air Force personnel. The Air Force Aid Society website provides information on and applications for the education grants offered by the Society.
(800) 429-9475 or (703) 607-3072
www.afas.org/education-grants
Army Emergency Relief
In addition to providing information on and applications for scholarships provided by the Army Emergency Relief to the spouses and children of deceased Army personnel, the Army Emergency Relief also maintains a listing of general financial aid links and scholarship search engines.
(866) 878-6378 or (703) 428-0000
www.aerhq.org/dnn563/Scholarships.aspx

Hope For The Warriors®

The mission of Hope For The Warriors® is to enhance quality of life for U.S. service members and their families nationwide who have been adversely affected by injuries or death in the line of duty. It has developed a number of advocacy, support, and educational programs.

Hope For The Warriors®

PMB 48

1335 Suite E, Western Blvd.

Jacksonville, NC 28546

(910)-938-1817 or 877-2HOPE4W

info@hopeforthewarriors.org

Intrepid Fallen Heroes Fund

www.fallenheroesfund.org

Marine Corps Scholarship Foundation

The Marine Corps Scholarship Foundation website provides information on and applications for scholarships offered by the foundation to the sons and daughters of current or former United States Marines, and to the children of current or former United States Navy Corpsmen who have served with the United States Marine Corps.

New Jersey Office—(800) 292-7777

Virginia Office—(703) 549-0060

https://my.mcsf.Org

Military.com

Military.com is a commercial, service-related organization that maintains a website offering a scholarship search function for dependents of service members as well as state-by-state education benefits listings.

www.military.com

Navy-Marine Corps Relief Society

The Navy-Marine Corps Relief Society maintains a website for information on and applications for educational grants offered and administered by the Navy-Marine Corps Relief Society.

(703) 696-4960

www.nmcrs.org

Reserve Officers Association

In addition to offering scholarship and loan programs to the families of its members, the Reserve Officers Association maintains a list of

military dependent scholarships and scholarships for the children of deceased service members generally.
(800) 809-9448
www.roa.org

Scholarships for Military Children

Scholarships for Military Children is a scholarship program that was created by the Defense Commissary Agency. Scholarships for Military Children maintains a website that provides information on and applications for scholarships funded through the manufacturers and suppliers whose products are sold at military commissaries around the globe.
(888) 294-8560
www.militaryscholar.org

OTHERS

Children of Fallen Heroes
www.cfsrf.org
Freedom Alliance
www.freedomalliance.org
Troops to Teachers
http://troopstoteachers.net

SERVICE SPECIFIC

Air Force Cross Roads
www.afcrossroads.com
Marines
www.marines.mil
Navy Personnel Command
www.npc.navy.mil
U.S. Army Human Resource Command
www.hrc.army.mil
U.S. Coastguard
www.uscg.mil

SERVICE SPECIFIC FINANCIAL ASSISTANCE

Air Force Aid Society (AFAS)
They also have a loan called the Falcon loan which is $500 or less for emergency needs.
www.afas.org
Army Emergency Relief
www.aerhq.org
Coast Guard Mutual Assistance (Active, Reserve, and Retired)
www.cgmahqmobile.org
Navy-Marine Corps Relief Society Financial Assistance
www.nmcrs.org

RELOCATION

Chamber of Commerce Locator
www.chamberofcommerce.com
Relocation Assistance Office Locator
www.militaryonesource.mil

MILITARY PERSONNEL PORTALS

Air Force Portal
www.my.af.mil
Army Knowledge Online (AKO)
www.army.mil/ako
Navy Knowledge Online (NKO)
www.nko.navy.mil
Travel and Per Diem Information
www.defensetravel.dod.mil/site/allowances.cfm
USA Travel Source
www.relo.usa.com

TRANSITION

Purple Star Veterans and Families
Provides resources for vets to ease their transition from military to civilian life.
www.veteransandfamilies.org

Sentinels of Freedom
Sentinels of Freedom's mission is to provide life-changing opportunities for service members who have suffered severe injuries and need the support of grateful communities to realize their dreams. Unlike any other time in history, many more severely wounded are coming home faced with the challenges of putting their lives back together. Sentinels of Freedom provides "life scholarships" to help vets become self-sufficient. Sentinels succeeds because whole communities help. Local businesses and individuals not only give money, but also time, goods and services, housing, and transportation.
www.sentinelsoffreedom.org

GENERAL TRANSITION-RELATED WEBSITES

Air Force Airman and Family Readiness Center
www.militaryinstallations.dod.mil

Army Career and Alumni Program (ACAP)
www.acap.army.mil

Coast Guard Worklife Division, Transition Assistance
www.uscg.mil/worklife/transition_assistance.asp

Department of Labor
www.dol.gov

Department of Veterans Affairs (DVA)
www.va.gov

Department of Veterans Affairs, Compensation
www.benefits.va.gov/compensation/

Department of Veterans Affairs, Locations
www1.va.gov/directory/guide/home.asp?isFlash=1)

Family Center, Chaplain's Office, and Related Resources Finder
www.nvti.ucdenver.edu/resources/militarybasestap.htm
Marines Career Resource Management Center (CRMC)/Transition and Employment Assistance Program Center
www.mccs-sc.com/support/crmc.asp
Marine for Life
www.marineforlife.org
Military Family Network
www.emilitary.org/
Military Home Front
www.militaryhomefront.dod.mil
Military Installation Locator
http://www.militaryinstallations.dod.mil/MOS/f?p=MI:ENTRY:0
Military OneSource
www.militaryonesource.mil
National Guard Transitional Assistance Advisors
www.jointservicessupport.org/ws/
Navy Fleet and Family Support Center
www.cnic.navy.mil/ffr/family_readiness/fleet_and_family_support_program.html
Operation Transition website
www.wilsonhcg.com/Operation-Transition
Temporary Early Retirement Authority (TERA) Program
www.dfas.mil/retiredmilitary/plan/retirement-types/tera.html

VETERANS AFFAIRS PROGRAMS

CHAMPVA for dependents
www.va.gov/purchasedcare/programs/dependents/champva/
Transition Assistant Advisors
www.taapmo.com
Veteran Affairs
www.va.gov
Veteran Business
www.vetbiz.gov

EMPLOYMENT

5 Star Worldwide
www.5starworldwide.com
American Corporate Program—Veterans Mentoring
http://acp-usa.org
Americas Heroes at Work
http://www.dol.gov/vets/ahaw/
Buckley AFB NAF Human Resource Office
http://m.military.com/base-guide/buckley-air-force-base/contact/naf-human-resources/6697
Colorado Department of Labor and Employment
www.colorado.gov/CDLE
Colorado Springs Help Wanted
http://regionalhelpwanted.com/colorado-springs-jobs
Colorado State Government Job Announcements
www.colorado.gov/pacific/dhr/jobs
DEERS/RAPIDS Locator
www.dmdc.osd.mil/rsl/appj/site?execution=e1s1
Enable America
www.enableamerica.org
Helmets to Hardhats
www.helmetstohardhats.org
Hire a Hero
www.hireahero.org
Hire America Heroes
www.hireamericasheroes.org
Hire Veterans
www.hireveterans.com
Job Bank
http://www.careeronestop.org/jobsearch/findjobs/state-job-banks.aspx
National Archives and Records Administration
www.archives.gov
Military Audiology
www.militaryaudiology.org

Military Coalition
www.themilitarycoalition.org
Military Connection
www.militaryconnection.com
Military Officers Association of America
www.MOAA.org
Recruit Airforce, Find a Recruiter
www.airforce.com/contact-us/recruiter-locator
Recruit Army, Locate a Recruiter
www.goarmy.com/locate-a-recruiter.html
Recruit Marines, Request Information
www.marines.com/request-information?ver=B
Recruit Navy, Find a Recruiter
www.navy.com/locator.html
Return 2 Work
www.return2work.org
To Transfer Military Occupation Specialty
www.OnetCenter.org
Transition Assistance Program (TAP)
www.dodtap.mil
USA Jobs
www.usajobs.gov
Veterans Green Jobs
www.greenvets.org
Vet Jobs
www.vetjobs.com

Index

About the Authors

Janelle B. Moore has spent the last fourteen years as part of a "think tank" consulting practice that provides executive-level advisory, planning, coaching, and training services for both the federal government and private firms. She resides with her family in the Tampa, Florida, area. She is coauthor of several Rowman and Littlefield titles in the Military Life series, including *The Wounded Warrior Handbook* (2009), *Life after the Military: A Handbook for Transitioning Military* (2011), *Special Needs Families in the Military: A Resource Guide* (2011), and *The Military Marriage Manual* (2010).

Don Philpott has been writing, reporting, and broadcasting on international events, trouble spots, and major news stories for almost fifty years. For several years he was editor of *Homeland Defense Journal* and *International Homeland Security* magazine. He is the author or coauthor of more than two hundred books.